COMMUNICATION RESEARCH METHODS IN POSTMODERN CULTURE

A REVISIONIST APPROACH

Larry Z. Leslie
University of South Florida, Tampa

Allyn & Bacon

Boston   New York   San Francisco
Mexico City   Montreal   Toronto   London   Madrid   Munich   Paris
Hong Kong   Singapore   Tokyo   Cape Town   Sydney

Acquisitions Editor: Jeanne Zalesky
Series Editorial Assistant: Megan Lentz
Marketing Manager: Suzan Czajkowski
Production Editor: Maggie Brobeck
Production Manager: Kathy Sleys
Manufacturing Buyer: Kathy Sleys
Full Service Project Management/Composition: Karpagam Jagadeesan/GGS Higher
   Education Resources, A division of PreMedia Global, Inc.
Design Director: Jayne Conte
Cover Illustration/Photo: Getty Images, Inc.
Cover Designer: Suzanne Behnke

Library of Congress Cataloging-in-Publication Data
Leslie, Larry Z.
  Communication research methods in postmodern culture / Larry Z. Leslie.
     p. cm.
  Includes bibliographical references and index.
  ISBN-13: 978-0-205-61564-3 (alk. paper)
  ISBN-10: 0-205-61564-3 (alk. paper)
  1. Communication—Research. 2. Postmodernism. I. Title.

P91.3.L47 2010
302.207'2—dc20

                       2008048572

10 9 8 7 6 5 4 3 2 1   13 12 11 10 09

Allyn & Bacon
is an imprint of

PEARSON

www.pearsonhighered.com

ISBN-10:   0-205-61564-3
ISBN-13: 978-0-205-61564-3

One more for Kelly Paige

CONTENTS

PREFACE

In many schools of communication at universities all across the country, the arrival of a new semester is an exciting time for students and faculty alike. A new semester heralds a new beginning, a chance for a fresh start, or at least a chance to perform better than we did last semester! A schedule of new classes will often invigorate even the most jaded student. However, this enthusiasm may be short-lived, especially if the student finds him/herself in a research methods class. "Students often [view] the methods course as one of those 'dreaded requirements' " (Ransford & Butler, 1982, p. 291). Professors who teach the research methods course are not much surprised by the dejected looks they encounter when they breeze into the room for that first class session. Students appear to be in pain and not a single word has yet been spoken. A cheery greeting and a comforting comment that the course will not be as terrible as expected do little to disperse an atmosphere of despair which has settled firmly over the room.

We soldier on. The syllabus is distributed, course goals and requirements explained, and questions answered. Professors who teach these sorts of courses generally like the material and are, more often than not, accomplished researchers themselves. Some feel that their enthusiasm for the material will eventually win the hearts and minds of a few students. Winning most of them is not a realistic goal. In short, research is something undergraduate education does not do well (Ellis, 1999, p. 1).

Of course, the argument should be made that such courses are valuable to students. In addition to learning how to do research, many students learn how to critically evaluate the research of others, a fairly useful skill in a high-tech, information-rich culture. Too, studying research methods can help students become more disciplined thinkers and planners. Again, these are valuable skills in today's world. A few students may come to use one or two of the methodologies taught (probably survey or maybe focus groups) in their jobs a year or two down the road, and so the course may eventually prove to be of some use to them. There are doubtless other ways such courses assist students and add to their growth and development as they prepare for careers in communication. "It is always useful to know what is true and what is not true. In the real world a large number of social variables are found to be interrelated . . . many explanations abound for the same phenomena" (Miller, 1991, p. 4–5). Still, students often remain unconvinced of the value of the course. But we professors are convinced. So, "professors labor through lectures on abstract concepts and the tedious details of research techniques" (Ransford & Butler, p. 291). Some professors add zest to methods courses by offering group projects, individual research activities, field trips to media research companies, and the like. Yet many agree with

Poindexter (1998) that "lectures, research textbook readings" plus a project are "insufficient for today's students" (pp. 25, 32). When the semester finally ends, everyone breathes a sigh of relief. It's over!

It is not my purpose to suggest that any of those involved in a research methods course, whether students or professors, are either right or wrong in their thinking and/or their methods. The assumption that today's communication students need the ability to understand research in an information-rich environment and need to be able to design and carry out a straightforward research project is not being challenged. Further, no quarrel is being taken with the many creative activities that professors use to assist students in mastering the material. I firmly believe that research can answer questions and concerns that arise in a media-saturated world. However, I do suggest that many research methods courses, especially those using traditional social science methodologies, are generally out-of-date and ultimately do an injustice to students by failing to prepare them for the sorts of research and thinking that will be demanded of them in the years ahead. The quarrel, then, is with the philosophical and theoretical foundations which inform our methodologies. We have failed to adjust our methodologies to a changing culture.

This textbook is designed for use in undergraduate research methods courses. It makes use of some traditional social science methodologies, albeit with some modification. It offers new ways students can use to answer questions they have about media and communication. It attempts to present research activity as a way to see and understand our present (postmodern) culture.

I would like to extend my gratitude to the following reviewers: John M. Barnum, Ph.D., Hawai'i Pacific University; Monica Brasted, SUNY–Brockport; Michael R. Frontani, Elon University; Dr. Matt Hamilton, Oklahoma City University; Dr. Karie Hollerbach, Southeast Missouri State University; Dr. Ellen Kanervo, Austin Peay State University; Irwin Mallin, Indiana University–Purdue University Fort Wayne; Andrea M. McClanahan, East Stroudsburg University of Pennsylvania; Patricia McCormick, Howard University; David R. Novak, Clemson University; Richard K. Olsen, University of North Carolina–Wilmington; Gregg A. Payne, Ph.D., Chapman University; and Raúl Tovares, Trinity University.

This book would not have been possible without the assistance of two colleagues: Dr. Kim Golombisky of the University of South Florida and Dr. Tim Bajkiewicz of Virginia Commonwealth University. They worked tirelessly on their chapters. They deserve more credit for their work than I am able to give them here.

Larry Z. Leslie
Tampa, Florida
May 2008

SECTION I

Foundations

This section of the text serves as an introduction to the world of communication and research. It provides a historical perspective on research, a picture of how communication research began and where it is today, and why changes are needed in our research practices.

You will also learn about postmodern culture and how it requires us to modify the way we do communication research. A communication model will be presented, as will information on research ethics and federal research regulations.

Most importantly, this section contains information on designing a research project.

CHAPTER 1

Introduction

If we value the pursuit of knowledge, we must be free to follow wherever that search may lead us. The free mind is no barking dog, to be tethered on a ten-foot chain.

—ADLAI STEVENSON

Throughout history, life has been somewhat unpredictable. One's life course has often been determined by the circumstances of one's birth. But a variety of other factors may also come into play: health, education, economics, experience, even random occurrences which cannot be predicted and over which one has no control. For each succeeding generation, life has become more complex.

It would be hard to argue that life in contemporary culture is simple. It is, in fact, quite complex. Many of our life activities involve social situations, that is, situations that involve other people or situations which speak to us uniquely because we are human. At work, at play, with family, even online, we are social beings. The relationships that arise in these situations make life complicated.

In today's multicultural society, a host of issues and problems compete for our attention: the global economy, the urban poor and other marginalized groups, the influx of immigrants—both legal and illegal—into the United States, the changing nature of American public schools, and the impact of technology on the educational process, among others.

Life is made richer and more meaningful if we understand ourselves and the complexities of our relationships with others. Understanding the actions, reactions, motivations, and consequences of our behavior can be useful facilitating growth and development. Of particular interest here are the social issues and concerns raised in life by our communicating behavior, especially our interaction with contemporary media.

Science has given us some tools to use in investigating the questions we have. Generally, these tools help us answer our questions in an organized, meaningful way. Scientists and scholars have been active throughout history, but some cultural periods have been more important than others in helping us answer our questions, particularly in terms of thinking and systematic investigation. Of course, the methods and materials of inquiry have changed substantially over time. Today, for example, high-technology machines assist those conducting research in medicine. Technology has been quite useful in helping us answer our questions about biological life.

But assessing the social aspect of life cannot be done satisfactorily by machines. Such inquiry still requires the human touch. Humans must frame and ask questions, record and analyze the responses, observe behaviors, and derive meaning from what is said or done. Previous historical periods have given us several methods for gathering information about the social aspects of life. These methods have been useful in revealing something of the human condition.

A BACKWARD GLANCE

The cultural period that seems to have made an important contribution to current thinking is the modern period. The term *modern* as used here describes a certain period in history, not the present day or what is happening now. "Human civilization has experienced many cultural periods. You don't have to be a student of history to be familiar with the Egyptian and Greek cultures. And, although you may not know exactly what happened in the Middle Ages or Renaissance, you have at least heard these terms applied to specific historical periods" (Leslie, 2000, p. 2). It is the nature of culture to ebb and flow, for one period to use and/or change the contributions of preceding periods.

The modern cultural period, which your author places between 1850 and 1965, owes much to the period immediately preceding it. The Enlightenment (1650–1850) awakened the human spirit and the human mind. Reason was emphasized and the resulting development of science had a dramatic impact on life and thinking. During the modern period, the Industrial Revolution took hold and many political and social changes occurred.

Although your author dates the modern period from 1850, Berman (1988) feels the modern period probably began in the sixteenth century and reflected the culture's groping for explanations, exploring new ideas, and developing new technologies. During these years, Berman holds, "society moved from the rather primitive to the spectacular, from the first printing press to regular space travel, for example" (Leslie, 1998, p. 113).

As the twentieth century arrived, a new organizing principle began to evolve. The modern period was ending and a new cultural period was beginning. This view was driven by the "notion that the modern period, while a time of enormous growth and progress, had failed to successfully deal with some important cultural and social issues: poverty; social injustice; the corruption of language, politics, and economics; among others." The new period has been called *postmodern,* literally "after modern." Those who believe we are now in this new cultural period acknowledge the contributions of the modern period, but believe that it no longer has the power to explain contemporary culture or to motivate positive change (Leslie, 1998, p. 113).

The new organizing principle, postmodernists say, is the discontinuity and growing ambiguity of contemporary life. Even if you don't realize it, "you will encounter it in your daily life, no matter who you are" (Postmodernism in Daily Life, 1996, p. 1). Others agree that this discontinuity is barely noticeable to the typical individual. In terms of some broad, overall applications, it can indeed be barely noticeable. Take history, for example. We no longer care much about what happened in the past. History now serves "to give voice to the silenced, or marginalized minorities." In literature, meaning is now derived not from what the author meant and wrote, but from what the reader constructs as his/her interpretation of the work. "What does it mean to me?" becomes the key question instead of "what did the author mean?" In education, teachers no longer transmit information but serve as facilitators so children can construct their own knowledge (Postmodernism in Daily Life, p. 1).

Of course, for many people, changes in history, literature, and education may not have great impact, but there are other characteristics of postmodern culture that can have a dramatic effect on the entire culture. Although no formal list of characteristics has been developed, some scholars feel that there are many aspects of contemporary life that promote discontinuity and ambiguity. For example, it could be argued that we have all been affected by the breakdown of the traditional structure of society. Our churches, families, and schools are no longer the institutions around which we organize our lives. In previous cultures, these institutions provided the venues that created communities. People had common goals and purposes. Today, however, church attendance is declining, families are fragmented, and schools seem to spend as much time coping with violence as teaching.

Our culture has been bombarded with information. There is more information available, not only in libraries but also on the Internet, than anyone can possibly fathom, much less read or even scan. Some of this is misinformation. Much of the factual information available to us is presented without context. Raw information is not all that helpful unless we know what to do with it. As Postman (1999) observes, "information is not the same thing as knowledge, and it is certainly not anything close to . . . wisdom" (p. 91).

To further complicate matters, there is a general confusion about what is right and wrong in contemporary culture. Ethics have become situational, relative to the individual. Individuals often avoid taking responsibility for their actions, preferring instead to blame others for what happens to them. Our courts are quite familiar with cases where individuals seek monetary damages from others for their own lack of common sense. Nevertheless, some scholars still feel this is the modern age, unable to see the many paradigm shifts which changed modernity at the edges rather than attacking its core. They see little or no validity in concerning themselves with postmodern thinking and its possible influence on the way one does research. For example, in the second edition of his research text, Babbie notes that "the postmodern view represents a critical dilemma for scientists" (2002, p. 9). While this statement may very well be true, he does not take the postmodern view very seriously. He notes that what Gertrude Stein said of Oakland, California, is also true of postmodernism, "There is no there, there." He seems to feel that postmodernism requires scholars to "totally step outside their humanness to see and understand the world as it 'really' is" (p. 10). This, he feels, is not possible; the only way to solve the problem of the postmodern view is to use "established scientific procedures" and to broaden the "range of possibilities for structuring our research" (p. 10). Thus, it is clear that the decline of modernism has been roundly rejected by some and has been "profoundly troubling to many . . . because most of our philosophical, religious, and political conceptions are grounded in it" (Davis & Jasinski, 1993, p. 14).

If modernity is dead or dying, shouldn't our attention turn to contemporary culture—to the postmodern era—and shouldn't we be exploring a host of questions and issues suggested by the new characteristics and new conditions present in the culture? Does all of this call for a change in the methods of inquiry we used in the modern period? Yes. Must all our present methods be discarded in favor of new, unfamiliar methods? No. But we will need to revise our thinking and modify our methods somewhat to be able to get satisfactory answers to the questions we have about communication, people, media, and contemporary culture.

A POSTMODERN PRIMER

The term *postmodernism* was probably first used in the 1870s by a British artist, presumably to describe his work. It surfaced again from time to time until the 1960s where it was applied not only to art and architecture, but also to "literature, social thought, economics, even religion" (Appignanesi & Garratt, 1995, p. 3). Connor (1989) notes that although a number of writers used the term in the 1950s and 1960s, "the concept of postmodernism cannot be said to have crystallized until about the mid-1970s [when it] began to harden within and across a number of different cultural areas and academic disciplines" (pp. 5–6). Today, the term is used in many areas of academic and political life, but in each case it carries the same basic meaning: we have "gone beyond the world-view of modernism—which is clearly inadequate—without specifying where we are going" (Jencks, quoted in Appignanesi & Garratt, 1995, p. 3).

Ironically, some of the philosophers whose ideas are now considered the "core beliefs" of postmodernism seemed generally unaware of, or at least unconcerned with, it. For example, Michel Foucault is considered a postmodernist, but not because he defined the term or tried to promote it as representing his ideas, but because some of his ideas fit the broad definition of the term, a definition generally developed by others. Among other things, Foucault questioned truth and power and their influence on knowledge. He was also concerned with ideas relating to sexuality, language, and politics. But Foucault acknowledged that his ideas on power, for example, really derived from Nietzsche who "specified the power relation as a general focus . . . of philosophical discourse" (Foucault, 1988).

In a 1983 interview, Foucault asked the interviewer to update him on postmodernism when the term came up in their discussion. The reviewer replied:

> Mainly it is the idea of modernity, of reason, we find in Lyotard: a "grand narrative" from which we have finally been freed by a kind of salutary awakening. Postmodernity is the breaking apart of reason. Postmodernity reveals, at least, that reason has only been one narrative among many others in history; a grand narrative, certainly, but one of many, which can now be followed by other narratives.

Foucault's question shows that he had not thought much about the term: "I feel troubled here, because I do not grasp clearly what that might mean," he said. He noted that he was skeptical about the disappearance of reason. "I cannot see any disappearance of that kind. I can see multiple transformations [but not] a collapse of any kind" (Foucault, 1998, pp. 447–449). Yet Foucault is still considered very much a part of the postmodernism movement.

In much the same way, Derrida did not consciously promote postmodernism, but those who read and interpreted him felt that he was very much a part of it. Derrida probably would not have agreed. Postmodernists, for example, question truth and meaning. Derrida believed "it would be literally non-sensical to attempt, or even wish, to abandon truth or meaning" (Howells, 1999, pp. 2–3). Still, many scholars feel that Derrida is one of the proponents of postmodernism, perhaps because he developed deconstruction as a way of understanding truth and meaning, and deconstruction is often seen as destructive. Derrida, however, felt that deconstruction may set out to "read between the lines," or "read against the grain," but it always attempts to read, and understand (Howells, p. 3).

Lyotard, on the other hand, does not hesitate to thrust himself to the forefront of postmodern thinking. He defines it as "the state of our culture following the transformations which, since the end of the nineteenth century, have altered the game rules for science, literature, and the arts" (Lyotard, 1992, p. 138). Thus, when one combines the various perspectives, postmodernism takes shape as a series of ideas suggesting that "all epistemological enterprises—including those of science and philosophy—are merely operative fictions" (Howells, 1999, p. 2).

Yet postmodernism has defied precise definition. In fact, several scholars have argued that too much attention has been given to the problem of defining the term (Strinati, 1995, p. 223). Our attention might be better directed toward determining what it means for life today, indeed perhaps *whether* it has any meaning for life today. Enough definitions exist for us to firmly grasp the concept and to see it at work in contemporary culture. Remember, postmodernism "speaks in diverse voices, so we must be cautious in making blanket assertions about what it is or is not, what it does or does not do" (Gubrium and Holstein, 1997, p. 75).

In general, postmodernism may be seen as "a descriptive term for all sorts of . . . shifts and changes in contemporary culture" (Ward, 1997, p. 1). More specifically, postmodernism is said "to describe the emergence of a social order in which the importance and power of the mass media and popular culture means that they govern and shape all other forms of social relationships" (Strinati, 1995, p. 224). Further, the patterns of thought and action resulting from this new social order "pass unnoticed like glasses on the nose" (Smith, 1989, p. 3). The structure of the family has changed, and so have our concepts of success, duty, right and wrong, among other things. Postmodernism is not "hell-bent on knocking down everything modernism took such a long time to build. Instead, what is going on involves a more subtle and elusive cultural shift" (Berube, 1994, p. 123). In short, postmodernism refers to "a new form of society, one that has been radically transformed by the invention of [media] into a visual, video culture. This transformation introduces a series of new cultural formations that impinge upon, shape, and redefine contemporary life" (Denzin, 1994, p. 184).

Of particular importance to many postmodern scholars is the loss of belief in an objective world. For modern man, an absolute or objective reality provided the order which held life together. Through reason, we were capable of discerning this order as it was revealed in nature. We derived knowledge and a certain sense of satisfaction by discovering the laws of nature and by utilizing or complying with them (Smith, 1989, p. 7). But postmodern man no longer has confidence in an absolute reality. Reality may not be ordered, and even if it is, we may not be able to grasp it. Thus, our "attention has turned from objective reality to the individual human personality struggling for self-realization" (Smith, p. 15). All of this has, of course, important implications for media. "The mass media were once thought of as holding up a mirror to, and thereby reflecting, a wider social reality. Now, reality can only be defined by the surface reflection of this mirror" (Strinati, 1995, p. 224).

But the nature of reality is just one aspect of postmodern thinking. In terms of things a typical person-on-the-street might find today, if he or she were a careful observer, the following list of characteristics can be useful in identifying some of the challenges of contemporary culture.

Postmodern culture can be said to be characterized by:

- a lack of common sense and clear, logical thinking;
- a breakdown of the traditional social institutions of marriage, family, church, and school;
- a general confusion about ethics and right and wrong behavior;

- a decline in personal responsibility and an alarming tendency to blame others for things that happen to us;
- an information glut and a decreasing ability to separate factual information from misinformation;
- a general attitude of indifference or apathy to events, issues, or people outside ourselves;
- increased efforts to accumulate material wealth as a measure of accomplishment and success; and
- increased use of and dependence on media and new media technology.

It is true that many of these characteristics can be seen in other cultural periods. But they seem more troublesome now because they appear to be more pervasive than ever before, largely because of the advance of technology, changing economic conditions, and an increasingly diverse racial and ethnic society. We are much more aware of the world today. Worldwide communication is instantaneous, not everyone in the culture looks like us, and there are marked differences in our economic and social well-being.

WHAT IS COMMUNICATION?

For most people communication means talking: sharing thoughts, beliefs, opinions, and information. Two people having lunch together might talk about their jobs, their personal lives, their goals, or perhaps sports or the latest news story. An individual watching television, listening to the radio, or reading a book is also involved in communication though he/she is on the receiving end of a message, and there is little opportunity for him/her to immediately communicate with the television, radio, or book. Communication does, of course, have a formal definition. Rubin, Rubin, and Piele (2005) define communication "as a process by which people arrive at shared meanings through the interchange of messages" (p. 3). This definition is useful because it fits most all communication situations, that is, those where one is actively participating in a message exchange as well as those where one is receiving but not sending a message.

As a field of study, *communication* has evolved down through the years. Today, the term is used to describe activities in journalism and mass communication, but also activities that were once found in academic speech departments. Public speaking, rhetorical criticism, discourse analysis, ethnography, and interaction analysis, among others, are now very much a part of a rather broad academic area that now comprises "communication." Communication scholars study not only media messages and practices but also interpersonal, group, organizational, and intercultural messages (Rubin et al., 2005, p. 4).

WHY RESEARCH?

Why does one do research? The simple answer is that research extends human knowledge by helping us see and understand our world. It can do this in any number of ways. Research can support, disprove, or modify what we know or think we know. It can verify, refute, or refine previous research studies. But generally, research is used to gather information for business, professional, or personal decision making.

Ragin (1994) lists seven goals of research. They are: (1) identifying general patterns and relationships, (2) testing and refining theories, (3) making predictions, (4) interpreting culturally or historically significant phenomena, (5) exploring diversity, (6) giving voice, and (7) advancing new theories (pp. 32–33). Ragin notes that "no research can tackle all seven goals at once" (p. 47). Researchers with a postmodern view would likely revise Ragin's list. Almost certainly, they would eliminate the goals dealing with theories and with making predictions. These goals would be seen as relics of the modern period and therefore of little use in doing anything except continuing to perpetuate the myth that modern social science can provide the answers to all our questions and the solutions for all our problems. In fact, postmodernists would suggest that the uncertainty and ambiguity of the human condition precludes the making of any generalizations about communication, media, technology, or life in the current era. A theory is often advanced with some authority, but it is merely the arbitrary imposition of a singular, systemic point of view and does not account for the differences or the contradictions often found both in life and in research.

In traditional social science research, scholars usually follow what is commonly called *the scientific method.* This method is based on five principles. First, scientific research is public. This means that methods are clearly reported so that others may duplicate the work, either verifying, improving, or refuting the original findings. Second, scientific research is objective. As humans, we cannot be totally without bias, but insofar as it is possible, scientific research follows strict rules and procedures designed to lead to a natural conclusion and not a conclusion manipulated or created by those doing the research. Third, scientific research is empirical. This simply means that we can experience things, take measurements, and draw meaningful conclusions about phenomena in the world around us. Fourth, scientific research is cumulative. Research activity should build on what is already known and add knowledge for others to use. Finally, scientific research is predictive. This does not mean that scientists can predict the future, but rather that scientists can design studies which are useful in determining what may happen as a result of a given set of conditions or circumstances. Clearly, "science is a highly public enterprise in which efficient communication among scientists is essential. Each scientist builds on what has been learned in the past, and day-by-day his or her findings must be compared with those of others . . . working on the same types of problems" (Nunnally, 1978, p. 7).

As you might expect, postmodernists have some difficulty accepting some aspects of the scientific method as gospel. For example, postmodernists believe that it is not really possible to be objective in research, particularly if one "builds" on the work of others. This "building" process in itself

suggests that one accepts what has been done before. This acceptance immediately constitutes a bias that will most certainly influence a new project. As
you will see as you progress through this book, there are other aspects of the
scientific method that are rejected by many postmodernists.

COMMUNICATION RESEARCH

The University of Pennsylvania offered the first curriculum in journalism
from 1893 to 1902; the University of Illinois dates its journalism program
from 1904. The first school of journalism was opened in 1904 at the
University of Missouri (Emery & Emery, 1988). Some writing and speech activities began in English departments, developed their own identities, and
later became separate communication departments. Journalism and mass
communication quickly became part of the academic landscape at many colleges and universities. The formation of academic disciplines was an outgrowth of the industrial revolution and the resulting need for individuals
trained (educated) in specific work areas (Brown, 1995).

The history of mass communication research is easy to trace. Czitrom
(1982) reports that "by the late 1930s an aggressively empirical spirit, stress-
ing new and increasingly sophisticated research techniques, characterized
the study of modern communication in America" (p. 122). Czitrom further
notes that "a diverse group of scholars, meeting under the auspices of the
Rockefeller Foundation, produced a lengthy memorandum outlining the
case for 'Research in Mass Communication' " (p. 131). Written in 1940, this
memo suggested communication researchers address four questions: who,
said what, to whom, and with what effect. Five research techniques were advanced as methods by which these questions could be answered. "These
[methods] included the poll, or short interview; the panel, or repeated interviewing of the same respondents over time; the intensive interview; community studies; and systematic content analysis" (Czitrom, p. 132).

The memorandum also called for a national institute to coordinate and
assist with communication research, and although no such institute was
ever established, "the four questions theme . . . who says what to whom
with what effect . . . became the dominant paradigm defining the scope" of
American mass communication research (Czitrom, 1982, p. 132). Of course,
our questions and our methods have changed somewhat over the years.
There has been some discussion in the journalism and mass communication
literature about how best to describe today's communication research. How
do researchers decide what to study and what methods do they use to carry
out their investigations? Blumler and Gurevitch (1987) believe that a research study can be motivated by any of the following: "sheer curiosity and
interest, a sense of a question unduly neglected, a sense of what is focusing
activity and controversy among prominent scholars, an awareness of . . .
problems requiring attention, [and] values relevant to . . . communication in
society," among others (p. 16).

In mass communication, research involves "the study of the mass media, the messages they generate, the audiences they attempt to reach, and their effects on these audiences" (Tan, 1981, p. 3). The mass media include not only newspapers, radio, broadcast, cable and satellite television, film, and some advertising and public relations activities, but also many of the communication avenues resulting from or relating to the Internet and other electronic forms of communication. Media play a large role in contemporary culture, and understanding these influential forces is important in helping us make a variety of life decisions. Research is one way we have of assisting us in knowing what media do and what impact they have on our lives.

In speech communication, research often involves studying some of the same messages mass communications scholars are examining, but it may also include—but is not limited to—the study of communication between two or more individuals, the gathering of told stories (narratives), a holistic examination of a cultural or subcultural group, and an analysis, interpretation, and evaluation of the impact of a persuasive message. Gender studies have also become popular among researchers.

Academic speech departments, like journalism and mass communication, also grew out of academic English departments. "During the later part of the nineteenth century and the early part of the twentieth century . . . some departments created 'Oral English' courses whose job it was to teach students the ancient art of elocution, that is, the physical movements, gestures, postures and vocal characteristics of people as they expressed various states of feeling" (Cohen, 1994, pp. 1, 27).

With the founding of the Eastern Public Speaking Conference in 1910, oral English became "public speaking," and a new academic department was on its way to being formed (Cohen, 1994, p. 29). Public speaking courses were widely offered. Colleges in Pennsylvania, Maryland, New Jersey, Delaware, and elsewhere were represented at the 1910 conference.

"After 1914 the profession became the National Association of Academic Teachers of Public Speaking, which had a national rather than a regional focus" (Cohen, 1994, p. 30). Today, the National Communication Association, formerly the Speech Communication Association, is seen as the oldest and largest association, a direct descendent of the 1914 group. Regional organizations still exist and are active in promoting communication scholarship and education in their respective areas. The Western States Communication Association and the Central States Communication Association are perhaps two of the better-known regional organizations. The International Communication Association is well-known all over the world and boasts more than 3,500 members in 65 countries. Like their counterparts in journalism and mass communication, speech communication researchers are committed to studying a variety of communication activities.

It seems appropriate at this point to end our detailed exploration of journalism/mass communication and speech communication as separate areas of research and study. There are differences in the two academic areas, to be sure, but there are important commonalities, too. At many universities, both journalism/mass communication and speech communication are part of the same academic department. At other universities, they are still in separate departments. Nevertheless, for purposes of exploring research methodology, it makes sense to consider all activities in journalism/mass communication and speech communication to be part of the broad field of "communication."

In terms of the methods used, it is a generally accepted notion that much communication research falls within the "social science" paradigm or pattern, and particularly the quantitative approach within that paradigm. In recent years, qualitative studies have increased in popularity. For the most part, our work today includes the quantitative methods of the survey, the experiment, and content analysis. Focus groups, historical/legal, ethnographic, and a number of other qualitative methods are used by a smaller yet increasing number of researchers.

Some scholars now believe, however, that the social, intellectual, economic, and technological changes that have resulted in the passing of the modern to the postmodern require us to change the way we conduct and report our research. Blumler and Gurevitch (1987) acknowledge this line of thinking by noting that critics have challenged American communication researchers "for adhering to a 'dominant paradigm' which . . . rests on shaky and outdated foundations" (p. 18). These critics have been quite specific about what they feel is wrong with communication scholarship: it is "crudely behaviorist and naively positivist;" it has been "overly preoccupied with individual-level audience phenomena;" it has "looked for evidence of media impact in the least likely and most trivial places;" and it has ignored the "more meaningful issues about the ideological role of the media, the location of media organizations in the nexus of power relations in society, the nature of the production process, and the values of media professionals" (p. 18).

While not all of what the critics say may be true, it could be argued that while the social science methods used during the modern period may have been appropriate for their time, times have changed. Postmodern culture has important implications for everything we do as communication practitioners, scholars, teachers, and students. Communication has always prided itself on being a cutting-edge, state-of-the-art discipline, a notion arising chiefly as a result of our ties to media industries. Media are technology-sensitive and are often the first to adopt and publicize their use of the latest technological advance. While media industries may be cutting edge, communication scholars often are not. For example, communication researchers have barely reacted to criticism of their scholarship. "A few bought the new approach more or less wholesale. . . . Some stoutly reasserted the claims of 'scientific' research models. . . . Some admired, even applauded, the new doctrines from afar, without modifying the essential thrust of their own strategies" (Blumler & Gurevitch, 1987, p. 18).

Change is never easy. It is much easier to resist attempts to update research methodologies, cling to the same old "modern" methods, and turn out research that many scholars feel is mediocre. Avery (1987) is disheartened by "the valuable time and energy that is invested in the rehashing of old issues, the restatement of old findings, and the rediscovery of old 'givens'" (p. 23). But McChesney's (1993) observation may be the most telling: "too many of us are simply producing inbred and unimportant work for a handful of colleagues who are doing the same" (p. 100).

EVALUATING AND RESTRUCTURING OUR RESEARCH PRACTICES

Although the early years of communication research are often viewed as being the best and most productive, McLeod (2000) argues that "there was no golden age of communications research" and that, in fact, many of the "great accomplishments" of the early years actually retarded research in the field. There was scant contribution to conceptual or theoretical development, and the research that was conducted showed little more than "clever research designs . . . large grant getting, policy politics, and mindless raw empiricism" (p. 1).

McLeod feels that scholars need to address some of the problems which are apparent in our research activities. These problems include (1) a narrow focus on micro variables and simple connections, (2) a resistance to complicated models which make connections to larger social systems or issues, and (3) a tendency to tap citizens' reactions to problems without getting at the root causes of the problems and without discovering how people might solve them (McLeod, 2000, p. 7).

Is there a common core of ideas and knowledge on which we can focus our research? Can we reemphasize clear writing and logical thinking? What should be our response to the collapsing of media boundaries, the transformation of news into an infotainment hybrid, and the resulting changes in the quality of public discourse? What impact is technology having on our ability to communicate with others? In short, McLeod asks, "what do we need to know in an uncertain, and rapidly changing world?" (McLeod, 2000, p. 7).

This question brings to mind one of the standard questions thesis and dissertation advisors often ask of their graduate students' research proposals: So what? A proposal may be clearly written and cleverly designed, but what does the research say about what we need to know in contemporary culture? For example, one published study concluded that "female scholars enjoy research as much as their male peers" (Dupagne, 1993). It could certainly be argued that this finding fails the so what test. Is this something we really need to know in a rapidly changing, uncertain, media-saturated culture? Is the issue of "enjoyment of research" worthy of research time and effort, or are there more important, more significant issues to be explored?

McLeod and others (and this text) are calling for an evaluation and a restructuring of the way we do communication research. A postmodern culture demands it. The twenty-first century is here, but it is not too late to make some changes in our thinking and our methods and thereby render communication research more important and more useful than ever before.

POSTMODERNISM AND COMMUNICATION RESEARCH

Postmodernism calls into question many of the foundations of communication research. Traditional communication research has sought significance, meaning, and a generalized application of its results. However, "postmodern thought tends to reject the idea of things having a single, basic meaning. Instead, it embraces fragmentation, conflict, and discontinuity in matters of history, identity, and culture" (Ward, 1997, p. 95). Moreover, "it is suspicious of any attempt to provide all-embracing, total theories. And it rejects the view that any cultural phenomenon can be explained as the effect of one objectively existing, fundamental cause" (Ward, p. 95). Thus, many social science methodologies—particularly the experimental method or any method that supposes to derive significant meaning, generalize from the small to the large, or draw conclusions about reality—have been set aside as having little importance in helping us understand contemporary life.

The shallowness of the research methods used and the claims made by many social science researchers today became quite evident in 1996 when "Alan D. Sokal published a famous hoax paper in the respectable journal *Social Text*. Sokal pretended to write about quantum gravity," but made absurd claims, got his facts wrong, and misrepresented several social theories. He took material from other sociological writers and wrapped his entire paper in jargon (Sardar & Van Loon, 1997, p. 98). In other words, the article had no merit whatsoever, yet was accepted by peer reviewers and published in a journal.

While Sokal felt he was exposing the flaws in postmodern approaches to research, he may well have exposed the flaws in all social science research. Misuse of scientific concepts and flawed research practices are problems for all researchers, regardless of their world view. Still, most critical theorists feel that postmodernists "are deeply hostile to genuine scientific methods and progress itself" (Sim & Van Loon, 2001, p. 14). This issue is discussed in greater detail in Chapter 2.

There has been no more vocal critic of the way research is currently done than Paul Feyerabend. He says it is not his intention "to replace one set of general [research] rules by another such set," but to convince researchers that "all methodologies, even the most obvious ones, have their limits" (Feyerabend, 1993, p. 23). Feyerabend asks (and answers) two important questions.

1. "What is science?"
2. "What's so great about science?" (p. 238)

Answering the first question, Feyerabend says that although "science" may be a single word, "there is no single entity that corresponds to the word" (1993, p. 238). In other words, there is such a wide divergence among individuals, schools, theories, concepts, and the like, in terms of approaches and practices, that settling on a single definition of the word is impossible.

The answer to the second question—what's so great about science—may be a bit surprising to some. Feyerabend notes that there are various degrees of greatness, but that "popularity" is one. He defines popularity as familiarity with the results of science and the belief that these results are important. To those who note that science is practical, Feyerabend would say "science sometimes works and sometimes doesn't" (1993, p. 247). Some sciences, he says, are in pretty "sorry shape." Other sciences are often regularly successful. However, "the fact that an approach is 'scientific' according to some clearly formulated criterion therefore is no guarantee that it will succeed. Each case must be judged separately" (p. 247).

Feyerabend concludes by noting that "there are many things we can learn from the sciences. But we can also learn from the humanities, from religion and from the remnants of ancient traditions. . . . No area is unified and perfect, few areas are repulsive and completely without merit" (1993, p. 249).

We have said that there are many different versions of postmodernism. But there are some common themes running through most of these versions. These themes tell us "what it means to live in our present times, and how best to go about describing them" (Ward, 1997, p. 5).

Broadly stated, here are the themes:

- "Society, culture, and lifestyle are today significantly different from what they were a hundred, fifty or even thirty years ago."
- Life today is heavily influenced by the *concrete* "developments in mass media, the consumer society, and information technology."
- "These kinds of developments have an impact on our understanding of more *abstract* matters, like meaning, identity, and even reality."
- "Old styles of analysis are no longer useful, and new approaches and new vocabularies need to be created in order to understand the present." (Ward, 1997, p. 5)

Thus, we see that postmodernism is a radically different cultural view involving a broad reconceptualization of how we experience and explain the world around us. It questions authority and "the arbitrary imposition of any singular, systemic, point of view . . . [and tolerates] different, even contradictory perspectives" (Rosenau, 1992, p. 13). It rejects the naive acceptance of science as the source of absolute truth and disputes the underlying assumptions of mainstream social science and its research product. For the typical individual, it presents a culture that has no unifying order, rules, or values, a culture dependent on appearance and image. There are no precise meanings for words, no definitive versions of a text, and no simple truths. The postmodern mind "lacks an embracing outlook." Surely this "signals the new chapter in intellectual history" (Smith, 1989, p. 232). As Capra (1982) notes, "cultural transformations of this magnitude and depth cannot be prevented. They should not be opposed, but, on the contrary, should be welcomed. . . . [we need] a deep reexamination of the main premises and values of our culture, a rejection of those conceptual models that have out-lived their usefulness. . ." (p. 33).

REVIEW QUESTIONS

1. Why is research important in contemporary culture?
2. List seven typical goals of research. Which one seems most important? Why?
3. Is there a difference between knowledge and wisdom? Explain.
4. What is communication?
5. What are the five principles of the scientific method? Explain what each means to a researcher.
6. What are some of the problems postmodernists have found with the way communication research is being done?
7. Is it important to evaluate our research practices? Why?
8. Why does postmodernism reject many of the processes and principles of traditional social science research?

SUGGESTED ACTIVITIES

1. Conduct an in-depth investigation into the Enlightenment cultural period (1650–1850). Find ideas developed during the era that are still influential today.
2. Ask other professors on your campus what they know/think about postmodernism. Compile your information and compare it to the information gathered by other students in your class. Develop your own "local" set of characteristics of postmodern culture.
3. Search for stories in newspapers and magazines, or online, that illustrate the complexities and ambiguities of contemporary life. Share these with your class or with other students.
4. Check with your campus's communication department to discover what specific communication areas are part of the department. Is the emphasis journalism/mass communication, speech communication, or some combination of the two?

CHAPTER 2

Knowledge, Culture, and Research

Science is built of facts the way a house is built of bricks; but an accumulation of facts is no more science than a pile of bricks is a house.

—HENRI POINCARE

All research practices are grounded in ideas which form the fundamental bases upon which a search for knowledge can begin. In some cases, these ideas may be concrete; in other cases, the ideas may be abstract, even philosophical, in nature. Nevertheless, a belief in the validity of ideas gives strength and direction to a research effort.

Let us now turn our attention to the business of determining just how research might be designed and conducted in contemporary, postmodern culture. In this chapter, you will find a general discussion of what knowledge is, how the modern period went about discovering knowledge, and how the qualities of postmodern culture contribute to what might be termed a *new research outlook*.

SOME IMPORTANT PHILOSOPHY

Epistemology is the "branch of philosophy concerned with the nature of knowledge, its possibility, scope, and general basis" (Honderich, 1995, p. 242). In practical terms, this means it "attempts to answer the basic question: what distinguishes true knowledge from false knowledge?" (Heylighen, 1993, p. 1). Research is essentially an epistemological activity, that is, an examination of discerned or discovered knowledge to see whether it is true or false. This is not as easy an enterprise as it might seem. "Philosophers have frequently been divided over the question of how knowledge is derived" (Flew, 1984, p. 109).

Although philosophers may argue among themselves about what constitutes knowledge, most people in the culture have a more practical—if somewhat less philosophical—belief in what knowledge is and how you get it. A typical person might be able to list six or seven ways of acquiring knowledge. This list might include things such as observation, experience, being told by a trusted friend or relative, reasoning, intuition, and perhaps even science. All of these have a rather practical, down-to-earth feel about them. For example, for most people, seeing is believing, so observation makes sense to them as a means to knowledge. Likewise, we tend to believe things we are told by individuals we regard as credible; we often have a "gut" feeling (intuition) about the truth or falsity of something, and so on. But for each of these practical methods to knowledge, a couple of questions arise: Is the acquired knowledge true or false? How dependable and reliable is the knowledge? Scholars feel that systematic study, that is, research, is often a better way to assess the validity, dependability, and reliability of gathered knowledge than any of the practical methods commonly used by the typical person.

Some scholars feel that the seventeenth and eighteenth centuries were *the age* of epistemology (Honderich, 1995, p. 242). Several important philosophers advanced theories during that time, theories that have been influential in our thinking about what knowledge is and how it is acquired. One of the most influential ideas was Descartes's belief (*Cogito ergo sum . . .* I think, therefore I am) that "the general basis for justification of claims for knowledge was to be found in the individual's own mind" (Honderich, p. 243). Descartes's notion led to a theory of knowledge called *rationalism*. Rationalists believe "that ideas of reason intrinsic to the mind are the only source of knowledge." On the other hand, those who believe in *empiricism* feel that "sense experience is the primary source of our ideas, and hence our knowledge" (Flew, 1984, p. 109). These two perspectives—rationalism and empiricism—dominated scholarly thinking in the late Renaissance period and have continued to be influential in every cultural period since.

Empiricism sees knowledge as a result of sensory experience and rationalism sees knowledge as a result of mental reflection. Of course, other points of view have been advanced, some in earlier cultures and some in later ones. One of the most popular can be found in the early twentieth century. The *pragmatic* approach, as a means to knowledge, rests on the notion that "knowledge consists of models that attempt to represent the environment in such a way as to maximally simplify problem-solving." Since no model can "capture all relevant information . . . [pragmatists] accept the parallel existence of different models . . . [and] the model which is chosen depends on the problem to be solved" (Heylighen, 1993, p. 2).

Other scholars see merit in the *reflection-correspondence* theory, a view which holds that "knowledge results from a kind of mapping or reflection of external objects, through our sensory organs, possibly aided by different observation instruments, to our brain or mind" (Heylighen, 1993, p. 1). Still others prefer *constructivism* which assumes "all knowledge is built up from scratch." This approach rejects givens, empirical data or facts, and the reflection-correspondence theory (Heylighen, p. 2).

Of course, there are numerous other theories of knowledge, but regardless of which theory one subscribes to, the natural tendency is toward *coherence*. In other words, knowledge that is inconsistent with the bulk of other knowledge will tend to be rejected, while knowledge that fits nicely with what we already know will be accepted (Heylighen, 1993, p. 2).

SOME ESSENTIAL HISTORY

As Capra (1982) notes, "between 1500 and 1700, there was a dramatic shift in the way people pictured the world and in their whole way of thinking" (p. 53). Prior to about 1500, the dominant worldview in most civilizations was *organic*, that is, based around living things. People lived in small, cohesive communities; they experienced nature in personal ways, subordinated individual needs to those of the community, and depended on their religious beliefs to give meaning and significance to things. But all this changed in the sixteenth and seventeenth centuries as science took hold. Copernicus, Galileo, Bacon, Descartes, and others were largely responsible for providing the intellectual bases for this change, but it was Newton who brought it all together, developing what is often called the *Mechanical World Paradigm* (Capra, p. 63).

As an outgrowth of the rise of science, the Enlightenment, and the Industrial Revolution, the Mechanical World Paradigm can be said to have the following characteristics:

1. the scientific method was accepted as the only valid approach to knowledge;
2. the universe was seen as "a mechanical system composed of elementary material building blocks;"
3. life was understood as a competitive struggle for survival; and
4. unlimited material progress could be made through continued economic and technological growth (Capra, 1982, p. 31).

These characteristics became the dominant assumptions of the modern period. "During the 19th century, scientists continued to elaborate the mechanistic model of the universe in physics, chemistry, biology, psychology, and the social sciences" (Capra, 1982, p. 69). Science and technology were "aimed at control, mass production, and standardization, and [were] subjected, most of the time, to centralized management that pursues the illusion of indefinite growth" (p. 44).

Some scholars feel it is time for a "deep re-examination of the main premises and values of our culture, a rejection of those conceptual models that have outlived their usefulness, and a new recognition of some of the values discarded in previous periods of our cultural history" (Capra, 1982, p. 33).

"Learning has become fragmented into tinier and tinier frameworks of study on the Newtonian assumption that the more we know about the individual parts, the more we will be able to make decisions about the whole these parts make up" (Rifkin, 1989, p. 263).

The notion that we cannot know the whole by examining its parts has long been a part of human experience. This is nowhere more obvious than in the famous Parable of the Elephant. There are many versions of this parable, but the message is always the same. One version of the parable goes like this:

> Four blind men, none of whom, of course, had ever seen an elephant, asked a learned man to let them touch an elephant and thereby learn the nature of the animal.
>
> The first approached the elephant and, reaching out, felt a tusk. He exclaimed, "This wonder of an elephant is very like a spear."
>
> The second man extended his hand and grasped the squirming trunk. "I see," said he, "the elephant is very like a snake."
>
> The third approached and seized the swinging tail. "I see," quoth he, "the elephant is very like a rope."
>
> The fourth blind man chanced to touch the ear. "Even the blindest man," he said, "can tell an elephant is very like a fan."

The parable's message, in all its versions, is, of course, that one must understand a whole, and that a whole is more than the sum of its parts (www.noogenesis.com).

Still, there is no question that the modern age was a time of significant accomplishments. The benefits of modernity included "drudgery relieved, health improved, goods multiplied, and leisure extended" (Smith, 1989, p. 6). For modern man, reason was the means by which he discovered the structure and order of his world. In other words, we determined that "there was an order to things and that order could be ascertained by mathematical formulas and scientific observation" (Rifkin, 1989, p. 37). Descartes once wrote that "all science is certain, evident knowledge. We reject all knowledge which is merely probable and judge that only those things should be believed which are perfectly known and about which there can be no doubts" (Capra, 1982, p. 57). The modern period was quite comfortable with this notion and with the role of science and reason as the primary means to knowledge.

But the postmodern age has ushered in a new way of thinking. Postmodern man is unsure that reality—at least the sort of reality that science and reason have discovered—is ordered, and even if it is, the mind may not be able to discern reality in any meaningful way (Smith, 1989, p. 16). In short, the postmodern mind "lacks an embracing outlook; it doubts that it is any longer possible or even desirable to have one" (Smith, p. 232).

Please do not misunderstand. We are not discarding everything science has told us. Some of the sciences, most notably medical science and the physical sciences, have made significant and important contributions to our understanding of life. For example, we would be foolish not to accept the law of gravity. The fundamental laws of physics, chemistry, geology, and similar sciences are not in dispute. What is in dispute are the "laws" of social science research.

This increasing distrust of reality, of science and reason as the only avenues to that reality, is further supported by the entropy law, sometimes referred to as the *second law of thermodynamics*. The entropy law dates from about 1868 and is considered a fundamental law of physics and chemistry. In simple language, it means that "everything in the universe began with structure and value and is irrevocably moving in the direction of random chaos and waste." Stated a bit more scientifically, it means that "matter and energy can be changed in only one direction, i.e., from usable to unusable, or from available to unavailable, or from ordered to disordered" (Rifkin, 1989, p. 20). Stated still another way, "any isolated physical system will proceed spontaneously in the direction of ever increasing disorder" (Capra, 1982, p. 73).

"The second law of thermodynamics is a powerful aid to help us understand why the world works as it does" (Lambert, 2005, para. 1). Although it is backed by a complicated theory and some mathematical equations, the typical person can see the law at work in everyday experience. "A rock will fall if you lift it up and let it go. Hot frying pans cool down when taken off the stove . . . ice cubes melt in a warm room" (A Student's Approach to the Second Law and Entropy, 2006, para. 3).

However, scholars have differing interpretations of the entropy law. All generally agree that the law is much in evidence in the world, but disagree on whether the law results in order or disorder. Lambert (2005) believes "the ideas of entropy and the second law have been almost hopelessly muddled by well-meaning but scientifically naive philosophers and writers of both fiction and non-fiction" (para. 5). He further notes that the order/disorder argument has been taken out of most [science] textbooks because the issue derives from a nineteenth century error and numerous misapplications since.

Other scholars, particularly those concerned about the *social rather than the scientific* impact of the law, believe the order/disorder argument has merit. To some, "entropy is no longer seen as a thermodynamic quantity; it has become a dark force in the universe" (Entropy, 1996). In other words, the entropy law may have different implications for the social world than it does for the world of chemistry and physics.

A rather convincing argument can be made that our social world, particularly in communication and in the use of technology, is becoming increasingly disordered. For example, certain uses of the Internet have contributed to disorder. The increasing number of child predators prowling MySpace and Facebook pages can be said to promote dangerous disorder for young Internet users. Millions of pieces of spam arrive in e-mail boxes around the world hourly. Viruses, worms, trojans, spyware, phishing, and pharming, as well as other time- and space-consuming elements result in the loss of both time and energy on the part of Internet users and contribute to a growing disorder in our work and personal lives (Hokikian, 2002).

This tendency to move toward an increasingly disordered state is everywhere evident in our daily lives. For example, has cell phone use by drivers made our streets and highways more ordered places to drive? Has the upsurge in terrorist attacks, both before and after 9/11, made life anywhere on the planet safer and more secure, that is, more ordered? Almost certainly not! Several research studies have found that a driver on a cell phone performs as though he/she were intoxicated. Furthermore, contemporary life has obviously become less ordered by the continued threat of terrorist attacks and the superficial security measures that have been put into place to thwart such attacks. There are numerous other examples of how our daily lives have become more disordered as we have progressed into the postmodern era.

Acceptance of the entropy law has significant consequences, particularly if one subscribes to what this text believes to be the *social application* of the law. In a chemistry or physics lab, scientists, as a result of their work, are free to say that entropy does not contribute to disorder. By the same token, in contemporary postmodern culture, social scientists, philosophers, writers, cultural observers, and others are similarly free to say that, according to the data they have gathered from the real world and their understanding of the entropy law, it does indeed contribute to disorder.

For one thing, it undermines the idea of history as progress. For another, it refutes the notion that science and technology are creating a more ordered world (Rifkin, 1989, p. 21). Energy is expended, and lost, in everything we do, including the learning process. "The Entropy Law is always at work in the collection of information, as in every other endeavor. . . . [challenging] the modern world view with a force of conviction that is every bit as convincing as was the Newtonian paradigm when it replaced the medieval Christian world view" (Rifkin, pp. 21, 182,).

ADDITIONAL FACTORS TO CONSIDER

"The appropriate reason for changing our outlook is not to create a better world or save the one we have. It is to see more clearly things as they are" (Smith, 1989, p. 210). One way change might be accomplished is to reformulate science, that is, revise or reinvent the processes and practices that lead us to knowledge and to its verification or rejection. As Rifkin argues, the first idea that must be abandoned is the notion that "specific phenomena can be isolated from the rest of the universe they are a part of and then connected to some kind of 'pure' causal relationship with everything else in a delicate and complex web of interrelationships" (1989, p. 259). The Newtonian Mechanical World Paradigm must give way to the notion that "everything is part of a dynamic flow." We can no longer treat all phenomena as isolated components of matter, because everything in the world is connected to other things and all of it is "always in the process of becoming" (p. 260).

In postmodern culture we cannot be objective, at least objective enough to generate dependable knowledge, because we cannot separate ourselves from nature, discover its inner secrets, and then use those secrets "as a fixed body of truths to manipulate and change the natural world" (Rifkin, 1989, p. 260). Objectivity, the basis of science, is not possible in contemporary culture and probably has not ever been possible in any culture. Shipman (1997) believes "it is easy to detect subjectivity in social research. It is impossible to confirm objectivity" (p. 18). Although some researchers would quickly assert that their intellectual detachment "places them in a position from which objectivity is possible," most researchers would probably agree that because humans are involved in social processes, "there is no detached position for neutral observation" (Shipman, p. 18). The best we can do is to submit research activity—from start to finish—to careful scrutiny. Although there will still be questions, if research assumptions, concepts, and methods are carefully examined and if the results are fully reported and appear to be sound, we probably have as much objectivity as we are going to get.

WHAT ABOUT COMMUNICATION RESEARCH?

"The grip of the [modern] scientific view remains strong. For more than 100 years, social scientists claimed they were in the business of explaining and hence predicting human behavior" (Shipman, 1997, p. 22). Although communication research dates from the 1920s, it is nevertheless squarely within the general social science tradition in terms of the concepts that inform its practices. "The concept of a science of human communication rests upon the optimistic assumption that behavior can be both understood and improved through systematic study." Research into communication behavior results in understanding, explanation, prediction, and control (Berger & Chaffee, 1987b, pp. 99–100).

Although Carl Hovland and Paul Lazarsfeld, among others, set both the philosophical tone and the basic approaches to communication research during the early years, communication research experienced its greatest period of development in the years following World War II. "The concentration upon survey and experimental research and the preference for quantitative data and statistical analysis . . . created a clear hierarchy of methods" that squeezed out other methodological approaches. Moreover, research methods texts used "to train the new generation of communication researchers concentrated almost entirely on survey, experimental, and statistical techniques" (Delia, 1987, p. 71). However, in recent years this powerful quantitative outlook has been modified somewhat and qualitative methodologies have been accepted as valid. Nevertheless, the quantitative approach remains powerful and the largest influence in the communications research field. Communication research, along with research in disciplines such as psychology, sociology, and political science, is squarely in the mainstream social science tradition, a tradition based on the Newtonian Mechanical World Paradigm.

Given what we know about the changes in thinking that result from postmodern culture, we must now question the very foundations of communication research. We must resist being "swept along by historical forces beyond [our] influence . . . the convincing appearance of social research is a warning to be cautious . . . laws explaining behavior are porous and prediction is perilous" in contemporary culture (Shipman, 1997, p. 23).

Communication opinion leaders have defined the field upon which researchers may work, and they have defined it quite precisely. A common definition of "communication science" is the following: "Communication science seeks to understand the production, processing, and effects of symbol and signal systems by developing testable theories, containing lawful generalizations, that explain phenomena associated with production, processing, and effects" (Berger & Chaffee, 1987a, p. 17). Setting aside for a moment the somewhat fuzzy and circular qualities of this definition, it should be noted that "most scholars in the discipline see a relatively close fit between their research and the view [the] definition advances" (Berger & Chaffee, p. 17). Still, there are some researchers "engaged in communication inquiry whose symbolic output of individuals or the media, for example, are not doing communication *science*," because their work is not "derived from any scientific theory." Further, "researchers whose job it is to make ethical or moral judgments about the communicative conduct of persons or institutions are not communication scientists" according to the earlier definition. "Neither are reformists who seek to change public policies" nor "analysts who seek to explain individual communication events in their own terms, without recourse to broader theoretical principles" (Berger & Chaffee, p. 17). In other words, a relatively small number of communication social scientists, all of them apparently following mainstream social science thinking, have defined the communication research field according to what they do, and since they conform to this definition, they are the sole arbiters of what constitutes appropriate research activity. This is intellectual thuggery. It is this narrow view of what communication science is, and the limits on knowledge gathering as a result of it that postmodernists reject as inappropriate and self-serving.

A NEW RESEARCH OUTLOOK

"There is little doubt that the human sciences are engaged in an extended and sometimes vociferous debate about research paradigms and methods" (Lincoln, 1998, p. 315). "If, for instance, as the postmodernists tell us, there is no single, ultimate reality on which social science must or can converge, then we are under some obligation to collect various versions of reality (or social constructions of reality)" (Lincoln, p. 317). As Leshan and Margenau (1982) argue, "we simply cannot have only one set of principles about how reality works" (p. 21). Lyotard (1984) holds that "scientific knowledge is a kind of discourse," but it does "not represent the totality of knowledge; it has always existed in addition to, and in competition and conflict with," other kinds of knowledge (pp. 3, 7).

It will not be easy to establish a new way of doing research, or even to modify some of the ways research is presently done. Current methods and practices are heavily ingrained in academic departments and the scholarly journals. Individuals who do research and those who hold powerful positions as editors of scholarly journals, together with those who claim research as their turf in academic departments, will not likely be willing to accept much change in the way things are done. This is a natural response. Although change is a universal constant, many people are unwilling to accept change if it means they must modify their own lives significantly. Nevertheless, change is sometimes thrust upon us, and we should often view it as positive, not negative.

"Postmodernism is Western civilization's best attempt to date to critique its own most fundamental assumptions, particularly those assumptions that constitute reality, subjectivity, research, and knowledge" (Scheurich, 1997, p. 2). Present communication/social science research attempts "to derive rigorous scientific rules for creating a one-to-one correspondence between what reality is and how it is represented in research so that the representation is untainted by researcher bias . . ." (Scheurich, p. 29). Present social science research, commonly called *positivism*, elevates science as the sole source of absolute truth. "For positivists, the rules for knowing (the positivist epistemology) guarantee or warrant the fact that the research representations of reality truly represent reality" (Scheurich, p. 29). Postmodernists feel this is wrongheaded because in contemporary culture, "reality is a staged, social production" (Denzin, 1991, p. ix), it is not really possible to eliminate researcher bias, and absolute truth probably does not exist.

Postmodernists see present research methodologies as mere *metanarratives*. According to Lyotard, metanarratives are "those universal guiding principles and mythologies which once seemed to control, delimit, and interpret all the diverse forms of discursive activity in the world" (Connor, 1989, p. 8). Lyotard urges us to be suspicious of metanarratives. They are, after all, just ways people have of organizing and deriving meaning from experience, and there is no clear evidence that any one metanarrative is better at doing this than any other. "Master narratives, once called 'theories,' . . . are now viewed as 'stories,' grand tales told about social life and linked with the perspectives and interests of their storytellers" (Gubrium & Holstein, 1997, p. 76).

It is easy to see how this concept works in communications research. Take, for example, the popular mass communications theory called *agenda setting*. This theory, based on the work of McCombs and Shaw (1972), suggests that although the media do not tell us what to think, they do tell us what to think about. In other words, when the media present an event, they influence the audience to see that event as important. This theory has been widely accepted by mass communication researchers and studies based on this theory (or some often obscure aspect of it) are published regularly. Postmodernists would call agenda setting "a grand tale" that tells us little of importance about the nature and quality of an individual's media experience and whether there are differences in thinking among media consumers, what these differences are, and what they mean, but it tells a lot about why the theory is so popular—it validates the work of mass communication researchers. What better way to gain acceptance of one's work than to present a story that purports to offer insight into the very work one is doing? The same criticism can be leveled, of course, at any media theory. They are all "master narratives"—stories told about media and tied to the perceptions and interests of the storyteller.

This is not necessarily a bad thing if we put it in perspective. We should acknowledge the conflict of interest here—between the "theory" and the interests of those proposing and "studying" the theory—and acknowledge the limits of any story that tries to explain or capture reality. For postmodernists, "the possibility of certainty must be regarded skeptically, if not rejected outright." Postmodernists doubt "the possibility of any totalizing or exhaustive theories or explanations" (Gubrium & Holstein, 1997, p. 75).

Nevertheless, a new research outlook does not mean that we are throwing out all the present ways we have of doing research, of conducting systematic investigations that attempt to answer questions we have about communication. But postmodern culture demands that we keep up with the times. Our methods and practices should be appropriate to the cultural times in which we live. This means realizing that a totally scientific world view might not be "an adequate guide for living life or for managing a [postmodern] society" (Harman, 1988, p. 122). After all, there have been some "very real changes in Western societies over the last thirty years" (Ashley, 1994, pp. 55–56). "The appropriate reason for changing our outlook is not to create a better world or save the one we have. It is to see more clearly things as they are. All other considerations are secondary" (Smith, 1989, p. 210).

Postmodern approaches essentially "dispute the underlying assumptions of mainstream social science and its research product . . ."(Rosenau, 1992, p. 3), so a new research approach might, for example, focus "on what has been taken for granted, what has been neglected . . . the irrational, the insignificant, the repressed . . . the rejected, the marginal, the accidental . . . all that which the modern age has never cared to understand in any particular detail, with any sort of specificity" (Rosenau, p. 8; Nelson, 1987, p. 217; Pfeil, 1988). Postmodernists often define everything as text and seek to "locate" meaning rather than to "discover" it. They rarely "reject, "but see themselves as "being concerned with," or "interested in" something (Rosenau, 1992, p. 8). A postmodern approach would involve a "coming together of elements from a number of different, often conflicting orientations." It might use some aspects of structuralism, romanticism, existentialism, hermeneutics, Marxism, critical theory, even positivism, among others. But it would not adopt any of these orientations as the one and only way to examine and understand cultural phenomena. In short, a postmodern approach would resist "the arbitrary imposition of any singular, systemic, point of view" but would accept "different, even contradictory perspectives" (Rosenau, p. 13). Research would no longer be a search for "truth," but rather a search for "clarity."

All this might seem to suggest changes that would be too extreme, too disruptive to research activity to be useful or meaningful. While one could take an extreme approach in applying postmodern thinking to research activities, such an approach might not be the best way to bring about positive change. There is disagreement among postmodernists about how much change is necessary, or to be a bit more specific, how much modification of current methods is needed to put research in step with contemporary culture. This disagreement hinges on one's worldview. *Skeptical postmodernists* have a rather negative, gloomy outlook on most aspects of contemporary culture. They often feel that fragmentation, disintegration, meaninglessness, and vagueness characterize life in contemporary culture.

On the other hand, *affirmative postmodernists* have a more hopeful, more optimistic view of the present age (Rosenau, 1992, p. 15). Affirmatives seek to *revise* rather than dismiss modern epistemology and methodology. They want to retain reason and rationality to some degree (Rosenau, pp. 172–173). It is this affirmative postmodern approach that will characterize the methods detailed in the coming chapters. In other words, our new research outlook will revise some of the present research methodologies and offer new approaches in an attempt to include postmodern thinking in mainstream communication/social science research activity. This would result in "a postmodern social science that would be broad-gauged and descriptive rather than predictive and policy-oriented." It would recognize the richness of difference in the culture and encourage interpretation. It would recognize personal meaning, but would not impose this meaning on others (Hirschman, 1987). It would draw its methods from a number of different orientations, but would not present any method or set of methods, or any set of philosophies, as the only ones able to locate and understand contemporary cultural phenomena.

People have many questions about communication. But a research study often begins with a single question about communication or an issue that you are curious about or something you have seen or heard and wish to know more about. One of the ways to answer the questions we have is to conduct a research study. A properly conducted research study often provides us with real-world evidence that can be used to answer our questions. Such real-world evidence is usually more persuasive than one's gut feeling about something.

POSTMODERN APPLICATION OF RESEARCH RESULTS

Interpreting research results in a postmodern environment will not be easy. The tendency of most researchers will be to place a study's results in the traditional social science paradigm. Since postmodernists believe this paradigm no longer holds, you will need to resist the impulse to do the following:

- generalize your study's findings to a larger audience;
- suggest that your findings represent absolute truth or a firm reality;
- connect your findings to any theory purporting to offer definitive explanations of any aspect of media or communication; or
- imply that your study's findings provide more than a temporary answer to any media or communication question.

Postmodern culture requires us to ask different questions about research results. The questions offered as research guidelines in Chapter 3 provide a starting place for interpreting research results in contemporary culture. We might ask the following questions about the research results:

- What do these results tell us about what we need to know in a rapidly changing world?
- Do the results help us see things more clearly as they are?
- What else needs to be explained or understood as a result of this research?
- Do the results show a particular reality or more than one reality?
- Do the results highlight the "richness of difference" in the culture?
- Are aspects of media or culture marginalized or ignored by the results?
- How are the results of this study related to or dependent on other things about communication that we know and observe in the culture?

Clearly, it may be difficult to provide answers to these questions. But the answers may well serve to indicate a particular quality (or several qualities) of life, communication, and experience with media in today's culture. If postmodernists are correct, you can expect to find ambiguity, discontinuity, multiple realities, and the like in a study's results.

It might be helpful to think of your study (and its results) as a picture, a snapshot, if you will. Taking a picture freezes a bit of life and experience in time. However, once that moment has been captured, it cannot occur exactly again. For example, if you and two friends are on vacation in New York and you take a picture of your friends near a tree in Central Park, you have captured that particular moment, and that moment only. Less than one second after the picture was taken, all sorts of things have changed. Your friends have changed their body positions and expressions, there may be different people or vehicles in the background, and even the position of the leaves on the tree has changed. You can take another picture that is somewhat like the previous one, but not exactly like it. In the same way, a research study is but a snapshot in time and is useful only to the extent that it tells something about the moment in time when it was done. You would not look at a picture taken on your vacation and claim that particular situation exists now. You should not look at a research study's results and say that, even though the data were gathered sometime ago, the results tell us what is presently going on.

THE COMMUNICATION PROCESS

Communication is usually an interactive process. People use and often interact with media; people interact with other people. Understanding the communication process is important if you are to conduct a research study that answers your questions about communication. There are several communication models in the scholarly literature. Some of these are quite complex, because, after all, communication is itself complex. But for our purposes, a simple communication model should provide enough information for us to understand the basic nature of communication.

Consider the four-step communication model in Figure 2.1. An originator sends a message through a medium to a receiver. This is really communication reduced to its simplest terms. It applies to all communication activities. If one student stops another student in the hall to ask about an upcoming class, one student (the originator) begins the conversation by asking a question (the message) which moves through the air (the medium) to the other student (the receiver). In a telephone conversation, we still have an originator (the one who placed the call) and a receiver (the one who answered the call), but the medium is different (telephone line or through-the-air cell phone signal), and, of course, the message can be almost anything.

This simple model can be easily applied to media. A newspaper, for example, contains a number of messages in the form of news stories, features, cartoons, photographs, and so on. The newspaper itself is the originator of these messages, although it may be the receiver of messages from reporters as part of an earlier communication process. The newspaper's medium is the printed page, and the receiver is the individual who reads the paper.

For purposes of designing a research project, one should consider each element of this communication model carefully. How the originator is defined or determined is important. An originator can be an individual working alone or for a large or small group, or the originator can be an organization. The characteristics of the message are important. A message may be oral, written, broadcast, or electronic. The medium, or the method or way in which the message is sent, can be something as common as the air (in personal conversation) or as complex as the Internet (electronic pulses in cyberspace). The receiver, like the originator, can be an individual—alone or part

Originator ⇒ Message ⇒ Medium ⇒ Receiver

FIGURE 2.1   A Communication Model

of a group—or the receiver can be a group of almost any size, and, of course, the receiver of some messages can be a mass audience.

RESEARCH ETHICS

Ethics can be defined as moral principles for living and making decisions. For most people, ethics simply means doing the right thing. But doing the right thing in postmodern culture is often difficult. For one thing, a part of any good ethical system is the pursuit of truth. Many postmodernists do not believe absolute truth exists, and even if it does, they feel we may not be able to grasp it. Postmodernists are often fond of noting that there are many truths in the culture, perhaps as many truths as there are individuals. Still, many people recognize that ethics deals with honesty and integrity as well as their reactions to a host of social and political issues such as abortion, gay marriage, gun control, and the like.

However, doing the right thing has rarely been rewarded throughout history. Yet we often expect progress from one cultural period to the next. Take the delivery of mail, for example. No one would be happy today with the old pony express mail delivery system. Although we often take it for granted, we expect daily mail service to our homes. Times have changed. As cultural periods have come and gone, we have made significant progress in most areas of life. In terms of the quality of life, we are certainly better off than we were 100 years ago. But are we more ethical than we were 100 years ago? Probably not. A highly competitive, self-absorbed, technology-rich culture has little time for ethics. As postmodern philosopher Michel Foucault noted, power is the operative force in the culture, and power results from economic and technological success. Many people use Machiavelli's "the ends justify the means" philosophy to achieve success in postmodern culture. But Machiavelli's philosophy is based on cleverness, viciousness, and surface appearances. These qualities bear little relationship to ethics.

It is little wonder, then, that most people don't worry much about doing the right thing because such behavior is almost never rewarded in postmodern culture. Bad behavior is regularly rewarded. For example, numerous celebrities and more than a few news makers have engaged in inappropriate and/or illegal activities, have been the subjects of continuous news stories or well-publicized trials, and—whether punished or not—have emerged from their situations to embrace multimillion-dollar book, movie, or television deals. Good behavior is rarely rewarded in a similar fashion. People recognize this and are often inclined to step over the ethical line because it is so widely done and because acting ethically has little cash value in postmodern culture. Check your daily newspaper for reports of individuals who were rewarded for their ethical behavior. You won't find many such stories. The one or two you might find during any given week will likely be lost among the many others reporting the financial rewards that have accrued to those who have acted inappropriately.

Do researchers face ethical problems in doing their work? Absolutely! Ethics should apply to all aspects of life and all human activity, including research. Being an ethical researcher is not all that difficult. An ethical researcher should be honest and show respect.

Let's take respect first. Respect in research often means dealing in a fair and straightforward way with the people involved in a research project. More than a few research methods require the researcher to ask people questions, conduct interviews, or interact with them in other ways. An ethical researcher may ask individuals to participate in a project, but should never force them to participate. Those who do participate should have their privacy protected, unless they otherwise agree to having their names or other specific information about them detailed in the project report. Protecting privacy is fairly easy. While a researcher may know a great deal about the participants in his/her project, this information should be kept confidential. Papers, notes, or other documents that could identify participants should be protected.

Additionally, participants in a research project should be informed about the purpose of the project and should be asked to give their informed consent to participate in it. A sample informed consent form is presented in Figure 2.2. Researchers should avoid lying to individuals in order to get them to participate. Researchers should follow through on their promises of confidentiality. If some aspects of the research are withheld from participants in order to avoid participant bias or withheld so as not to jeopardize the project in some other way, researchers should debrief participants, that is, fully explain what was withheld and why, and when the project has been concluded.

The second ethical concern for researchers is honesty. Honesty in research requires that the researcher adhere to a set of rules. These rules are appropriate for use in postmodern culture; although postmodernists often resist rules, the ones listed here can be used with confidence that you are acting ethically:

1. Select a research design (plan) that is appropriate for the project.
2. Faithfully carry out the research design.
3. Take accurate notes; record data or other information correctly; preserve and keep this information confidential.
4. Avoid tossing out information that you disagree with.
5. Do not change the study design to fit the results.
6. Do not change the results to fit a project sponsor's needs.
7. Write a clear and concise report about the project.
8. Do not plagiarize the work of other researchers.
9. Do not attach your name to a project in which you did not participate.

These rules appear to be forthright and reasonable and not all that difficult to follow. However, more than a few researchers have admitted to violating one or more of the rules. A *Washington Post* report in the summer of 2005 indicated that while "few scientists fabricate results from scratch or

Research Project Name:
Binge Drinking Among College Students

Project Sponsor:
ABC University and Professor L. V. Baber

Project Purpose:
To determine the extent of binge drinking among college students at ABC University

Project Activity:
A questionnaire will be distributed to a random selection of students at ABC University; after completing the questionnaire, students will participate in a focus group session where the issue of binge drinking will be thoroughly explored.

Privacy Issues:
Complete confidentially will be maintained for those participating in the project; individual participants will not be identified; questionnaire responses and focus group comments will be reported as overall summaries.

Participant Consent:
By signing this statement, I acknowledge that I understand the general nature of the research project and that I am a willing participant. I have been given the opportunity to decline participation without penalty.

_____   _____

           Participant Signature   Date

_____

           Project Director Signature

FIGURE 2.2   Sample Informed Consent Form

flatly plagiarize the work of others . . . a surprising number engage in troubling degrees of fact-bending or deceit." The report was based on a survey of scientific behavior funded by the National Institutes of Health and involved 3,247 researchers.

If you are looking for a more detailed treatment of a researcher's ethical responsibilities, the American Psychological Association (APA) has an ethical code worth reading. It can be accessed through the association's Web site at www.apa.org.

FEDERAL REGULATIONS

In order to insure that participants in research projects are not harmed, the U.S. Department of Health and Human Services (HHS) developed a set of guidelines that require research projects to be submitted for review to safeguard the rights of individuals involved. Institutional review boards (IRBs) were established at many hospitals, medical schools, universities, research centers, and other institutions. These boards meet regularly and examine the details of research projects for problems relating to human subjects. A few projects are exempt from these reviews, particularly those involving classroom (academic) learning/instructional projects or those using existing public data. Each IRB operates in a slightly different way. If the research project you propose involves human subjects and your organization has a review board, you will have to submit your proposal to the board for review before you carry out the research study. The board may want to see an outline of your project and whether you intend to provide participants with an informed consent form, and so forth.

Some communication researchers are annoyed by the IRB requirements. They point out that the kinds of research they do have been done for more than 50 years and that there has not been an instance of anyone being harmed by a survey or a focus group. Still, the law is the law, and you should comply with the rules and regulations for research set down by your institution.

REVIEW QUESTIONS

1. What is the Mechanical World Paradigm and what are its characteristics?
2. What is the Parable of the Elephant and how does it support the notion that the Mechanical World Paradigm is not appropriate as a fundamental basis for communication research?
3. What is the "new research outlook" proposed in this chapter?
4. What are metanarratives and why are postmodernists skeptical of them?
5. What is the difference between skeptical and affirmative postmodernism?
6. Explain each part of the four-step communication model.
7. What steps should a researcher take to insure that his/her research project is being conducted in an ethical fashion?
8. Why are some research projects required to have the approval of an IRB?

SUGGESTED ACTIVITIES

1. Find examples of events or situations that appear to contribute to disorder in the culture. Then find examples of events or situations that appear to contribute to order in the culture. Based on your observations, would you say the entropy law results in order or disorder? Wait a week and find additional examples of order and disorder in the culture. Has your opinion changed about the entropy law?
2. Develop a timeline that illustrates the development and growth of communication research.
3. Find precise definitions for the following terms:

   rationalism   romanticism
   behaviorism   hermeneutics
   structuralism   critical theory
   positivism

4. Contact the IRB on your campus. Ask about the requirements and responsibilities of a person doing communication research. Report your findings to the class.

CHAPTER 3

Getting Started

*I admit that twice two makes four is an excellent
thing, but if we are to give everything its due,
twice two makes five is sometimes a very charming
thing too.*

—FYODOR DOSTOEVSKY

It is not the purpose of this text to abandon all the present ways we have
of doing research. Our goal is to modify some present methods and add
new ones so that research can be more revealing and useful in helping us
see and understand our world. With this in mind, let's take a look at some
key terms and concepts.

BASIC TERMINOLOGY

Researchers often speak of their project's *methodology*. What is methodology?
Methodology is simply "how one goes about studying whatever is of interest; it relates to the process of inquiry, but does not tell us what to expect to
find" (Rosenau, 1992, p. 116).

Current social science methodology, at least in communication studies,
is often placed in one of two general categories: quantitative or qualitative.
Quantitative methodologies usually result in numerical data that can be organized and analyzed using mathematical operations. Qualitative data tend
to be language-based and do not lend themselves easily to mathematical
models, but do lend themselves to other sorts of analysis. It seems useful to
retain these categories as general descriptions of the type of information derived from research activities. You will find that Section II of this text reflects
this approach.

Let's first look at some terms and concepts used in quantitative research. We may use some of these in the methodology chapters (Chapters 5
through 10), or we may later ignore some of these terms and concepts if they
have no application to a particular research project.

In most studies, researchers concern themselves with variables. A *variable* is an event, an experience, or some other phenomenon that a researcher wishes to examine. Variables can often be measured, and some can be manipulated. Take, for example, the temperature in a college classroom. Let's say, for the purpose of illustration, that the room temperature is 73 degrees. The instructor can, by adjusting the thermostat on the wall, either raise or lower the temperature in the room. Room temperature is therefore a variable that can be both measured and manipulated. Researchers call this an *independent variable.* The student reaction to the raising or lowering of the temperature is also a variable. If the temperature is increased in the room, students may begin to sweat; some might doze off; others might remove a sweater or jacket. These behaviors can be observed and depend on an individual's reaction to the increased temperature. The response to the increase in temperature is a *dependent variable*, that is, it depends on how high the temperature goes and how an individual responds as a result.

Variables need precise definitions. We need to be sure our measurements and observations are accurate. In order to do this, we must be quite sure that we are seeing what we think we are seeing. Do not depend on common definitions to provide you with the specific information you need. For example, some terms in use in the language these days have several meanings, or at least different meanings for different people. If a student says he/she is "burned out," does that mean that he/she is physically exhausted by schoolwork? Intellectually drained? Overly stressed by a tight work and class schedule? Annoyed with his/her classes to the point of disinterest? A researcher must, therefore, provide a precise definition, called an *operational* definition, for each of the variables involved in a research study.

In order to measure variables, quantitative researchers have employed a number of measurement methods down through the years. One of the most common is the 1 to 10 scale. Almost everyone is familiar with the way this works. It is often used in real life. More than one young man, returning from a blind date, has been asked by his roommates to rate his date's looks and personality. If the young man was extremely well-satisfied with his date's appearance and the date was enjoyable, he might say, "She's a 9." Of course, if things did not go well on the date and expectations were not met, he might say, "She's a 1." This sort of female-rating activity derives from the 1979 movie *10*, starring Bo Derek and Dudley Moore. Derek was considered by many at the time to be the perfect dream-girl.

The 0 to 100 scale is another measurement tool that has been widely used. This is much more familiar to most people in the United States. Our money is based on this scale. One dollar is 100 pennies. We know that an item priced at 75 cents costs three times as much as an item priced at 25 cents.

Probably one of the most popular ways to measure variables in social science research is to use a Likert Scale. Developed by psychologist Rensis Likert, this scale is usually a five- or seven-step set of responses expressing

various degrees of agreement or disagreement to a list of declarative statements. Look at the following example:

Statement:

    I am excited about taking this research methods class.

    _____ Strongly agree (5)

    _____ Agree (4)

    _____ Neither agree nor disagree (3)

    _____ Disagree (2)

    _____ Strongly disagree (1)

A student would mark the response that best represents the level of his/her
excitement about the class. Quantitative researchers usually assign a numerical value to each response—noted in parentheses in the previous example—
in order that mathematical operations can be performed on the entire set of
responses to the item. A qualitative researcher, on the other hand, might ask
an open-ended question: "Are you excited about taking this research methods class? Why or why not?" A question of this sort would yield a verbal
response which could be compared to the verbal responses of others who
answered the question.

    There are other ways to measure responses to a question, of course.
Some research items require a simple "Yes" or "No" response from those
participating, but many researchers feel that these simple responses do not
provide enough information. Some researchers devise their own measurement systems, ones that fit their particular projects.

    Regardless of what type of measurement a researcher uses, he/she is
faced with several questions about the measurement process: Does the measurement scale actually measure what it is supposed to measure? How do I
know? Does the scale provide consistent responses at different points in
time? How do I know? These issues relate to what researchers call *validity*
and *reliability*. For example, suppose you are engaging in target practice with
your favorite hunting rifle. Observing all safety rules, you take careful aim at
the center of the target and squeeze the trigger 10 times. You fire the same
number of shots at a second target. You retrieve the targets and examine
them. Look at the illustration in Figure 3.1.

    What conclusions can you draw? Well, your shots certainly missed the
target's bulls-eye, and all the shots are clustered in the upper right portion of
the target. In research terms, you could say that the gun (or your shooting of it)
had *reliability* because it hit the same part of the target on repeated occasions,
but that it did not have *validity* because it clearly missed the center of the target
where you were aiming (Brown, Amos, & Mink, 1975, pp. 107–108). Thus, reliability can be defined as *giving similar, consistent results for each use*. Validity can
be defined as *being true and accurate*. There are ways to assess reliability and
validity, and these will necessarily vary from one research method to another.

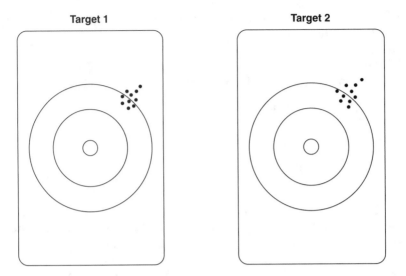

FIGURE 3.1   Reliability and Validity Illustrated

Some researchers feel that a research project should be connected in some way to a _theory_. A theory is simply a statement or a set of statements that specifies the relationship among variables and provides us with a concept or set of concepts about how reality works. Of course, we are talking here about current social science research practices. Postmodernists are not generally fond of theory since they believe that reality is itself variable and probably socially constructed. A theory is, therefore, arbitrary and of little use in explaining anything in today's postmodern culture.

RESEARCH GUIDELINES

Because postmodernists believe that mainstream social science methodologies no longer have the power to explain contemporary culture or to motivate positive change, we will need a new organizing principle and a set of guidelines to help focus our research. The old Newtonian Mechanical World Paradigm (MWP) will not always work in today's complex culture. The MWP's emphasis on control, mass production, standardization, and prediction is misplaced in today's culture where the second law of thermodynamics (entropy law) holds sway. In other words, science and reason are not the only avenues to reality in contemporary culture. The culture is not becoming more ordered, as the MWP suggests, but more disordered, as the entropy law suggests.

So here is the new organizing principle for communication research in the postmodern era: _the purpose of research is to help us see and understand the interrelatedness and interdependency of people, communication, and media in contemporary (postmodern) culture, a culture that is marked by discontinuity and_ *ambiguity*. Postmodern communication research does not advance new theories or make predictions. It acknowledges the difficulty, if not the impossibility, of conducting objective research, and it is more interested in exploring connections to larger social systems or issues than in observing and reporting behavior at the individual level. It may or may not make use of mathematical operations to assist in understanding what is happening.

This new research approach resembles, in several ways, the *systems view*. According to this particular approach, one "looks at the world in terms of the interrelatedness and interdependence of all phenomena—physical, biological, psychological, social, and cultural" (Capra, 1982, p. 47, 265). "A system can be defined as a collection of interrelated parts that work together by way of some driving process" (www.physicalgeography.net). This notion can be traced back to 1928 and Hungarian biologist Ludwig von Bertalanffy. He felt that Descartes's idea that "a system could be broken down into its individual components so that each component could be analyzed as an independent entity, and the components could be added in a linear (i.e., progressing from one stage to another) fashion to describe the totality of the system" was wrong; instead, a system is characterized *by the interactions of its components* (emphasis added) and the components probably do not progress in an orderly fashion from one stage to another (Walonick, n.d., para. 1).

However, there is presently "no well-established framework, either conceptual or institutional, that would accommodate the formulation of the new paradigm, but the outlines of such a framework are already being shaped" (Capra, 1982, p. 265). Applied to communication research, this means that we should be "gradually formulating a network of interlocking concepts and models . . . [that] will go beyond the conventional disciplinary distinctions . . . to describe different aspects of the multi-leveled, interrelated fabric of reality" (p. 265).

Here are some questions which can be used to guide communication research in today's postmodern culture:

- What do we need to know in an uncertain and rapidly changing world?
- What are the root causes of problems and how might they be solved?
- How can we more clearly see things as they are?
- What needs to be understood and explained?
- Can we find several versions of reality, or social constructions thereof?
- What can be said of the "richness of difference" in the culture?
- Can personal meaning be located and how is that meaning developed?
- What has been taken for granted, neglected, rejected, or otherwise ignored?
- What can be discovered about interrelatedness and interdependence, specifically as they relate to media and communication?

Of course, these are very broad, general questions. But if we are going to change some social science practices, we must replace a few mainstream "rules" with rules of our own. However, postmodernists would probably reject the notion of "rules" for research, so the questions just mentioned must be offered only as guidelines for doing communication research in a post-modern environment.

Since this text's approach is based essentially on affirmative postmod-ernism, some mainstream social science concepts and methods may be re-vised and put to good use. For example, we will retain reason and rationality to some degree; we may even submit some information to a few mathemati-cal operations just to see if such activity assists us in any way in achieving our goals. If the postmodernists are right and everything is indeed part of "a dynamic flow," of an interrelated and interdependent system, we should be able to see how our research contributes to an understanding of that system and flow.

REVIEW QUESTIONS

1. What does a researcher mean when he/she speaks of a project's "methodology?"
2. What is the difference between a qualitative methodology and a quantitative methodology?
3. Researchers often study and measure variables. Why are some called indepen-dent variables and others called dependent variables?
4. Why should each variable in a study have an operational definition?
5. Why are research questions which generate a simple "Yes" or "No" response often seen as inadequate?
6. What is the difference between reliability and validity? Why are both important for a research study?

## CHAPTER 4

Designing a Research Study

Scientific discovery consists in the interpretation for our own convenience of a system of existence which has been made with no eye to our convenience at all.

—NORBERT WIENER

A research design is simply a step-by-step plan for how a research study will be carried out. The plan is usually highly specific and includes all aspects of a project from the beginning research questions to the reporting of results. In order to assist you in designing a research study, a flowchart, or pictorial plan, has been developed to show you what to do and in what order (See Figure 4.1). Using the flowchart will help you design projects in a systematic fashion and will help you in gathering evidence that will answer the questions you have about media and communication.

THE FLOWCHART PROCESS

Let's take a look at each step in the flowchart. The flowchart begins by asking you to *state the problem or issue you wish to study*. This step is important because it asks you to put into words the aspect of communication you have an interest in studying. Different researchers will have different interests, of course, but whatever interests you should be the focus of your research study. The issue you select could be almost any issue relating to media or communication.

You are next asked to *state the problem or issue as a question or series of questions*. It will be the goal of the research study to answer these *research questions*. They are, in fact, the questions that guide the study and influence the method or methods used to answer them. How many questions do you need? That depends on the issue and what you want to know about that

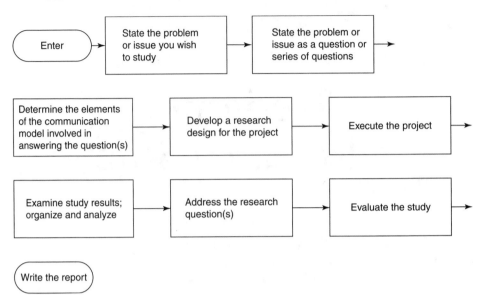

FIGURE 4.1   Research Flowchart

issue. One question might be enough, but many researchers find that a series of questions, say three or four, are often needed to fully address the concerns they have about the communication issues they are studying.

At this point in the flowchart process, it might be useful to consider *which element(s) of the communication model will be involved* in answering the research questions. At least one element of the communication model should be involved in your research study. For example, if you are interested in finding out what viewers think of television's reality shows, you'd want to gather information from television viewers who, in this case, are the *receivers* in the communication model. Of course, a study can involve more than one element in the model. You could, for example, compare news reports in newspapers and on television and you'd be involving the *medium* and *message* elements of the model.

The next step in the flowchart is both important and complex. You are asked to *develop a research design for the project.* As noted earlier, a research design is simply a step-by-step plan for conducting the study. This part of the process has a number of subparts, each of which must be faithfully carried out. These subparts are as follows:

- Discuss the problem.
- Search the literature.
- Revise the research question(s).
- Select a research method and justify your choice.
- Develop a detailed plan for employing the method.
- Handle logistical details.

Let's take a look at each of these important subparts. Proper attention to each of these is necessary to insure the success of the project.

Discuss the Problem

Discussing the problem with friends, colleagues, or others who might have an interest in the issue or problem you are studying may take the form of brainstorming and is intended to expand, or perhaps reduce, the concerns you have about the problem or issue. Hearing how others feel about the issue or what they think about the problem may help you focus your study.

Search the Literature

This is a necessary but often painful process. It involves visiting libraries, searching databases, and finding other sources for information on work that has been done by others and work that relates to the issue or problem you wish to study. Although some postmodernists feel it is not necessary "to build on the work of others," there are other important reasons for examining the work of others. First, if the project you envision has already been carried out by other researchers, and your research questions have already been answered, you may wish to reconsider your project. Some scholars do not think it useful to "reinvent the wheel," that is, to do a study that has already been done. You could, of course, repeat the study. A *replication*, as it is sometimes called, might reinforce the findings of the original study, or it might refute them, or it might in some other way modify them. Such a study could be useful. However, most researchers want to do a project that has not already been done; they want something unique and original, and only by searching the literature on your issue can you be sure that you have selected an area where you can make an original and unique contribution. Also, by examining what others have done, you can note the strengths and weaknesses of those studies and utilize that information in designing your own study. Here are some questions that you can use to guide your review of the literature:

- What research methods were used in previous studies on this issue or problem?
- What did previous studies find?
- What suggestions do the researchers make for further study?
- How does my proposed study fit in with others that have been done?
- What has not been investigated?

So far, so good, but exactly how does one go about searching the literature? Computers and the Internet have made this part of the process somewhat easier. You should begin by searching all available databases that might contain information on your problem or issue of interest. Obtain hard copies of studies that relate to your project. Keep a record of where you got each piece of information. This record is called a *reference citation* and it includes the following information: author, title of article, place and date of original publication (if first published elsewhere), URL (Web site) address, identification of Web site owner, and date of download. These elements are placed in specific order in a reference list which will become part of the final report. Information on reference style can be found in Section III of this text.

Your search in electronic databases should be as exhaustive as possible. Begin, of course, with LexisNexis, the newspaper database. But search business databases as well as those cataloging scholarly (academic) work. A university library's home page is a good place to begin. Often there will be links not only to the available databases, but also to other sources of information.

To find information of a general nature available on the World Wide Web (www), you can use a search engine, such as Google or Yahoo!. But you should be aware that not everything you find online is accurate information. A Web site is fairly easy to create, and all sorts of information can be posted on Web sites. But most of this information has not been examined by others for truthfulness and/or accuracy. If your author has a Web site, he could post information that says he is the great, great grandson of Thomas Edison. Not true, of course, but how would you know? The information would appear on the screen, and you would have no way of judging its accuracy. As you look at information online, you might ask yourself a few questions: Has this information likely been examined by others? Has this information been published first elsewhere and thus may have passed through the hands of editors or publishers? Is there any way for me to determine whether this information is accurate? If you are satisfied that the information you have is indeed accurate, then you may wish to include it in your review of the literature (with proper citation, of course).

When you have completed searching the databases for information on your issue of interest, your next stop is the library. Not all the information you need is available through your computer. You will need to visit a good library. Public libraries often have limited resources and limited holdings, so visit a university library. If you are a student, there is a library somewhere on campus. Find it and get acquainted with the various librarians who work there. Treat these professionals with respect; they may be useful to you if you have a question or are unable to find certain materials. If you are not a student, make arrangements to visit the nearest university library even if you have to drive several miles to get there. In a literature search, there is absolutely no substitute for the resources available at a good university library.

Once inside the library, the work really begins. The old card catalog system has been replaced in most libraries by an electronic library catalog. The library's holdings may be accessed at any one of a number of computer terminals, often scattered throughout the library. Searching the electronic catalog usually involves entering the name of an author or the title of a book. If you know this information, this is certainly the way to go. But in a usual search of the literature, you have no specific author or title information and must resort to a search using general terms or keywords. Entering a set of keywords relating to your communication issue or problem often yields a wealth of information, including the call number and location of books and other materials relating to your keywords. Some items listed may be peripheral in nature, but these can be easily ignored. Concentrate on those materials that you feel directly relate to the issue or problem you are preparing to study. Take complete notes which, in addition to the call number, include the author and title of the publication, as well as any other information that might appear in the library catalog.

It is now time for what some researchers call "donkey work." This is a reference to the work donkeys do in some parts of the world where they are used as "beasts of burden." The poor creatures are often loaded down with pounds and pounds of baggage and required to carry this baggage for many miles. Sometimes, when the animals seem disinclined to participate in this difficult work, they are struck repeatedly with a stick to encourage them to move on. It won't be quite like that for you in the library stacks, but you will most likely not have an easy time locating the books you need, collecting them, and then carrying them to a nearby table for closer examination. If you leave the electronic library catalog with a list of 12 books you think you need to look at, you will likely find half that many. Some of the books you need will be checked out, some may have been recently returned and are awaiting reshelving by library staff, some may have simply been misplaced on library shelves, others will have been lost or stolen. Not finding needed materials has discouraged more than a few researchers. If you do manage to find 6 of the 12 books you need, that's an armful, but you can manage to get them to a nearby table or study area and begin to examine them for information useful to your project. If you are extremely lucky, you might find all 12 books. And, yes, it will be a struggle to get them all to the table, but, like the donkey, you should persevere.

If the books are from the circulating collection, you may wish to check out those that are of particular interest and take them with you for study and examination. However, it is possible to skim many of the books quickly and identify what you need from them. You can take notes or copy whole sections of a book. Most libraries have several photocopy machines available for just this purpose. Reference books do not circulate, so information from them should be photocopied. Again, remember to keep a careful record of the authors, titles, pages, and publication data of each source from which you gather information.

Don't expect to complete your library work in one trip. It will likely take several trips to complete the task. You may have to order some materials through interlibrary loan, and this process takes some time. No matter how many books or articles you find, it will not be possible to examine them all at one sitting. Plan on doing your library work over several days. Remember to look at the reference lists of those books and articles you find useful. These lists will lead you to other sources of information. Take frequent breaks and approach the task with a positive attitude. You will always learn something in the process.

Once all the materials have been examined, you should write a brief summary of what you have discovered in the literature search. This summary will later become part of the project report. To give you an example of what this summary might look like, here is a snippet from a literature review examining representation and image of the elderly in prime-time television programming.

> One study noted that older men were represented in proportion to the population statistics at the time, but that older women were under represented. The image of men was considered "generally favorable" (Tycer, 1977, p. 573). This study's methodology seems questionable. The researcher failed to establish firm criteria for identifying elderly people, and used relatively vague attribute pairs such as "nice/awful" to measure image.
>
> White (1974) examined 2741 characters in prime time television programming and reported a negative image of the elderly as well as an under representation of elders overall (4.9%). Only 40% of older characters were portrayed in a positive manner, described as successful, happy, and good.
>
> Kline (1975) examined the portrayal of elderly characters in both programming and commercials, and reported negative representations in both. The elderly appeared in true proportion in commercials (10.6%) to existing census figures, but appeared in a slightly lower proportion (8.3%) in programming. No figures support the under representation of older women in either instance. The authors found the elderly to be one-dimensional, undeveloped characters.
>
> Several studies have indicated that the elderly are slightly over represented in daytime serial dramas, often called soap operas (Colby, 1981; Brooks, 1982; Michaels, 1982). Still, the overall image of the elderly was shown to be . . . .

Notice the way in which a study's findings are reported and the way in which those findings are tied to a reference citation. Of course, a complete reference citation for each of the studies examined would appear in the reference list.

Revise the Research Question(s)

Once the literature has been searched and similar and/or useful studies have been identified, read, and summarized, you are ready to take a second look at your research question(s). It is possible that, given what you now know about work that has already been done in the area and where that work has both succeeded and fallen short, you may need to revise your research question(s). You may need to broaden them, or refocus them, or in some other way sharpen them to meet your specific needs. You may want to add a question or eliminate one. Take some time to examine and revise your questions before continuing.

Select a Research Method

With the research questions clearly stated, it is now time to determine which method of gathering the information or evidence—or *data*, as it is sometimes called—you need to answer the questions is most appropriate for the study. You will need to acquaint yourself with each of the methods described in this book in order to make a proper decision. Examine each method and evaluate its usefulness in gathering the information you need. Researchers typically use only one method, but some projects might require the use of a second method. You'll want to carefully consider which method, when properly applied, will provide the needed information and enable you to provide clear and convincing answers to your research questions. You might be wondering exactly what you will be recording, in other words, what are data? Data "can be bits and pieces of almost anything. They do not necessarily have to be expressed in numbers. Data can come in the form of words, images, impressions, gestures, or tones which represent real events or reality as it is seen . . ." (Qualitative Social Science Methodology).

Once you have selected a method for gathering information, you need to justify the selection of that method. Why was the method selected? How will it provide the information you need? How is it better than the other methods? As part of the justification, you should acknowledge both the strengths and weaknesses of the method. No research method is perfect, and no research study is perfect. Each method and each study have limitations, and these should be recognized.

Develop a Detailed Plan

Developing a detailed plan for employing the selected research method is the next step in the flowchart. Think of this plan as a road map, if you will. It should clearly explain how, when, and where the method will be applied. Be as specific as possible. Provide enough information so that if for some reason you were unable to conduct the project, a friend could take your plan and, without explanation or revision, carry forward the project.

Handle the Logistics

The final step in designing a research study is handling the logistical details. Logistics may be defined as gathering, organizing, and placing the people and materials needed to carry the project forward. The key to logistical activity is the budget. A budget is simply a list of anticipated expenditures. Every research study should have a budget. If you are a student, it will be helpful to know about how much it will cost you to complete the project. If you are working in the outside world, your project may be funded by your company, or it may have external funding. In any case, it is a good practice to develop a budget for a research study. Depending on the nature of your study, your budget may have some or all of the major categories of anticipated expenses: personnel, materials, facilities and equipment, travel, and miscellaneous.

If your study requires another person or two, often called *research assistants*, to assist you in conducting the study, it would be appropriate to pay these individuals for their services. In some cases, particularly if there is external funding, you may want to include an amount for yourself, because, after all, you are the principal researcher for the project, and the one who will do the most work on it.

It is not likely that any project can be completed without some materials. Materials, in this case, usually means office supplies, that is, paper, pencils, paper clips, staplers, scotch tape, and the like. Some projects may require the purchase of current or back issues of newspapers or magazines, or the purchase of blank videotapes, CDs or DVDs, or the like. Most items in the materials category are consumables, that is, they will be "used up" by the project.

Your research study may require specialized equipment, such as CD/DVD players, VCRs, televisions, radios, computers and monitors, film projectors, and so forth. These items are usually rented, but there is, of course, almost always a rental fee involved. In terms of facilities, are special rooms needed for the project? Would a conference room or a classroom be more appropriate? Is there a fee for room rental? Are telephone or Internet connections needed?

Some projects may require travel, and travel is expensive. Airfare, hotels, tips, and meals will add many dollars to a budget. Finally, it is always a good idea to have a modest "miscellaneous" line item for those unanticipated expenses sure to present themselves.

How much money should you allow for each of the categories in your budget? This will, of course, depend on the nature of the research study and on current prices for goods and services in the outside world. Your figures do not have to be 100% accurate. After all, a budget is only an estimate of what it will cost to complete the project. But the estimate should be as close to the real costs as possible. It may be necessary to inquire about certain costs, such as airfare, hotel arrangements, room rental, or telephone service. But some other costs can be reasonably estimated without a lot of trouble. Presented next is a budget from a student who proposed a survey project to study binge drinking on her campus.

Personnel:

     Three research assistants, $30 per day, five days $450

Facilities/Equipment:

     Computer lab rental, use of Excel & Word 100

     Photocopy machine (300 copies @ $0.30/copy) 90

     Classroom for planning & organizing 0

Materials/Supplies:

     Paper, pencils, pens, etc. 50

Miscellaneous:

     Food for research assistants (soda, pizza, sandwiches, etc.) 85

Total Budget for Proposed Project $775

Seven hundred seventy-five dollars is a lot of money for many of us, particularly for college students. Few students could afford to carry out a project that costs that much. In the outside world, projects may cost many times more than that. In any case, the previous example should give you an idea that research is neither free nor cheap. The student who presented the budget in the previous example was only required—as part of an assignment—to design a research study and propose a budget. She did not have to carry out the project. However, some graduate students, particularly those whose graduate work requires a thesis, may indeed have to conduct a research project at their own expense.

You can easily see from the budget that part of the logistics process will involve employing research assistants, arranging for a computer lab and a classroom, obtaining the necessary office materials, and so forth. Do not neglect this part of the research design. A project cannot be successfully completed unless someone has handled all the details.

Execute the Project

If you have carefully designed the project according to the guidelines discussed so far in this chapter, you should have little difficulty carrying it out. You already have a step-by-step process to follow. This means, for example, that if your project involves interviewing individuals, you should begin the interviewing process. If your project involves examining historical documents, then you should begin that examination. Remember to take good notes. Accurately and completely recording the information you gather is important. This information is, in fact, the evidence that you acquire in the research process. This evidence will be used to answer the research questions; therefore, you must keep excellent records.

Record keeping is not as easy as it might appear. There are many different ways to preserve the information you collect. The way you select to record information may depend on the nature of your project and your own personal preferences. For example, if your project involves interviewing individuals, you might wish to consider using a tape recorder or a video recorder so that you can replay the interview sessions and check to see whether you have gleaned all the information you need from them. Of course, you'd have to get the participants to agree to having the sessions recorded, but this is not often a problem if the individuals have consented to be interviewed in the first place. If your project involves examining and evaluating printed materials, you may wish to take notes in a notebook of some sort. This is where a researcher's preferences are important. Some researchers use spiral-bound notebooks; others prefer using legal pads. Some projects will require one or more sheets of paper to be filled out by the research participants, by research assistants, or by others. These sheets should be handled carefully and systematically stored (perhaps in a three-ring binder) for later examination and analysis.

For many researchers these days, pencil-and-paper record keeping has been replaced by computer record keeping. Desktop computers can be used, of course, but most research work will be done away from your desktop location. This means that data must often be recorded by hand or some other means and then typed into a file on your desktop. If you have a laptop, you can usually take it with you to almost all research locations and type the information you gather directly into a file. Remember, too, that electronic equipment can be a bit touchy at times—hard drives can crash or important files can be mistakenly deleted—so keep a backup copy of all your research files. Tips on recording and preserving the information you collect can be found in each of the methods chapters (Chapters 5 through 10) which follow in this book.

Organize and Analyze Study Results

There are several ways to organize and analyze your study's results. These ways vary according to the research project and the nature of the information you have collected. Each of the methods chapters (Chapters 5 through 10) in this book has a section on organizing and analyzing your project data.

Address the Research Question(s)

Once you have a grasp of what your data mean, you can answer the research questions you posed at the beginning of the project. Your answer to each question should be supported by the evidence you have collected. If you are unable to answer a question because the information is insufficient to provide an answer, do not be afraid to say so. If the answer to a question also raises additional questions that need answers, do not hesitate to pose these new questions so that other researchers can see what work remains to be done in the area of your study.

Evaluate the Study

Although you are nearing the end of the flowchart, do not neglect the final two steps in the process. Evaluating the study means you should take a critical look at all aspects of the study and point out the project's strengths and weaknesses. What was done that was successful? What was not done that perhaps should have been done? What difficulties did you encounter in carrying out the project? Were the logistical details handled well? Was the budget sufficient to meet the needs of the project? What new questions were raised by the project that might inspire additional research?

Write the Report

This final step in the research process is an extremely important one. If you had internal or external funding for the project, the individuals who provided the money will want to know about the project and its findings. These findings may be used by them to make economic or policy decisions. A final report is important for others who might be doing research in your area of interest. These individuals will need to know what you did, how you did it, what you found, and what it all means. The best way to communicate this information is in a written report.

How do you write a final report? That often depends on the nature of the project, the report's intended audience, and the researcher's writing abilities. Nevertheless, at a minimum, a final report should have the following sections: title page, introduction, research questions, literature summary, methodology, results, discussion, and reference list. The title page should contain the project's title, the name of the researchers, the date of the report, and other pertinent information, such as the name of your company or the funding agency, and so forth. The introduction should present the problem or issue to be studied and should be followed by the research questions. A brief summary of what others have done in this area is usually appropriate. This information is readily available from your search of the literature. The project's methodology should be thoroughly explained. This portion of the report should be highly specific. Include dates and times, if appropriate. Remember that a reader of the report will want to know in some detail just how you applied the research method(s) you used. The results section details the evidence you found or the information you collected. This should be presented in a logical, organized fashion. Tables and figures may be used to illustrate some of the findings. In the discussion section, you will need to address the research questions and acknowledge the project's strengths and weaknesses. It is also often useful to suggest additional research that might be needed. In any case, you should not fail to say what the study means in terms of media and communication. Finally, a reference list should be provided. This list will provide detailed information about each of the studies presented in your literature review.

REVIEW QUESTIONS

1. Why is the design of a research study of particular importance?
2. Why should a research project always begin with the statement of a problem?
3. What is to be gained by discussing the problem with others?
4. Why is a literature search an important part of any research project?
5. What difficulties could one be expected to have with a literature search?
6. What cautions should be observed when searching literature on the Internet?
7. How do research questions actually "guide" a research project?
8. What is meant by the term *logistics*, and how does it apply to research?
9. Why is a proposed budget of importance when designing a research project?
10. What is a final research report? What information should it contain?

SECTION II

Methodologies

In this section of the text, you will find detailed information and directions designed to help you plan and conduct a research project using quantitative and qualitative methods. Remember that these methodologies, even though they may have the same names, will likely differ somewhat from mainstream social science quantitative and qualitative methods. We are, after all, modifying present methods to make them more appropriate for postmodern culture.

There are a variety of methods discussed and explained on the following pages. No one method is superior to any other method. Each has its strengths and weaknesses. A researcher should follow the research flow-chart presented in Chapter 4 of this text and, at the appropriate time, determine which method is most appropriate for his/her needs.

## CHAPTER 5

Focus Group Research

Every judgment in science stands on the edge of error, and is personal.

—Jacob Bronowski

A *focus group* brings together a relatively small number of people for a group discussion. Quite popular among market researchers, focus groups use "group interaction to produce data and insights that would be less accessible without the interaction found in a group" (Morgan, 1988, p. 12). Some researchers call this group interviewing, but the method really involves more than interviewing. Interviewing is often done one-on-one. This is the case with a telephone survey, for example. A researcher calls an individual, asks a series of questions, and records the individual's responses on the study questionnaire. Questions are usually closed-ended and allow for little or no explanation. However, in a focus group, questions are usually open-ended, and explanation, amplification, and additional comments are encouraged. Members of a focus group will participate in a moderately structured discussion led by a research moderator who is a trained research discussion facilitator.

A focus group is usually composed of 6 to 12 individuals who have agreed to participate. Its purpose is "to understand how people feel or think about an issue, product, service, or idea" (Krueger & Casey, 2000, p. 4). To get participants for a focus group, it is usually not necessary to use a sampling procedure; however, you may want to have a variety of individuals in the group, so it may take some effort to recruit individuals who have the qualities you need. For example, if you are studying children's daily exposure to television and you wish to conduct a focus group, it would probably not be worth your time to recruit adults whose children are grown and gone from home. However, if you are studying television use in general, you could recruit from all age groups. It depends on your topic and the qualities you require for your participants to provide meaningful information.

Some researchers believe that you may not be able to get all the information you are seeking in one focus group session. It is usually advisable to conduct several focus groups, each with 6 to 12 different participating individuals. Multiple focus groups will allow you to compare results across all sessions. Must the group have 12 members, you might ask? Can it have fewer than 6? You can conduct a productive focus group session with 12 participants, but large groups are sometimes difficult to manage. Conducting one with fewer than 6 will probably not provide you with as much information as you may be seeking.

Nevertheless, if fewer than six people show up for a session, you almost certainly will conduct it with however many show up. Participants have taken the time and effort to come be a part of the research activity, and you should not send them home without following through on your commitment to have them be part of the focus group. Your author's experience suggests that 8 to 10 participants is ideal. A group this size is easy to manage, and you can involve all participants in answering questions and offering comments about the topic under study.

Focus groups often have two uses. They are commonly used as a preliminary activity to another, more detailed research study. For example, if you wish to conduct a telephone survey concerning Internet use among senior citizens, you might want to hold a focus group session or two to identify some of the issues, practices, or concerns that you will need to consider as you develop a questionnaire for the survey.

A second use of focus groups is to provide information for immediate use in decision making. Although we know that the opinions and ideas advanced in a focus group session do not necessarily represent the opinions and ideas of other individuals, the information you get from the focus group session may be all you really need to make a decision. Suppose, for example, that you wish to know whether the 2,000 employees of a certain company would read a monthly newsletter if one were to be developed and regularly given to each employee. You could, of course, survey all 2,000 employees, but this might be somewhat difficult and time consuming. A reasonable course of action might be to conduct three focus group sessions with 10 participants in each, drawn from all company operations. You could present them with an example of the first newsletter issue and engage them in a discussion about it. You might find that most members of the focus groups are excited about the newsletter and would eagerly read the document each month. You might then recommend to your supervisors that the newsletter is worth trying as a means of communicating with employees. On the other hand, if there were a general consensus that the newsletter would simply be another piece of company propaganda and that most employees would toss it into the trash unread, you might recommend that some other way be found to communicate with employees. It is true that the opinions of the focus groups might or might not represent the opinions of all the employees, but if you need some information in order to make a quick decision, focus groups may be the way to go.

A POSTMODERN PERSPECTIVE

Focus groups will not be changed much by a postmodern approach. Sampling is usually not an issue in focus group research. Results from a focus group session are not generalized to a larger population, nor are they usually used to support or refute some communication theory. Postmodernists would be comfortable with focus group practices. In fact, focus group activity—as it is commonly practiced in communication—could provide answers to some of the questions postmodernists think ought to be addressed by research. For example, a focus group might well provide an answer to this question: Do the results help us see things more clearly as they are? Or this question: Do the results highlight the "richness of difference" in the culture? In general, focus group research is typically used to provide quick, practical information relating to a specific issue, often business related. Although action may be taken on the results, such action is rarely presented as applicable to any situation other than the one the focus group was specifically convened to address.

ADVANTAGES AND DISADVANTAGES

Like all other research methods, focus groups have advantages and disadvantages. One distinct advantage is that a focus group can often be conducted quickly. If you can identify and get the cooperation of the participants, you can often plan and conduct the session within a week or two. A second advantage is that a focus group is a relatively low-cost way of gathering information. However, there are often some costs involved, including paying the focus group moderator, research assistance, travel expenses, refreshments, and taping and transcribing the sessions. Nevertheless, compared to the cost of some other research activities, the cost for a series of focus groups will likely be somewhat less.

Getting in-depth explanations of opinions and ideas is a third advantage. As noted earlier, most focus groups involve a group discussion of a series of open-ended questions. The research moderator can probe for additional information or explanations. This provides more information than you would get by having someone complete a questionnaire. Finally, a focus group allows you to be flexible. If the research moderator identifies an issue or concern that is not related to the questions he/she had planned to ask but knows that an exploration of that issue or concern could be of some use to the study, the issue or concern may easily become a part of the group discussion. In other words, in a focus group, you can depart from your set of predetermined discussion questions and consider new questions or new ideas. You cannot easily do this with some other types of research and most certainly not with survey research where procedures require that you not deviate from the prepared questionnaire.

There are a few disadvantages to the focus group, but many researchers believe these can be overcome. One problem that often arises in a focus group is that the group may contain an individual who is so full of opinions and ideas, he/she will try to dominate the discussion. He/she is often the first to respond to a question and will often respond at length. This sort of behavior usually leaves little time or opportunity for other members of the focus group to offer their ideas and opinions. Some may even feel intimidated by the aggressive way in which the "opinion leader" voices his/her opinions. On the flip side, there may be those who say little or nothing in the session. They often listen carefully to what others say but are hesitant to offer their own views. Or they might agree with what someone else has said and believe that saying about the same thing does not add much to the discussion. A good research moderator can overcome these problems. He/she must simply guide the discussion in such a way that one person does not dominate it and that each person contributes regardless of whether he/she agrees or disagrees with what has been said. It takes both skill and courtesy to verbally restrain a dominant group member, and it takes a different type of skill and courtesy to get the reluctant talkers involved.

Another disadvantage is that the group discussion will often get off track. In other words, participants may begin to talk among themselves or relate stories that have no bearing on the issues under consideration. Again, a strong research moderator can get the discussion back on track. A third disadvantage is that some participants may object to having the session recorded. Focus group sessions are often recorded on audiotape so that researchers do not have to depend on writing down every comment correctly. With audiotape, researchers can have access to all the comments made during a session. Some participants may object to having their voices recorded, but the research moderator can usually get their cooperation by promising that their voices will not be identified in any way and by informing participants that the goal of the session is to get their exact comments and ideas on important issues and the best way to be precise is to tape record the session. In rare cases, focus group sessions may be videotaped. This is a little more risky than audiotaping. Some participants do not wish to be videotaped, particularly if they are offering opinions on sensitive issues.

BASICS

You begin planning a focus group session in the same way you begin other sorts of research activities: complete the basics. This means that you follow the preliminary steps in the research flowchart. You will then need to *discuss the research topic, conduct the literature search*, and *revise the research questions*. Finally, you will need to *develop the series of questions* that you will use to stimulate the focus group discussion. These discussion questions should be linked directly to the study's research questions. In general, they should be open-ended questions which can be clearly understood by group participants. They should be short, interesting questions; the research moderator should use words that the participants themselves might use. Questions should be put in conversational language to the degree possible (Krueger & Casey, 2000, p. 40). Remember, the goal of the questions is to stimulate the exchange of ideas and opinions about the topic of your research study.

LOGISTICS

As with any research project, there are dozens of details that must be attended to in order for a focus group to be successful. The first and most important task, after completing the basics, is to find and/or train the research moderator who will lead the discussion. As noted earlier, a good research moderator will be able to overcome many of the problems that plague focus groups. There are no particular gender or age requirements for a moderator. A good moderator will be a skilled and courteous communicator who understands the focus group process and understands your project.

You may need a number of research assistants to assist with data recording. If you are planning to audiotape the session, your research assistants may be charged with the task of acquiring several tape recorders, purchasing batteries and blank audiotapes, and placing the recorders in appropriate locations in the focus group room. Recorders should be monitored closely during the session to insure that they are operating properly.

Pay special attention to the date and time of a proposed focus group session. Avoid awkward times such as 8 a.m. or 5 p.m. Some people do not like early 8 a.m. activities; others might be anxious to get home at 5 p.m. after the business day. Mid-morning, mid-afternoon, or early evening (7:30 p.m. or so) are usually workable times. Selecting a date for the focus group can also be problematic. Weekends are out; no one wants to do this sort of "work" on Saturday or Sunday. Some people have difficulties with Monday (first workday of the week for many) and Friday (last workday of week). Remember, too, to keep focus group sessions away from special calendar days such as holidays, elections, major sporting events, and the like. You can't please everyone, of course, but you will need to think carefully about the proposed day and time of your session.

Recruiting participants may or may not be difficult. It often depends on the nature of the project. If you are doing a focus group for a medium-market radio station, you'll want to try to reach members of that station's target audience. This is often determined by the station's format. A station with a Top 40 format will likely have an audience different from a station whose format is oldies. Still, an effort should be made to recruit as wide a variety of participants as possible.

If you are recruiting from the general public, your task will be somewhat more difficult. Many people may not be able (or may not want) to give several hours of their time to your research project. In any case, whether your participants are easy or difficult to recruit, you should contact them in person. Cards, letters, and e-mail messages are usually not as effective in soliciting participation as personal contact. Although your focus group may last only an hour or so, considerable time may be spent by participants in preparation and travel. If possible, you should offer participants some sort of incentive or reward for coming to your focus group session. Cash is always welcomed, but this sort of reward can increase a project's costs. Sometimes gift certificates for free meals or free services will suffice. Obtaining these will not likely be "free" for the researcher and if you are working from a small budget, these sorts of things may not be possible.

You can often get individuals to agree to participate by convincing them that the discussion topic is one that is important. If possible, link the discussion topic to something that may be important to participants. For example, if you are studying late-evening television use by teenagers, you could probably make a convincing argument that a parent with one or two teenagers in the house might like to know the ideas and opinions of other group members who also have teens at home. Mention, too, any incentive (cash payment, gift certificate, etc.) that will be awarded to those who participate in and finish the session.

If you are conducting a focus group for a business or some other organization and the focus group needs to be composed of employees of that business or organization, the recruiting task is somewhat easier. Participants may often come to a session during some part of their normal workday. In some cases, supervisors may require attendance, but this is not recommended. A focus group works best if participants are willing—not forced—to attend.

Other important details include reserving a room where the session will be held and providing refreshments. Obtaining a room is usually not all that difficult. Motels, universities, public schools, and some businesses often have conference rooms that may be rented for your focus group session. If you can get a room without cost, so much the better. The room should be easy to find, and parking should be readily available. Participants may not be familiar with the area or building in which the room is located, so clear directions (and perhaps a few large, hand-lettered signs at appropriate locations) will enable your participants to find the session location. The room should be large enough to easily accommodate all parties, both participants and researchers, comfortably, but not so large that the group appears to be lost in some large cavern. A room can be too small, of course. These may seem like obvious considerations, but these are details that cannot be taken for granted.

Refreshments should be available at no cost to the participants. Researchers have found that "eating together tends to promote conversation and communication within the group" (Krueger & Casey, 2000, p. 104). The type of refreshment will, of course, depend both on the time of day and your budget. A 9:30 a.m. focus group might appreciate juice, coffee, and light pastries of some sort. A 3 p.m. focus group or a 7:30 p.m. focus group might appreciate coffee, soda, bottled water, and a snack tray of vegetables, cheese, and crackers. Refreshments need not be terribly expensive if you do not overdo it. It would not, for example, be financially prudent to provide focus group members with filet mignon sandwiches and expensive wines. Remember that the purpose of the session is to gather data for your research project, not to get participants together for a social hour. Refreshments should serve the purpose of keeping your participants alert and comfortable.

CONDUCTING THE SESSION

You are now ready to conduct the focus group. The research moderator should begin by introducing him/herself and welcoming the participants. Some researchers feel it is important that participants introduce themselves. Others feel that name tags are sufficient, particularly if there has been some group interaction at the refreshment table before the session. The moderator should next make a brief statement about the nature of the research project and note that refreshments are available. The moderator should then explain how the session will work. This includes noting that the session will be tape recorded but that confidentially will be maintained (or that participant comments will be written down by the research assistants, placed strategically throughout the room). The moderator may also tell participants that some personal information is needed from them. A short questionnaire asking for demographic information, that is, age, gender, educational level, annual income, and so forth should be given to each participant. This sort of information is not necessarily a requirement, but it often helps to know some things about the group providing the information. After collecting the questionnaires, the moderator should encourage everyone to participate in the discussion. Participants should be told not to be afraid of offering a different opinion about an issue or agreeing with what has already been said. The moderator should then ask the first question.

A skilled moderator will know how to use silence to his/her advantage. In some instances it might be useful for the moderator to say nothing for a few seconds after a response. This period of silence will often prompt some other participant to speak up. Also, the moderator will already know, by looking at the session questions, which ones may require him/her to probe for additional information. The moderator should maintain eye contact with participants and nod his/her head occasionally to indicate that he/she is hearing what is being said. Avoid too much head nodding as this may be interpreted by participants as agreeing with a comment. A moderator must not be seen as taking sides with regard to any issue (Krueger & Casey, 2000, p. 113).

Once the discussion has covered all the questions the moderator has in hand plus any new questions or concerns that arose during the course of the session, the moderator should thank the participants and, if appropriate, present them with the cash payments or "gifts" that they were promised when they were recruited.

SOLVING POTENTIAL PROBLEMS

Krueger and Casey (2000) note that a number of unanticipated problems may pop up and require attention. If it is necessary to cancel your focus session (bad weather, ill health, and the like), you should contact all participants and let them know the session has been cancelled. Tell them you'll be calling them again soon to reschedule.

If some of your participants bring their children, you may have a significant problem. Some children are well-behaved; others are out of control. Children of any sort are often detrimental to the focus group research process. If you can provide child care (this can be expensive), the problem may be easily solved. Otherwise, puzzles and games in a far corner of the room, or videos in an adjoining room (supervised by a research assistant) may be possible solutions. One way to head off this problem is to indicate, at the time of recruitment, that child care will *not* be available during the session and that there will be nothing available to maintain a child's interest during the session.

What if some uninvited participants show up? Suppose Bill and Susan Citizen decide to bring Aunt Maude to the session. Aunt Maude has plenty of time on her hands. Why not include her in the activities? Krueger and Casey (2000) feel that you should thank the uninvited person for his/her interest, perhaps offer to get in touch later on a different project, and excuse the individual from the session.

On the other hand, what if nobody shows up? This is every researcher's nightmare. A great deal of time, effort, and money has been expended in planning the focus group. If no one shows up, you will probably need to get your research assistants (and any others involved in the project) together and try to find out what went wrong. You'll have plenty of time to do this right there in the empty room, and you'll have plenty of refreshments, too. So get busy redesigning the project, solving problems, and moving ahead with planning another focus group session.

ANALYZING THE DATA

If the data have been tape recorded, you will need to create printed transcripts from the tapes. This means someone (or several people) will have to listen to the tapes and write down precisely what is on the tapes. Your research assistants might be able to do this, or the tapes may be placed in the hands of a professional secretarial agency that specializes in transcribing material. In any case, you will need hard copies of all the comments made during the focus group session.

Once the data are in hand, you are ready to start examining the information with a view toward answering your study's research questions. Some researchers feel that analyzing focus group data is difficult. To be sure, it is not as simple as assigning participant comments a numerical value and computing averages and the like. Each participant's comments will be a little different and more likely very different from the comments of any other participant. However, you can use the process outlined in Chapter 6 for analyzing field interview data. You should probably follow these steps:

1. Organize the responses by question
2. Find commonalities
3. Note the range of comments
4. Sort the comments by some variable
5. Identify themes and patterns
6. Summarize your findings

Begin by *organizing the responses by question*, that is, arranging all participant comments according to the question answered. This can be readily accomplished but may require some extra organization. You will need a large workspace, perhaps a conference table or a series of card tables or the like. From the transcripts, cut out each individual response to each question and place the response on the table underneath a plain sheet on which only the question appears. For example, if your focus group session involved 15 questions, you'd have 15 different sheets, each with a single session question; participant responses would then be placed under the appropriate sheet. If you have held more than one focus group session, you may want to print the session transcripts on different colored paper so that you can easily identify from which session a particular comment came. You can also use colored markers or highlighters to distinguish among groups. Krueger and Casey (2000) also advise making two copies of each transcript, one to cut up and one to retain intact for your files.

Next, you will need to *find commonalities* among the comments. This requires that the verbatim comments of the participants be read and evaluated carefully. Are some comments *exactly the same* as others? Are some *almost the same*? If not exactly or almost the same, do the comments appear to be expressing essentially similar ideas or opinions? Can similar comments be comfortably grouped together? Does the preponderance of opinion seem to point in one direction?

Now, search the comments under each question and *note the range of comments*. This means identifying what might be called "extreme" opinions on the question. Can the extreme positions regarding the question be identified? Where do the other comments fall relative to the extremes? For example, responses to one question might be a simple "yes" or "no," in which case locating the extremes would be easy. Some participants said "yes," so these would be placed together; other participants said "no," and these comments would be grouped together. There may be some comments between these two extremes, but leaning more toward one than the other. Some questions might not have such direct and easily placed extreme comments. It should be noted that the word "extreme" is not being used here in any negative sense. It is used to help describe the breadth of comments on any particular question. In other words, we are trying to establish a spectrum of comments and to do this, we need to identify comments that should represent the ends of the spectrum.

You might want to *sort the comments by some variable*. Demographic variables can be very useful in sorting data. For example, for a given question, did males have opinions different from females? As near as you can tell, did younger participants differ markedly in their responses from older participants? The ability to sort data by some variable will depend on the degree to which transcribers and/or research assistants can correctly assign a particular comment to an individual participant. Gender should not be much of a problem. You can almost always tell the difference between a male voice and a female voice on the audio tape. Age can be problematic. It is sometimes not all that easy to distinguish younger and older voices, but it might not be all that difficult. It all depends on the group's makeup. In any case, you should be careful here and make decisions about demographic characteristics only when you have solid evidence.

Identifying themes and patterns is an important part of the data analysis process. Once the data have been organized, commonalities found, and the range of comments noted and sorted, you are ready to step back from the data and ask yourself whether the data seem to reflect themes or fall into certain patterns. For example, returning to our earlier example of the company newsletter focus group, you might find that almost all comments about most of the questions were negative. Perhaps a few participants thought the newsletter worthwhile, but most indicated they wouldn't read it, didn't have time for it, was company propaganda, and would divert financial resources that could be better used elsewhere in the company. You could safely conclude that one overall theme emerging from the focus group was that employees did not think much of the newsletter idea. A focus group session may result in a number of different themes or patterns, but each should be based on a solid foundation of participant comments.

It may not be necessary to *summarize your findings*. In some cases, identifying themes and patterns may serve the summarizing function. However, in some cases, you may want to provide a more complete, detailed summary which reports on each step in the data analysis process.

Data analysis is, of course, hard work. There is no easy way to take dozens and perhaps even hundreds of focus group comments and make some sense of them. You will derive the most benefit from having held the focus group if you systematically and vigorously evaluate all participant comments.

ADDRESSING THE RESEARCH QUESTIONS

You are now ready to answer your study's research questions. This is an important part of the research process. You have questions about your topic, and now you have information that may provide answers to those questions. Remember that, in all likelihood, some of the questions may not have satisfactory answers, that is, the data may not provide enough information for you to answer a question completely. In that case, the data may raise new questions. However, in many cases, if the focus group has been conducted properly, you will be able to address most of your research questions.

EVALUATING THE STUDY

At this point you should take a critical look at the study you have just completed. What were its strengths and weaknesses? What would you do differently next time and why? Did the focus group sessions generate enough data for you to answer the questions you had about the topic? What was the overall quality of the data gathered? What advice would you offer to others who are considering a focus group project?

WRITING THE REPORT

This is the final step in the research process. Report writing is covered in detail in Section III of this text.

REVIEW QUESTIONS

1. How is a focus group discussion different from, say, a discussion you might have in one of your classes?
2. Why are open-ended questions often most useful in a focus group?
3. Focus groups usually have two uses. What are they?
4. Why is group size important in focus group research?
5. What do you think is the greatest advantage to a focus group? The greatest disadvantage?
6. Why is the role of the research moderator extremely important?
7. What scheduling difficulties sometimes arise with focus groups?
8. How does one record the "data" from a focus group session?
9. What techniques can be used to analyze data from a focus group session?

SUGGESTED ACTIVITIES

1. Search the literature in the scholarly communication journals for a study utilizing focus groups. How and why was the study conducted? What were the study's results and how were they used? What problems, if any, did the researchers encounter?
2. Find out whether a researcher somewhere on your campus is conducting a focus group. Ask for permission to attend the session as an observer. Take careful notes about the way the session is handled and analyze the session for its strengths and weaknesses. Share your findings with your class.
3. Identify two or three issues on your campus that you feel would be appropriate topics for focus group research. Develop a set of questions that might be asked of a focus group for each issue.

## CHAPTER 6

Survey Research

The pressure of public opinion is like the pressure of the atmosphere; you can't see it—but all the same, it is sixteen pounds to the square inch.

—JAMES RUSSELL LOWELL

S urvey research is one of the most popular ways of gathering informa- tion. It is so easy; almost anyone can do it. All you need is a page full of questions, a copy machine to duplicate dozens (perhaps hundreds) of copies of the question sheet, and people to fill in the answers to your ques- tions. Right? Well, not quite. Good survey research is a bit more complicated than that.

DEFINITION AND USES

A survey can be defined as a detailed investigation of the behavior, atti- tudes, values, opinions, beliefs, and/or personal characteristics of individ- uals. Some researchers believe there are two types of surveys. "A descriptive survey attempts to describe or document current conditions or atti- tudes—that is, to explain what exists at the moment. . . . An analytical survey attempts to explain *why* situations exist" (Wimmer & Dominick, 2006, p. 179).

Survey research is widely used today by professional polling organiza- tions, by media companies, by advertising agencies, by educational institu- tions, and by major business firms. We have an almost insatiable need for information in today's culture, information that can be used to make social, economic, or political decisions. Survey research is sometimes called *polling*, though, technically, not all survey activities are polls. In any case, we use surveys to determine the key issues of the day, and public opinion about those issues. Politicians often use this information in conducting their election campaigns. Two of the most popular polls are, of course, the presidential preference poll and the exit poll. During a presidential election campaign, people often want to know who is ahead in the race for the nation's most important job. After voting, some people are part of an exit poll which asks which candidate they just voted for. Some polls ask what issues voters consider most important in the coming election. Results from all these polls are widely reported in the media. Otherwise, media organizations are mostly interested in gathering information about who is using what media, when, and for how long; occasionally, media may also want to know what we think or feel about the programming we see or the media products we use.

Businesses and other organizations may use surveys for market research in order to determine individuals' product preferences and the degree to which they are satisfied with the products they purchase and use. Survey research can also be used to evaluate the performance of products, services, or even organizations. Educational institutions often use survey research to determine the degree to which graduates are satisfied with the education they received as well as whether they were able to find employment in their chosen fields.

There are probably many other ways survey research can be used to answer some of the questions we have about business, politics, education, and communication. It has proved to be a rather durable way to gather information. Survey research is an important part of today's mainstream social science research activity.

A POSTMODERN PERSPECTIVE

In general, postmodernists would probably recognize the necessity of some types of survey research. Certainly market research can be valuable in gathering a variety of information on consumers and products. Political polling can be useful, too, if done in a meaningful way. However, survey research can be of most value when it addresses or is at least related to one or more of the research guidelines presented in Chapter 3. Almost any survey can be placed under the question, "What needs to be understood and explained?" "What do we need to know in an uncertain and rapidly changing world?" is another question that would likely catch a number of survey activities. Nevertheless, surveys might have a bit more difficulty relating research activity to a question such as, "What can be said of the 'richness of difference' in the culture?" Of course, a survey research project does not have to relate to all the guidelines in Chapter 3, but it should clearly be connected to one or more.

There will be other things about survey research that a postmodernist will want to change or modify. These include the way people are selected to participate in a survey project as well as how survey results are interpreted and used. These issues will be discussed in some detail in this chapter.

ISSUES AND PROBLEMS

There are a number of issues and problems you need to consider if you are planning to conduct a survey. First and foremost, survey research is not cheap. You will have to spend some money, regardless of what type of survey research you are doing. Often the cost of a project is related to its size, and costs can sometimes be reduced by limiting the scope of the survey. However, conducting a smaller-than-planned survey may not meet your needs. It would be wise to develop a budget for your proposed survey project. Information on developing a budget was presented in Chapter 4.

Each of the survey methods discussed in this chapter has its own set of issues and problems. Some attention will be given to these as each survey method is presented. But, in addition to the cost, another important issue is that of participation. Americans are very busy people and, increasingly, fewer and fewer of them are willing to take time to participate in a survey. Many feel survey activities are intrusive; some people do not like getting phone calls when they are doing other things around the house; still others do not like survey questionnaires "cluttering up" their mailboxes.

A continuing concern among researchers is the quality of the responses. Are survey participants reporting what they really do, think, see, and believe, or are they merely providing the answers they think you want in order to get through the questionnaire and on to other things? Since there is no way to accurately assess whether respondents are telling you the truth, we have to assume that they are, in fact, giving you an appropriate response. In other words, self-reporting can be problematic. It is one thing for a researcher to observe a behavior directly; it is quite another for a researcher to be told about a behavior by the person who may (or may not) have engaged in that behavior.

Survey research has, in recent years, received something of a bad reputation due to the number of organizations who "pretend" to be conducting survey research, but are in fact interested in something else entirely. The American Association for Public Opinion Research (AAPOR) has for years exposed organizations that use surveys or polls as "facades" for fund-raising appeals. Down through the years, some fairly well-known organizations have combined survey research with fund-raising activities. Most of the time, the survey research data are of little or no interest to the sponsoring agency, but the funds raised in the process are of extreme interest. Some organizations that have engaged in this practice in the past include the following: American Foundation for AIDS Research, American Society for the Prevention of Cruelty to Animals, Mothers Against Drunk Driving, National Parks and Conservation Association, National Space Society, Seniors Coalition, and the Union of Concerned Scientists, among others. These organizations are probably composed of individuals who are concerned about some of the issues and problems that confront us, but their use of survey research to disguise their fund-raising activities is deceptive and unethical.

The deceptive use of survey research is not limited to public organizations composed of concerned citizens. It is also used by government organizations, even educational enterprises. For example, your author received an interesting piece of mail just as this chapter was being written. A large, blue and white envelope arrived, marked "Priority Delivery . . . Urgent! Time sensitive material enclosed." The return address showed it was sent by the Smithsonian Institution in Washington, DC. The face of the envelope indicated that a survey was inside, that your author had been specially selected to participate in the survey, that two gifts were enclosed, and that the postmaster should return the envelope if the recipient's address had changed.

Inside, your author found the free gifts: 30 return address labels for his personal use and information on how to get a free copy of the *Smithsonian* magazine. If the survey was returned promptly, your author would be entered in a drawing and might win one of 50 free digital cameras to be given away. The "Smithsonian Institution Official Survey" contained eight items, was postcard-size, and was attached to the main information page. Instructions for completing the survey assured that all information provided would remain confidential and that "your knowledge would be helpful to us."

According to its Web site (www.si.edu), the Smithsonian is the world's largest museum complex. The organization has 19 museums, ranging from the African Art Museum to the Natural History Museum. There is even a Postal Museum. The Smithsonian also operates nine research centers. It appears to be a well-respected institution. Many visitors to Washington, DC make it a point to spend time at the Smithsonian.

But sadly, the Smithsonian has apparently fallen victim to the practice of raising money by conducting a "pretend survey." As noted earlier, your author was offered a free copy of the institution's official magazine, *Smithsonian*. However, the free copy was offered in conjunction with a "free trial membership." Of course, the membership would be cancelled if the word "cancel" was written across the regular membership fee bill (which would arrive sometime after the free trial membership had expired). The cancelled bill would then need to be returned to the Smithsonian. This is a common tactic in the business world and is found quite frequently among book and record clubs. Perhaps we should not judge the Smithsonian too harshly on this sales effort. However, we cannot be so forgiving about the survey.

The questionnaire contained eight items. Not one of the items appears to require any "knowledge" on the part of the respondent. It is difficult to see how the responses to the questions would be at all helpful to the Smithsonian. Knowledge is often defined as the sum or range of what has been seen, discovered, or learned. But the questions appear to ask for the respondent's preferences, not his/her knowledge. A preference is something chosen or desired and does not require any particular knowledge.

Let's look at some of the survey questions.

1. Which of these great men would you choose to have dinner with?
   A. Ben Franklin   **B.** Martin Luther King
   C. Jonas Salk   **D.** Theodore Roosevelt

2. Which of the following most symbolizes America?
   A. The American Flag   **B.** Constitution
   C. Statue of Liberty   **D.** The Liberty Bell

3. If you had the opportunity to live the life of a Revolutionary War hero, who would it be?
   A. Benjamin Franklin   **B.** Thomas Jefferson
   C. Paul Revere   **D.** George Washington

These, and the other five questions, are rather harmless inquiries. But a researcher might be a bit puzzled. What larger research question or questions will be addressed by the responses to these items? Real survey researchers reject speculative questions or questions not related to the real world. Yet almost all of the items ask "fantasy" questions. No one living today will ever have the opportunity to have dinner with Franklin, King, Salk, or Roosevelt. Why ask such a question? No one will ever have the opportunity to have the life of Franklin, Jefferson, Revere, or Washington. Why speculate on an impossible and useless situation? Even if a majority select one of the offered responses, it really doesn't mean much. In short, this questionnaire fails to ask questions that will tell us anything we really need to know about our world. Will the museum open new exhibits based on the survey responses? Will some exhibits be closed because of survey results? Will the results be summarized and published? Will the results tell us anything we need to know about life in postmodern culture? Will the results tell us anything we need to know about history?

In short, this pretend survey does not give the respondent the opportunity to share his/her knowledge with the Smithsonian. The questions do not ask for knowledge. Clearly, the Smithsonian is not searching for knowledge but rather searching for new magazine subscribers. Using a pretend survey to accomplish this sales goal is an inappropriate use of research by an institution that prides itself on operating nine research centers.

These sorts of activities have given survey research something of a bad name. Sometimes you can easily identify a real piece of research from a fake one. One of the first indicators can be found in the terminology. The word *survey* refers to an entire research process; the document one is asked to fill out and return is called a *questionnaire*. So the Smithsonian's "official survey" is really a questionnaire. Apparently, someone with imprecise knowledge of survey research assisted in the preparation of the material. If someone says, "Please fill out this survey," you know you are dealing with an amateur.

If someone says, "Please fill out this questionnaire," at least you know the person has his/her terminology correct.

Of course, a very clear indicator that the material you have in hand may not be "real" survey research is a request for money. Real survey research never asks for money of any kind, either as a subscription to something or as a contribution to any cause. Here is a good rule of thumb: if they want money, it is not real survey research.

There are some additional problems and issues that you will need to consider if you are planning a survey research project. Most of these are related to specific survey methodologies and will be discussed just ahead.

BASICS

As noted earlier, several types of survey research will be covered in this chapter. Regardless of which method you plan to use, there is a set of basic activities that must be completed before launching into the actual survey itself. Begin by following the research flowchart presented in Chapter 4. The first three steps in the process are important in helping you focus your project. You should then complete the first steps in the research design process: *discuss the problem, search the literature,* and *revise the research questions.* You are encouraged not to take these activities lightly by rushing through them. You are probably anxious to begin the actual "survey," but poor preparation often leads to poor results. Take the time to complete each step of the research design process in a thorough manner. It is not appropriate to go back and "fix" something about the research questions or to change the focus of the problem once the actual survey has begun.

For survey research, an important basic activity is selecting the individuals from whom you wish to gather information, that is, the individuals who will be filling out the questionnaire themselves (if by mail) or answering the questionnaire items posed to them by interviewers (if by phone). This selection activity is called *sampling.* Please remember that sampling is not a research method. It is a tool used in survey research, as well as in some other methods.

It is with sampling that we will see our first major break with traditional, mainstream social science methodology. It has always been a social science cardinal rule that if you take a random sample of a population (an extremely large group of individuals from whom you are interested in gathering information), you can examine the sample in some detail and draw conclusions, not only about the sample but also about the population from which it came. Social scientists call this "generalizing." There is some error in doing this, social scientists admit, so they stress that the larger the sample, the smaller the margin of error. For example, a random sample of 1,000 individuals would be better than a random sample of 100 individuals from the same population. Some researchers believe that "sampling error is generally much larger than it may seem" (Zukin, 2004, para. 3).

To most people, sampling makes sense. After all, there are many practical, real-world applications of this random sample principle. For example, suppose you are making homemade vegetable soup. You assemble the ingredients and add them to a large cooking pot on the stove, according to the recipe directions. You simmer the soup until it is done. You don't have to consume the entire pot of soup to know how it tastes. You can simply stir the soup, withdraw a typical spoonful, and taste it. The degree to which you get an accurate impression of the taste will often depend on the degree to which you stirred the mixture and came out with a portion of it that represented all the elements in the pot. You are essentially trying to draw a random sample of the soup and taste it. If your sample spoonful is too salty, you may conclude that the entire pot of soup is too salty. You are able to generalize to the entire pot by tasting a small portion of your soup.

In survey research, the practice of studying a sample of individuals and then generalizing the findings to the larger population may have once worked well. It is, postmodernists would say, no longer valid. Sampling has two major flaws. First, the practice is clearly a cornerstone of the mechanical world paradigm view of the world, that is, the notion that we can learn about the whole of something by examining its parts. Postmodernists reject this worldview as no longer viable in explaining anything we need to know about contemporary phenomena. There is a second flaw in sampling: the random sample. It is not possible today to get a "real" random sample. A random sample is not possible in telephone survey research because of the nature of postmodern telephone technology. Most homes have caller ID, and an incoming call can be ignored if the homeowner does not recognize the phone number or the name of the caller. Some people, particularly people in their 20s and early 30s, have selected cell phones as their only telephone service. They do not have regular, landline telephones in their apartments or condos. One researcher estimated that perhaps 6% of American households are "cell phone only" (Zukin, 2004). Since cell phone numbers are not available to survey researchers, a substantial portion of the American population is unavailable to participate in a phone survey project. Additionally, another 5% of households have no phone service of any type. Survey researchers can't get a real random sample without those people!

Well, survey researchers say, we'll just do the same thing with them that we do with individuals we reach but who do not wish to participate; we will substitute. At first glance, this might seem to work well, and your author is sure some mathematician could provide an equation to show how a substitute number is just as good as an original number. But this is a difficult sell from a practical standpoint. Remember that science and math are merely metanarratives and are not infallible.

Let's return to our example of the pot of soup. If your soup has some green beans in it, and your spoonful does not contain a green bean, then the spoonful is not truly representative of the soup. You might substitute a red bean for the green bean, but it would still not be representative. You need that green bean. In other words, the substitute is never the same as the original.

You might dip around in the soup until you find a green bean; you can't dip around in a batch of telephone numbers looking for an exact substitute for a number that has refused to respond, or one you can't reach. No two people on the other end of any phone are alike. Yet for years, even decades, social scientists have continued to use a variety of sampling techniques that are, at best, convenient, and, at worst, dishonest. But modern culture taught us not to question science. We were sold the mechanical world paradigm and all its minions as the ultimate source of truth. Postmodernists say there may be many versions of the truth, and we should not accept any one as the only one.

Let's look a little more closely at the idea of randomness and consider it from a different point of view. Scientists often use the term *random occurrence* to describe an event or phenomenon that cannot be predicted. Social scientists like random samples for their research activities because such a sample makes it more likely to correspond with reality and less likely to be a sample designed to yield a particular result.

But suppose that "randomness is only the appearance, not the reality . . . [and] just because we cannot predict an event that doesn't make the event *unpredictable*, it just makes *us unable to predict it*. French statistician Abraham De Moivre believed that chance was an illusion . . . that nothing ever happened by chance—every seemingly random event could actually be traced back to a physical cause" (Fawer, 2005, pp. 231–232).

Scientists are fond of using a coin flip as an example of the unpredictability of randomness. If a coin is flipped, they'd say that whether it comes up tails or heads is a matter of pure chance. "But just because we can't measure the factors [controlling a coin flip] doesn't mean the result of the coin flip is determined by chance. It only means that we, as human beings, don't have the ability to measure certain facets of the universe. Hence, events may *appear* random even though they are entirely determined by physical phenomena" (Fawer, 2005, pp. 231–132).

How is this possible, you might ask? Well, one explanation rests on some of the concepts of quantum mechanics where physicists have discovered that all matter is made up of 12 quarks and 12 leptons, but that "only a handful exist in our universe, the rest don't exist or disappear after a nanosecond." Some physicists believe that "the rest do exist in other universes—parallel universes, or nonlocal realities, that coexist alongside our own with different properties" (Fawer, 2005, p. 358). Could what we call randomness or chance events in our universe be predicted in other universes or other realities? Or imagine our universe with dimensions other than the one in which we live. String theory suggests there are probably at least 10 dimensions—9 of space and 1 of time. Is it so far-fetched to think that what we call random events, that is, chance events that we cannot predict, may very well be clearly understood and quite predictable in other dimensions, or other realities? Perhaps we take ourselves a little too seriously when we accept science, or anything like a master story, or a metanarrative as the definitive answer to our questions.

So what now? Your telephone survey research project cannot, in all likelihood, call every member of the population, so who do you call? The answer is quite simple. Continue to take a sample from the population. Make it fit the needs of your project. Gather information from that sample and report the study's findings. But *you should not generalize to any larger population*. You should simply indicate that your results show that such-and-such was true of the group of people you contacted at the time you talked with them. It might or might not be true of those people now, and it might or might not be true of all those individuals you did not contact.

Some researchers might ask, "If I can't generalize to a larger population, of what use is survey research?" Survey researchers should be more concerned with exploring why respondents answered as they did; they should be concerned with how the results relate to other aspects of life, experience, contemporary culture, or communication behavior. In other words, they should be analytical and explore the interrelatedness of the results to a variety of other variables or real-world experiences.

Similar sampling problems are likely to arise with a mail survey. Assuming you draw a random sample, you'll need to get the participation of each member of that sample in order to have valid results. This most certainly will not happen. Many potential respondents will discard the questionnaire; others may intend to return the questionnaire, but just never get around to doing it. As just another piece of paper on a person's desk, the questionnaire may soon be forgotten or discarded. The return rates for a mail survey are abysmally low. One researcher estimates that the response rate for a mail survey ranges from 1% to 4%. Phone survey response rates are somewhat better at 19% to 75% (Wimmer & Dominick, 2006, p. 205). Anything less than a 100% response rate invalidates the random sample. Generalizing the responses of a 4% return mail survey to a larger population is sheer folly. You would be examining an increasingly smaller element and trying to apply the results of the smaller part to the larger whole. In other words, you would be following the mechanical world paradigm notion that we can learn about the whole by examining its parts. But how small can these parts be? Remember our pot of soup? Will tasting 4% of your sample spoonful give you a clear idea of what the entire pot tastes like? Doubtful.

Please do not misunderstand. We are not saying that everyone should stop doing survey research. We are saying that it must be done in a more honest fashion, particularly when it comes to interpreting and applying the results of the survey activity. Continue to conduct both phone and mail surveys, but realize that the results you get will be of limited use in making comments about any larger group of people.

SOME SAMPLING TECHNIQUES

There are numerous ways to draw a sample of people (or items or objects) from whom you want to gather information. An *available sample* uses people who are at hand and who can easily be conscripted to participate in the research activity. A college professor conducting a research project might use one of his/her classes as the sample. These students could easily be used as subjects in the research project; the professor would simply make the activity part of the course requirements. Students might be asked to volunteer to participate in the research project, giving you a *volunteer sample.*

If you were studying gender issues, you might want to involve only women in your research study, and you might wish only to gather information from women who are 18 to 25 years of age. Locating and involving these individuals would give you a *purposive sample,* in other words, a sample required for a specific purpose (in this case a gender issue). If you wanted a sample that reflected the percentage makeup of a larger group, you might take a *quota sample.* If your larger group was composed of 60% women and 40% men, you would draw a sample that reflected those percentages. Some researchers still conduct research activities in a shopping mall setting. Stopping individuals as they stroll through a mall and getting them to participate in your research project would give you a *mall-intercept* sample.

If none of the methods discussed so far meets your needs, and that could certainly be the case if you are planning a state, regional, or national survey, you will likely have to depend on some other method of obtaining a sample. One of the most popular methods of getting a sample for a telephone survey project is *random digit dialing.* In this method, a computer program is used to generate telephone numbers. Researchers would then call these numbers and gather information from those individuals who answered their phones. However, a computer-generated list of telephone numbers will likely include numbers not in service, numbers that belong to businesses, or even numbers that do not exist (numbers yet to be assigned to anyone). Researchers might make several calls before getting a "working" number. This wastes project time and effort. It seems useless to call numbers that have little chance of success.

This problem is easily solved by obtaining the services of a professional sampling company. For a fee, the company will provide you with a list of telephone numbers drawn from your population. These numbers can be screened so that business numbers and disconnected numbers are eliminated. Although not perfect, this type of sample is quite efficient in getting a good set of working numbers. It will likely save research assistants time and effort.

If you are conducting a mail survey, a similar service offers the names and addresses of individuals to whom survey packets may be sent. Check your local yellow pages for local companies who provide this service. Your author's experience has been that the names and addresses provided in this way are somewhat less valid than a sample of screened telephone numbers. However, if you are doing a mail survey, telephone numbers are useless, and obtaining a mailing list from a local company is probably the way to go.

In some cases, you can get a list of names and addresses (and sometimes telephone numbers) from organizations or institutions that are allowed by law to release such information. For example, if you are conducting a survey on political issues, you can get a list of all the registered Democrats, Republicans, and Independents in your county. You can then select individuals from each of these groups and send them your mail survey packets. Sometimes telephone numbers are provided, and you could use these if your political survey is a telephone survey.

Suppose you have a list of 1000 individuals who are members of a charity organization. Also suppose that your research budget does not allow you to mail (or phone) all 1000 of these individuals. How do you select whom to contact? Traditional social science researchers would likely suggest a *systematic random sample*. If your budget allowed you to contact 250 of these individuals, you would, according to traditional sampling methodology, contact every fourth name on the list, beginning from a random starting point. This would give each individual on the list a chance of being selected (4 multiplied by 250 equals 1000) and would, according to tradition, give you the ability to generalize to the larger group. However, remember that we are not concerned now about generalizing from the small part to the whole. Nevertheless, it does no harm to attempt to involve individuals from the entire list. Our approach here would be to draw the systematic random sample and gather the needed information, but, for reasons already explained, we would make no attempt to generalize from the sample to the whole.

In general, as a researcher, you should vigorously attempt to involve as many individuals in your project as possible as well as select a variety of individuals for participation. Do not take the easy way out. Work hard to get a good sample of individuals who can provide the information you are seeking. Use traditional social science sampling methodologies if you wish. But remember, you will be interpreting your findings in a smaller context. You will not be generalizing to a larger population, but you will be exploring the ways your findings might be related or connected to a variety of other variables.

TYPES OF SURVEYS

Telephone Survey

Here is a step-by-step process for conducting a telephone survey. It is assumed that you will, at this point, have finished with the basic activities noted earlier (discussion, literature search, revision of research questions, and sampling). Once these basics have been completed, you are ready to follow the plan outlined here for conducting the telephone survey activity.

1. Develop the questionnaire
2. Pretest and revise the questionnaire
3. Handle logistics
4. Make the calls
5. Follow-up

6. Examine responses
7. Analyze and interpret results
8. Address research questions

Let's take each step and fill in some specific details that will be necessary to complete the step successfully.

In order to *develop the questionnaire,* you must have a good set of research questions. Sometimes projects flow from a single research question, but many projects have several research questions that need answers. Begin by writing each of these research questions at the top of a blank page. Then, for each, write a series of questions that you think will provide the answer to the research question. You should broaden your focus a little in order to gather the widest possible range of information that relates to the original research question. For example, suppose you are studying computer use among college students. One of your research questions might be this one: To what extent do students use their computers for academic work? The series of questions that you could write to provide information to answer this rather broad research question might include the following:

- Do you use your computer to transcribe handwritten class notes?
- How often do you transcribe notes?
- Why do you transcribe your class notes?
- Do you use your computer to study for exams? How?
- Do you use your computer to gather information for a class paper? For a class project? How do you gather this information?
- Do you use your computer to communicate with other members of your class? With the class instructor? What do you discuss with other students? With the instructor?
- In what other ways do you use your computer in your academic work?

Of course, these questions will need a bit of tweaking to sharpen the language, and each will need a set of response options. The first question in the previous list is rather easily answered; respondents are given a "yes" or "no" choice. If the answer to the first question is "no," the respondent would skip to the fourth question in the list. If the answer to the first question is "yes," respondents would proceed to the second question which will need a more varied set of possible responses. "How often do you transcribe notes?" requires that you offer the respondent several choices from which he/she may select the appropriate one. For example, the question might have the following response options:

_____ After each class session

_____ At the end of each class week

_____ Sometime before the next exam

_____ Whenever I can get to it

_____ Other (Please explain) _____

Some researchers prefer not to restrict the possible range of answers and might simply supply a blank line next to the question so that the respondent can provide his/her own answer. This is acceptable, but you should know that it will take longer to complete the questionnaire if responses have to be written out in some detail. This might not be a bad thing; detailed answers are often quite revealing. However, experience tells us that most respondents do not want to take a lot of time answering questions about a subject in which they may have little or no interest. In a mail survey, giving them a questionnaire with blank-line-after-blank-line may not inspire them to complete it. There are many things that may influence the degree to which a respondent completes a questionnaire and answers honestly in the process. In a telephone survey, your research callers will need to have the ability to quickly and accurately record everything the respondent says. Many people talk rapidly and often not in complete sentences. These sorts of responses are difficult to write down. It is sometimes more efficient to provide a set of response options, as shown previously, and include an "other" option that can be used for answer choices not provided. Social science researchers have terms that describe the two types of questions common to questionnaires. An *open-ended question* requires the respondent to come up with his/her own answer. A *closed-ended question* requires the respondent to select a response from the choices given.

You will need to take the series of questions you have generated for each of the original research questions and determine which should be open-ended and which should be closed-ended. If closed-ended, you will need to provide a set of response options. You may want to review the information on measurement and response scales in Chapter 3 before you develop response choices for each question. Be especially careful not to offer response choices that overlap. You need what researchers call *mutually exclusive categories*. For example, suppose you ask this question: How much time do you spend watching television each day?

Your response options might be as follows:

_____ None

_____ Less than 1 hr

_____ 1 to 3 hr

_____ 3 to 6 hr

_____ More than 6 hr

At first glance, this might seem like a good set of response choices. But suppose a respondent watches 3 hr of television daily. Which choice would he/she check, the third or the fourth? Both these items contain the number "3." If you allow overlapping choices on your questionnaire, you will end up with inexact results. You may not be able to address the original research questions and you will most certainly have wasted time and effort (and probably money) in conducting a project that does not meet your needs. A better set of response items might look like this:

_____ None

_____ 1 to 3 hr

_____ 4 to 6 hr

_____ More than 6 hr

You are well on your way to developing your research questionnaire. You have a series of questions with response options. These questions are linked to the study's larger research questions. You will now need to add an additional set of questions. These questions are designed to give you a profile of the individual who is responding to your survey. Researchers call these sorts of items *demographic questions*. These questions generally relate to issues such as gender, age, education, annual income, religious preference, and the like. Do not neglect this portion of the questionnaire. These are important questions and the answers will help you analyze and derive meaning from the study results. Be especially careful in developing response choices for demographic items. Some people are hesitant to provide too much specific information about themselves; researchers have found that providing categories works well. For example, if you are asking about a respondent's age, you could simply ask this question: How old are you? Some people are sensitive about age and may not give you an accurate answer. They are more likely to give you an accurate answer if you provide them a range of ages and ask which range applies to them. For example, ask this question: In which of the following age categories do you fall?

- Younger than 18 years
- 18 to 25
- 26 to 35
- 36 to 45
- 46 to 55
- 56 to 65
- Older than 65

A set of response choices like this one provides two benefits. The categories are mutually exclusive, and respondents usually do not object to selecting the correct response.

Now collect all the questions you have written, the demographic items as well as the items you generated from each of the overall research questions. Arrange them neatly and in some logical order on fresh pages. You now have a working draft of your questionnaire, or data-gathering tool, as some researchers call it. The next step is *pretesting the questionnaire*. The purpose of the pretest is to see whether there is a problem with any of the questions. Are some confusing, or overlapping, or poorly written? A pretest will help you find problem areas and correct them before going on to the actual survey activity. Pretesting is fairly simple. You need to find about 10 individuals who are willing to complete the questionnaire and then talk with you about it, pointing out things about the document with which they might have had problems. If problems are found, you should, of course, revise the questionnaire to eliminate or minimize those problems.

The next step in the phone survey process is probably the most complicated. Once the questionnaire is complete, you are ready to *handle the logistics*. This is complicated because it requires you to pay attention to a multitude of details. Attending to numerous details may require you to multitask, that is, handle several aspects of the project simultaneously. You will need telephones and telephone lines placed in a room where your research assistants can make their calls. You will need office supplies: paper, pens, paper clips, staplers, wastebaskets, Post-it notes, and the like. Most importantly, you will need to hire and train your research assistants. Even individuals who know something about research will likely need to be trained in order to successfully conduct a phone survey project. The success of a telephone survey research project may very well depend on having good callers, or interviewers as some researchers call them. Callers will need to follow a specific set of rules in performing their duties. The purpose of the training session is to provide callers with the information and skills they will need to successfully carry out their part of the survey project. Suggestions for training can be found in Figure 6.1.

You will also need to write the script the researchers will use to introduce themselves to the individuals they reach on the phone and get their agreement to participate. An example of a caller script can be found in Figure 6.2. You may also want to arrange for lunch or refreshments for your research assistants if they will be working long hours or working around a mealtime. If you are paying your research assistants, you will need some way to keep track of their time so they may be paid appropriately. A sign-in and sign-out sheet, with dates and times, will usually suffice for keeping time. You will also need to arrange for one individual to serve as call-room supervisor. This person's job will be to circulate within the calling room and provide assistance to your research assistants. The supervisor can answer questions, provide advice, and encourage callers to apply their best efforts to the task at hand.

With everything now in place, you are ready to turn your research assistants loose to *make the calls*. Remember that all the calls will not likely be completed in one day. Most phone survey research projects will need to make calls at different times of the day and over a period of several days. The design of the project should indicate how many calls you need to complete, that is, how many completed questionnaires you need to adequately answer your research questions.

Be aware that if you are conducting a nationwide survey, the United States has different time zones. You will need to schedule your callers at appropriate times. In other words, if you are calling from California at 9 p.m.,

1. **Screen Callers.** Callers must be willing to devote the time and energy needed to carry out their responsibilities. Callers must have a good voice, that is, they must be fluent speakers and able to be heard clearly and distinctly on the telephone. Callers need not be of any certain age or gender. Callers often need a certain "attitude." This quality is difficult to identify. It simply means that the best callers are the ones whose voices can be said to reflect confidence, helpfulness, understanding, and friendliness. Callers should not use improper grammar or slang language.

2. **Learn the Questionnaire.** Callers must be thoroughly familiar with the questionnaire. There can be no hesitation about asking the questions or about the pace that must be established in order to successfully complete the questionnaire. Callers should also be familiar with the overall goals and objectives of the project.

3. **Learn the Rules.** Callers must know the interviewing rules established by the project director in order to carry out their interviews in a consistent and nonbiased fashion. These rules include the following:
   - Read the questions precisely as they appear on the questionnaire.
   - Do not explain a question. Repeat a question if respondent is confused or asks to repeat.
   - Do not suggest an answer to a question.
   - Do not provide supporting comments such as "right," "good," "okay," and the like.
   - Do not allow respondent to get off track by telling stories, arguing about the question, asking what caller thinks about the question, and so forth.
   - Record respondent answers exactly. Do not change the wording of a response.
   - Be courteous and friendly at all times, but also be businesslike.
   - Thank the respondent for his/her time and cooperation.

4. **Practice.** Callers should practice making calls and asking questions until their delivery is smooth and professional. Try role-playing to find problem areas.

FIGURE 6.1 Suggestions for Training Callers

you would not want to call a number in the Eastern Time Zone where it is midnight. People who are awakened late at night (or anytime, for that matter) are not likely to want to help you with your research project. In general, survey researchers have found that calling between 7 p.m. and 9 p.m. is useful, but some projects have found individuals willing to participate at midmorning or in the afternoon. The key to successful calling at times other than the evening is finding people at home during normal workday hours.

Once the calling process seems to be winding down—you are running out of numbers to call or you have reached your goal of completed questionnaires—it is often useful to have a short *follow-up* meeting. This meeting

"Hello, my name is _____ and I'm calling from _____ .
This is not a sales call. Your number was selected at random. I am calling
as part of a research project and would like to get your opinions on
several important issues. Your responses will be kept confidential. I know
your time is valuable, but your opinions will help us answer the questions
we have about _____. Are you ready for the first question?"

(If respondent says, "yes," go to first item on questionnaire. If respondent
says, "no," say "Thank you for your time," hang up, and go to the next call.)

Note to callers: Respondents sometimes ask questions about the project. If
they do, answer the question and return immediately to the questionnaire.

Common questions: Who is sponsoring this research?
What will you do with my answers?
May I get a copy of the results?
May I speak with your supervisor?

FIGURE 6.2   Sample Caller Script

would be attended by all the research callers, the call supervisor, and by others who are working on the project. The purpose of the meeting is simple: to
assess the success of the project to this point, to find and correct problem
areas, and to determine whether additional calls need to be made, either
from fresh numbers or from numbers that have been tried but have not yet
been answered (*call backs*, which include busy numbers, answering machines, and the like). If necessary, your research assistants can return to the
call room and make the additional calls. You might decide that you have
what you need and that it is appropriate to proceed to the next step: *data
analysis*. This activity is described in some detail later in this chapter.

Mail Survey

A mail survey project has many of the same requirements as the telephone
survey project discussed earlier. There are important differences, however.
For one thing, a mail survey requires a researcher to send a complete survey
packet to a potential respondent. In a phone survey, the respondent never
sees the questionnaire; the respondent's connection to the project is through
the caller who fills in the given responses. With a mail survey, there is no direct human contact. The questionnaire is placed in the hands of the potential
respondent by mail. A mail survey asks a respondent to do a lot of the work:
complete the questionnaire and return it in the mail. As noted earlier, many
potential respondents may consider the survey packet junk mail and throw
it away. Others may keep the packet with the intention of completing the
questionnaire but just never get around to doing it. Still others will complete

the questionnaire as requested and mail it back. We'll deal with some of these issues shortly, but let's begin as we did with the telephone survey by providing a step-by-step process for conducting a mail survey project.

Like the phone survey project, a mail survey requires you to *complete the basics* first. This means that, in addition to following the first several steps in the research flowchart, you will need to discuss the issue you are studying with appropriate others, conduct a literature search on the issue, and revise your research questions. You will also need to draw your sample, that is, obtain the names and addresses of those individuals to whom you will be sending your mail survey packets. Finally, you will need to develop, pretest, and revise the questionnaire. These activities are much the same as those for a phone survey project.

When you are ready to *handle the logistics*, you will find that the process is quite different from the phone survey. You will need to *assemble the survey packets*. These packets will be sent to the individuals in your sample. A mail survey packet should contain the following:

- A letter of introduction and explanation
- The research questionnaire
- A pre-addressed, postage-paid return envelope

Let's take a look at each of these items. The letter of introduction and explanation is important. It provides information to the potential respondent about the research project, who is sponsoring it, the importance of returning the completed questionnaire, and the confidential nature of the respondent's answers. It should also contain a return-date deadline along with a word of thanks for the respondent's participation. A well-written letter can be a motivating factor in a respondent's decision to complete and return the questionnaire. Of course, the packet will also need to contain the questionnaire. It should be neatly printed on plain paper and specific in what it is asking of the respondent. Finally, a postage-paid pre-addressed return envelope should be included. Respondents should not be expected to write in your address. Neither should you expect them to pay the return postage. It will be difficult enough to get their cooperation if you have done these things for them. They will almost certainly not participate if you ask them to do too much.

You must, of course, purchase the envelopes that you will use. These are usually of two types. You will need a large (9×12) manila envelope and a regular white business size envelope for each packet. If you have a limited budget, you can probably, by folding carefully, fit the letter, questionnaire, and return envelope in a standard business size envelope. Each envelope will have to be properly addressed and the right amount of postage will need to be affixed to it. As noted earlier, response rates in a mail survey are not high and you need to do everything you can to maximize your return rate. Some researchers feel that if the original packet has a handwritten address and the cover letter has an original signature, respondents are more likely to complete and return the questionnaire.

Others believe that using real stamps, rather than metered postage, on all the envelopes improves the return rate.

Once the packets have been assembled, the next step is to *mail them*. While the project is in the mail, or in the field, as some researchers say, there are other things you need to do. For example, as the completed questionnaires arrive, you will need a central location, with appropriate office supplies, to process the incoming mail. Once the return deadline has passed, some researchers have found it useful to send a postcard reminder to the sample, asking those who have not yet completed the questionnaire and returned it to do so within the next day or two. This usually results in a few more returned questionnaires.

When the return deadline has passed and you have completed any planned follow-up activities, and when you are fairly sure that no more completed questionnaires will be coming in, you are ready to proceed to the *data analysis* step.

Other Types of Surveys

There are, of course, other types of surveys that a researcher can use. Two of these other types, the *Internet survey* and the *field survey*, are used enough these days to merit some attention. Internet surveys are fairly easy and are becoming more popular. The initial procedure for conducting an Internet survey has some similarities to other survey methods. You need to complete the basics (discussion, literature search, revision of research questions, and develop and pretest the questionnaire), but an Internet survey has several advantages over the more traditional mail and phone surveys. For one thing, an Internet survey is faster. You can create a questionnaire, distribute it to your respondents, and get the data back in a fraction of the time it would take you to do the same tasks for a mail or phone survey.

Another advantage is cost. It will cost less to do an Internet survey because you will not need to print multiple copies of the questionnaire, hire and train callers, or assemble and mail survey packets, or record the incoming data by hand.

The logistics for an Internet survey are somewhat different from those required by other survey methods. The main logistical activity will be managing the electronic nature of the project. You may be able to get important help for this part of the project. There are several online survey services which can design your survey, collect responses, and analyze the results. One of the most popular services is SurveyMonkey. Prices vary according to survey size, of course, but for a small monthly fee, you can get up to 1,000 responses per month for a survey with an unlimited number of questions. A variety of support features are also included in the package (surveymonkey.com). There are other online survey services: infosurv.com; surveyconsole.com; surveycompany.com; and surveywriter.com, among others. You can use an Internet search engine to find the names and Web sites of other online survey companies. Some services offer a free trial. Visit company Web sites, read the information carefully, and decide whether these services are appropriate for your project.

Of course, this survey method is not without a few problems. An e-mail message announcing that the receiver has been selected to participate in a survey may simply be ignored, lost among all the other messages the typical individual receives, or mistaken for spam. It doesn't take much effort to delete a message, whether read or unread. Also, there is the problem of who responds to the questionnaire. If the questionnaire is targeted to adult women, you have no assurance that the person who completed the questionnaire was indeed an adult woman. If the e-mail address is, for example, kellysmith@abcnet.com, unless you have some other sort of identifying information, you will not know whether this person is male or female. Kelly is a common name for both men and women. Even if you do have information that this person is female, you will not be able to identify exactly who completed the questionnaire. Was it Kelly herself, or a friend, or a spouse, or a significant other, or a child?

Some scholars feel that "not all populations are candidates for Internet survey research. The general consumer population is often a poor fit," in part because of the danger of cyberstalkers and con artists who often use fake surveys to gather personal information from Internet users (Watt, 1997, para. 6). A screened sample is often preferred by many researchers. Respondents are screened according to some characteristic: gender, income, occupation, geographical region, membership in a professional organization, and the like. E-mail addresses are obtained from the sample and used to distribute the questionnaires.

A *field survey* is another matter entirely. Field work is so named because the data gathering activity occurs in the real world, in natural settings, rather than in a laboratory or a room, or in some other location where it is obvious that individuals would not normally be there except for the fact that they are participating in a research project. Some researchers prefer to call this sort of activity field research; others call it field observation or field interviewing. The process for designing and conducting a field interview is fairly straightforward. You begin, of course, by completing the basics (discussion, literature search, revision of research questions, development of the questionnaire).

Field surveys have never been highly popular largely due to their cost. They are used infrequently these days precisely because the world has become an increasingly dangerous place. With heightened fears of terrorism and the crime rates in some neighborhoods, many people simply do not want to talk to strangers or invite them into their homes. People often find in-home interviews too intrusive. In-home interviews may not be all that welcome by your research interviewers either. These individuals will have to walk through strange neighborhoods, knock on doors, and avoid angry dogs. Also, what time is most appropriate for these sorts of interviews?

Early afternoon? Late afternoon? Evenings? What if you can't find anyone at home? Do you return later or earlier?

One way to address some of these problems is to contact potential interviewees in the context of some organization of which they are members. For example, if you are interested in getting information on parental control of children's Internet use, you might get the cooperation of a local parent-teacher organization. Working through such an organization might go a long way toward getting interviewee cooperation and easing some of the fears they might have about meeting and talking with strangers.

Another way to avoid the problems associated with in-home interviewing is to conduct your field interviews in a public area such as you might find at a sports event or a concert. Interviewing in the parking lot of a football stadium or in the common areas of a concert venue can often meet with success. But remember, you will need to get the approval of those who own or control the property on which you will be conducting the interviews. Do not just show up at a Friday night football game at a local high school and start interviewing people. You will need to contact the local school system and the high school principal to get approval for your research activity. Approval is not guaranteed. School officials often want to know what the project is about and how intrusive it will be to those attending a school-sponsored event. Some schools have a blanket policy against such activities; others permit them under certain conditions. Even man-on-the-street interviews often require approval from city or county government officials. Do not neglect this aspect of your research project.

Recording interviewee responses, or—in research language—recording the data, is extremely important and will require interviewers to be on their toes. Sometimes responses can be tape recorded for later transcription, but not all interviewees will consent to having their voices recorded. Your research interviewers will probably be required to write down responses and write them down exactly. This may not be all that difficult a task if you can provide your interviewers with laptop computers. Computer Assisted Personal Interviewing (CAPI) is gaining in popularity. Researchers simply record responses by typing them into a file on a laptop computer. This will enable your interviewer to *probe* a response, that is, to ask the interviewee to clarify or elaborate on a response. A probe often results in a flood of additional information. Field research usually involves a certain amount of travel. Arranging transportation and scheduling both the interviewers and the interviewees at mutually convenient times will present logistical problems, but these problems are solvable.

A final word on all survey activities: ethics. Remember to plan and conduct your survey research project in an ethical fashion. A strong sense of ethics is particularly important in conducting field research. Your research interviewers should be friendly and businesslike and should refrain from commenting about any individual's personal situation. This includes an individual's appearance, home, property, children, spouse, or the like. It is not the job of a research interviewer to provide social comment on such things; it is the job of the interviewer to conduct the interview in an ethical fashion and to gather data for the project.

ANALYZING THE DATA

The information you gather in any research project, including all types of survey research, is called *data*. The word *data* is plural and takes a plural verb. The singular form of the word is *datum*. You now have lots of data in hand and are ready to make some sense of it. You should proceed to the next step in the research flowchart: examine study results, organize, and analyze.

If you have completed a telephone or mail survey activity, the information will be contained on the completed questionnaires which you now have in hand. You should begin by assigning each questionnaire an identification number. If you have completed 425 telephone interviews, you would begin by numbering the first questionnaire 001. The second would be numbered 002, and so on until you reach 425. Identification numbers will help you organize your results.

Next, you could transfer the information from each questionnaire onto a spreadsheet or put it in some similar format. For example, your entries might look something like this:

ID	Gender	Age Range	Education (years)	Watch TV News?	Newspaper?
001	F	26–35	14	No	No
002	M	56–65	08	Yes	No
003	F	36–45	16	No	Yes
. . .					
425	M	18–25	16	No	No

Once you have all 425 entries organized and recorded in this or some similar manner, you are ready to begin analyzing your results. You should begin by determining the frequency of each response and then the percentage that response is in terms of all the responses to that item. This is almost always the first step in the analysis of any data set. You might find, for example, that 301 of your respondents were women, and 124 were men. This means that 79% of your respondents were women, and 29% were men. You could draw a few conclusions from this simple analysis. Since, according to the most recent census, the U.S. population consists of approximately 51% women and 49% men, you could conclude that your respondents were not in the same proportion as the overall population. This does not invalidate your study; it simply means that you have interviewed more women than men and that there are likely other women and many other men in the country who may have the same or different opinions about the questions you asked. Remember that we are not trying to characterize the whole by examining its small parts.

Here is another example. Suppose you asked whether the respondent regularly reads a daily newspaper. Suppose also that your results showed that 70% said "no" and 30% said "yes." This might not be as much information as you want to know about newspaper reading. You might then look at the responses by gender. How often did men answer "no?" How often did women answer "no?" Or look at the responses by age. Did individuals age 56–65 answer "yes," more often than individuals age 25–36? In other words, you could do some comparisons according to gender, age, education, and the like. You could compare any two (or more) items. Were those who watched television news more or less likely to read a daily newspaper? You may want to display your analysis of the data in tables, charts, or graphs of some sort.

At this point, mainstream social science researchers would be inclined to submit the data to one or more statistical tests. Their purpose would be, of course, to generalize the findings or draw conclusions about a larger population. But remember that we have abandoned the mechanical world paradigm and the notion that one can know about the whole by examining the parts. A survey examines a part of the whole and we can draw some conclusions about what we have found, but these conclusions must be tempered by the context of postmodern culture, as well as by the variety and interrelatedness of life and experience.

Frequencies and percentages will sometimes provide you with enough information to address the research questions you have posed. In some cases, you may want to analyze the data in a slightly different way. You could assign a numerical value to a particular response for a given question. Look at this example:

How satisfied are you with your local newspaper's coverage of crime news?

_____ Very satisfied (5)

_____ Satisfied (4)

_____ Neither satisfied nor dissatisfied (3)

_____ Dissatisfied (2)

_____ Very dissatisfied (1)

You could give each response a numerical value such as the one indicated in parentheses after each response option. By adding the numerical values for all the respondents and dividing by 425, you could determine the average response (the *mean*). Since you have frequencies and percentages for this item, you already know which response was given most often and which was given least often. By determining the mean, you now know the average response. Sometimes that information is useful, sometimes not. In point of fact, any number has only as much meaning as we humans give it. For example, we have decided that the symbol "7" has more numerical value than the symbol "1." This is purely arbitrary. The symbols have much in common, but one is tilted slightly and has a longer extension to the left. Does this make it more important? No, it is more important numerically because we have agreed that it is more important; in other words, we have assigned these symbols meanings, and this assignment has no deeper significance than convenience (the convenience of having a standard system understood by all). We could just as easily have had a system like this: 0, 7, 2, 3, 4, 5, 6, 1, 8, 9 to indicate an increasing amount or number of something. The symbols by themselves have no meaning; humans have given them meaning. It is therefore a little dangerous to place one's total faith in numbers as if they hold the magic clue to understanding life, experience, culture, and the like.

Please do not misunderstand. Your author likes numbers. They are often useful. For example, he especially likes large numbers on his paycheck, though he sees very few large numbers there. However, paycheck numbers do not speak to one's character, experience, personality, or worth. The business world would have you believe that you get paid according to your worth. This may be true in some cases, but it is nonsense in other cases. There are numerous examples of highly paid CEOs who have failed miserably to revitalize their companies. Many of these individuals have been fired and given multimillion dollar payoffs. Some have remained with their failing corporations, have been given a bonus, and have ordered cuts in employee jobs and/or pension systems to address company revenue shortfalls. Meanwhile, lower paid employees continue to do their jobs daily without much recognition or financial reward. The real success of a company often depends on those who actually do the work!

Social science researchers have long played fast and loose with their numerical data. Krenz and Sax (1986) believe that "statistics lessons have . . . been learned badly. So many statistical errors can be found in published studies that one can only imagine the number occurring in the theses and dissertations that fortunately never leave the library" (p. 62). Furthermore, "it is hard for researchers to develop a feeling for the data . . . when they are surrounded by mechanical and electronic gadgets that often serve little purpose—except perhaps to help them exchange what is important for what can be obtained with the least effort and most money" (p. 62).

In short, numbers tell us some things, but they do not tell us all we need to know about life and its meaning. In postmodern culture, we will need to find additional ways to analyze the information we gather and determine its significance and usefulness in helping us answer our questions, understand our culture, and find meaning in our lives.

If you have completed a field survey or a field interview activity, your data may not be on completed questionnaires. The responses to your questions may be on audiotape or they may be in the form of written notes. It is possible, of course, to complete a questionnaire while conducting an interview, but researchers generally want more information, that is, explanations as to why the respondent answered a question the way he/she did. After being given a response to a question, a researcher will often ask, "Why do you feel that way?" or "Why do you think that?" There are other questions that might result from a respondent's answer to an item. The point is that a one-on-one interview situation gives a researcher the opportunity to explore issues, questions, and responses in depth. In-depth answers need to be recorded in some fashion, either by hand or on audiotape. Writing by hand is often slow, so many researchers ask for and get permission from the respondent to tape record the session. The researcher should, of course, remind the person being interviewed that his/her name will not be used or associated with any answers. Audiotapes must be transcribed, that is, every word spoken in the session must appear on a transcript of the session. Transcripts should also identify who is speaking, but in general terms. For example, individuals might be identified as researcher, adult family member #1 (female) and adult family member #2 (male), perhaps also young female child #1 or youngest male child or the like. Great care must be taken in transcribing information from audiotape to the printed page.

Once you have a hard copy of the information from all the field interviews you have completed, you are ready to organize and analyze the data. You should follow these steps:

- Organize the responses by question
- Find commonalities
- Note the range of comments
- Examine unusual responses
- Sort the comments by some variable
- Identify themes and patterns
- Summarize your findings

Begin by *organizing your responses by question*, that is, arranging all respondent comments according to the question answered. This will usually require some careful organization. You will likely need a large workspace, perhaps a conference table or a series of smaller tables or the like. From the transcripts, cut out each individual response to each question and place the response on the table underneath a plain sheet of paper on which only the question appears. For example, if your interview involved a dozen questions, you'd have 12 different sheets, each with a single question written on it; cut out responses would then be placed under the appropriate question sheet. Krueger and Casey (2000) advise making two copies of each interview transcript, one to cut up and one to retain intact in your files.

Next, you will need to *find commonalities* among the comments. This requires that you carefully examine the verbatim comments of those you interviewed. Are some comments exactly the same as others? Are some comments almost the same? Do the comments appear to be expressing essentially the same idea or opinion, though not necessarily in the same words? Can similar comments be grouped together? Is there a consensus of opinion about a particular item or issue?

Now, search the comments under each question and *note the range of comments*. This means identifying what might be called *extreme* opinions on the question. Can the extreme position regarding the question be identified? Where do the other comments fall relative to the extremes? For example, responses to one question might be a simple "yes" or "no." Locating these extremes would be easy. Some respondents may not have answered "yes" or "no," saying instead "sometimes," "it depends," or some other response that would fall somewhere between the absolute "yes" and "no" answers. Some interview questions may not have such direct and easily placed extreme answers. Please note that we are not using the word "extreme" in any negative sense. We are using it to describe the range or expanse of responses to a particular question. In other words, we are trying to establish a spectrum of comments. In doing so, it is necessary to determine the "ends" or extreme points of the spectrum.

It is often helpful to *examine unusual responses*, the ones that are insufficient, obscure, or in some other way incomplete. They may or may not appear to be very useful in helping you address your research questions. Nevertheless, each and every response is a piece of data and, as such, cannot just be thrown out because it doesn't fit somewhere. Look at these sorts of responses and try to see what meaning, if any, they might have.

Next, *sort the comments by some variable*. Demographic variables can be useful in sorting data. For example, for a given question, did men have opinions different from women? Did younger respondents differ markedly in their responses from older respondents? In order to sort the data by a variable, the interviewer must have recorded enough information about the respondent(s) so that responses can be accurately assigned to a particular individual.

Identifying themes and patterns is an important part of data analysis. Once the data have been organized, commonalities found, the range of comments noted, and the data sorted by some variable or combination of variables, you are ready to pause and ask yourself whether the data seem to reflect themes or fall into certain patterns. Certain themes or patterns may emerge from the data analysis. If, after examining your analysis, there do not seem to be any themes or patterns, do not twist the data or in some other way manipulate it in order to find themes or patterns that are not readily apparent.

If you have identified several themes or patterns in the data, it may not be necessary to *summarize your findings*. The statement of themes or patterns may suffice as a summary. However, in some cases, you may want to provide a more complete, detailed summary of the data analysis, one which reports on each step of the analysis process. Each summary point should be supported by the data. In other words, if you are asked to explain why you made such-and-such a summary statement, you should be ready to show that you have the actual words of those interviewed and that these comments, taken together, seem to point toward a general summary statement that reflects the true nature of the combined comments.

It should be obvious that analyzing data is not an easy task. There is no easy way to take dozens, perhaps hundreds, of interviewee comments and make some sense of them. Nevertheless, you will derive the most benefit from having conducted the interviews if you systematically and vigorously evaluate all the data.

If you have conducted an Internet survey, your data will likely have been recorded in real time. You can see graphs and charts, or "dig down to get individual responses . . . [or] download a summary of your results in multiple formats . . . [or] download all of the raw data you've collected either as a spreadsheet, or in a database format" (surveymonkey.com).

ADDRESSING THE RESEARCH QUESTIONS

You are now ready to take the next step on the research flowchart. You have your study results in hand and you should now be able to answer the research questions you proposed (and revised) earlier in the project. In general, if a research project has been carefully designed and carried out, the data you have in hand will enable you to provide answers to your research questions. In some cases, however, the data may fail to adequately answer a research question, and, more often than not, the study results will raise additional questions. This is to be expected. No research project guarantees that all its questions will be answered. Many projects generate new research questions that are often the basis for additional research activity. In any case, be specific in your answers to the research questions and rely on the data to support your answers, but don't be afraid to say what you think the data mean in terms of our overall understanding of communication and of life in contemporary culture.

EVALUATING THE STUDY

It is now time to take a critical look at the study you have just completed. Determine the study's strengths and weaknesses. Freely admit mistakes and errors and indicate what was done to correct them. Comment on aspects of the project that went extremely well. Offer advice to other researchers who might be interested in conducting a similar project.

WRITING THE REPORT

The final step in the research flowchart is writing the report. This activity is covered in some detail in Section III of this text.

REVIEW QUESTIONS

1. What is the difference between a descriptive survey and an analytical survey?
2. In what ways might businesses use survey research?
3. How has survey research received something of a "bad reputation" as a result of its use by some well-known organizations?

4. Why is sampling important in survey research?
5. What do postmodernists say about generalizing survey results? Why do they feel this way?
6. Why is random digit dialing one of the most popular methods of getting a survey sample?
7. What are some of the problems researchers encounter with telephone surveys? With mail surveys?
8. Why is the development of the questionnaire an extremely important part of survey research?
9. What is the difference between an open-ended question and a closed-ended question?
10. Why is it important to train the individuals who will be doing the calling for a telephone survey?
11. Why is a caller script necessary for a telephone survey?
12. What are the advantages and disadvantages of an Internet survey?

SUGGESTED ACTIVITIES

1. Examine other research methods books for the formal definition of a survey. Compare the definitions and select one that you think best describes the process.
2. Investigate the AAPOR. Find out the goals and objectives of the organization, who its members are, and when they meet. What contributions is the organization making to quality survey research?
3. Try to find examples of "fake" surveys, that is, surveys whose purpose is to raise money, get a subscription, or the like. Determine whether these surveys are really interested in the data they presume to gather and what use might be made of the data.
4. In the library (or online) find several examples of survey research in the communication literature. Determine what kind of sample was selected. Does the sample seem appropriate for the survey project? Explain.
5. Find examples of survey questionnaires. Many organizations circulate questionnaires asking for their customers' input on their experiences with the organization. Analyze these questionnaires for proper form and function.
6. Assume you are assigned to conduct a telephone survey of the most recent 200 graduates of your communication department. You are interested in determining whether these graduates were satisfied with the education they received from your college or university. Develop a line-item budget for this project.
7. Engage in a little role-playing with a fellow student. Assume one of you is the research caller and the other the respondent. Develop a caller script and one or two demographic questions. Hint: the respondent should be a little uncooperative. This activity should challenge both the caller and the respondent.
8. Visit the SurveyMonkey Web site (or some similar Web site) and learn the specific kinds of help offered by these organizations.

CHAPTER 7

Historical Research

Over the three decades that I have been working as a historian, I have learned that a historian works like a detective. If a historical controversy captures your attention and you want to find out "what happened," you have to do a lot of investigation. First, you read what other historians have written. Then you carefully review their evidence, examine primary sources, and begin to shape your own conclusions—your own explanation of what happened.

One asks, again and again, How do I know this is so? Is it logical? What is the evidence? Sometimes your inquiries will confirm the conventional account; in other cases you may be able to find new ways of interpreting the same well-known facts. That is the fun of doing history. It requires patience, some ingenuity, a love of research, and a modicum of irreverence toward the received wisdom. After all, if you are willing to accept unquestioningly what "everyone" says, then the story is over before the investigation begins.

—DIANE RAVITCH

H istory is not a subject that excites many students. There are some history lovers out there in classrooms, of course. But, for the most part, students often see history as names and dates to be memorized for upcoming exams. It is true that history includes names and dates, but it is much more than that. History is a record of the past, and the past includes a multitude of other facts beyond names and dates. The past also involves events and, quite likely, a host of economic, social, and political situations that may be little understood in present day culture.

Shafer (1980) notes that "history is one of the most powerful studies for engendering empathy, an understanding of the motives, beliefs, frustrations, culture patterns, and hopes of other people" (p. 6). In a general way, studying history prepares us for what to expect in life, whether from "human greed, cruelty, and folly [or] from nobility and courage and wisdom" (p. 7).

Wilson (1999) believes that history "is both a subject, or what has happened, and *the process of recounting and analyzing that subject*" [emphasis added] (p. 1). If one is to recount (or retell, if you will) what happened in the past and analyze information and materials that facilitate that retelling, then history essentially becomes a method we can use to answer questions we have about the past in general, and about communication and media, in particular.

DEFINITION AND USES

History has many definitions. Most people believe it to be what happened in the past. Some might rely on a dictionary definition. But if we are to use history as a method of research, our definition must be much more specific than those offered either by conventional wisdom or by any dictionary. Let's define history this way: *History is the written or spoken record, or physical artifact, or interpretation, or study of all that has happened up to the present time.*

There are many reasons to study history beyond knowing what happened in the past. More broadly, history can help us understand and adapt to change, realize the significance of time and place in life, and enrich our knowledge and perspective about others who were (or are) different from us.

In an earlier chapter, we noted that much early research in communication was guided by the principle of determining "who said what to whom in what channel with what effect." We can use a paraphrased version of this as a guiding principle for investigating problems, ideas, and issues of concern using history as a research method. We can ask the following: What happened to whom, where, why, with what effect, and with what meaning for our present culture?

Historical methods are used by scholars in a number of academic fields, including sociology, anthropology, and political science, among others. Scholars use a variety of terms to describe their specific research activities. Historical study can include the following: historical criticism which "examines how important past events shape and are shaped by rhetorical messages;" historical case studies which "examine texts related to a single, salient historical event to understand the role played by communication;" biographical studies which "examine public and private texts of prominent, influential, or otherwise remarkable individuals;" social movement studies which "examine persuasive strategies used to influence the historical development of specific campaigns or causes" (Frey, Botan, & Kreps, 2000, pp. 231–232). Historical research also includes oral history which "investigates spoken, as opposed to written, accounts of personal experiences to understand more fully what happened in the past" (Frey et al., p. 231). Oral history research has become increasingly popular in postmodern culture. This particular historical method deserves a more detailed treatment. You will, therefore, find a complete discussion and presentation of oral history methods in Chapter 8. The case study method is often used by historical researchers, although it can be used in connection with other methods, too. A description of the case study method may be found later in this chapter.

Other historical methods exist, of course, but our purpose here is not to survey all possible historical methods but to establish a method that can reasonably be used to answer some of the questions we have about communication and media.

A POSTMODERN PERSPECTIVE

Does contemporary culture influence history? Could postmodern culture change the way we study history, or at least how we interpret it? Nord (2003) believes that "historians and philosophers have long pondered the question, Is history a form of science or a genre of literature? The arrival of postmodernism rendered that question considerably more fundamental and urgent, for at the radical extreme, postmodernism seemed to say that history is indeed fiction— but, then, so is science" (p. 363). Clearly, postmodernism rests on "the multiplicity and elusiveness of meaning in human affairs . . . [yet] humans live their lives in a world of words and interpretations that draw meaning from other words and interpretations" (p. 364). Some say postmodernists delight in obscurity and obfuscation, particularly when they "deny that one objective reality exists" (Wilson, 1999, p. 112). How can an historical study deliver an accurate picture of the reality of a past time, person, or event if there is no such thing as reality? Does one create a new reality in the process of knowing history?

If history is built on the known facts of the time, are those facts "different from what we believe or know today?" But "historical 'facts' are what the historian happens, or chooses, to find and may change if he or she learns more about the subject" (Stacks & Hocking, 1999, p. 104; Wilson, 1999, p. 1). Nord (2003) notes that Becker "drew a sharp distinction between history as the actual past and history as our reconstruction of the past . . . even so-called facts [may be] relative" (p. 365).

Still, postmodernism may not have impacted history all that much. "Historians still churn out articles and books that build arguments with empirical evidence, just as if the Enlightenment were alive and well" (Nord,

2003, p. 366). Nevertheless, "to know what people did we must know what they meant; and meaning is necessarily situated in the contexts of time and place" (p. 366). This makes historical research important.

So what is demanded of the postmodern researcher who selects the historical method to gather evidence aimed at answering questions he/she has about communication? An historical study must, first of all, be a quest for knowledge. It must seek solid evidence that can be used to address important research questions. Second, it must rigorously follow a set of rules and procedures for gathering that evidence. Third, it requires the researcher "to take on, mentally, the circumstances, views, and feelings of those being studied, so that the researcher can interpret their actions appropriately" (Weber, cited in Babbie, 2002, p. 334). Finally, an historical study must find meaning; that meaning must be expressed in terms of what it meant in its time and what it means in our time.

BASICS

If you are planning to use the historical method of research, you most likely have identified a problem or area of interest about something or someone in the past. Our research flowchart suggests you state the problem or issue you wish to study. This problem statement is, of course, followed by a question or series of questions that need to be answered. Rousmaniere (2004) believes that historians begin their research with a question, usually a simple one such as, "What happened?" followed by more complex questions . . . (p. 43). It is often helpful to determine the elements of the communication model likely to be involved in answering your questions. For historical research, this could be any (or all) of the model elements.

With a question or series of questions in hand, you are now ready to develop a research design for your project. The first step in this process is to complete the basics, that is, the activities that are common to any research method. You should *discuss the problem* with others, *search the literature* for information about the problem, and *revise the research questions*. Please do not rush through these activities. They are important. Most researchers are anxious to get their projects started, that is, to begin the actual data gathering. Data gathering (or collecting evidence, if you will) is important, and it will come along at the appropriate time. But now, you should give your full attention and effort to clarifying the problem you wish to study, reviewing what others have found and written about it, and revising the questions that will guide your study. "Refining and clarifying a historical question is a key first step" in historical research (Rousmaniere, p. 43).

USING QUALITY SOURCES

As you develop plans to talk with individuals and examine historical documents and artifacts, keep in mind that there are degrees or levels of importance in the quality of information you will receive from your sources.

Historical researchers should first use *primary sources*. These sources are those individuals who were actually involved in the event or situation you are studying. In other words, they have first-hand information. They've seen it with their own eyes or experienced it. Individuals are extremely important sources of primary information. Gubrium and Holstein (2003) feel that "everyone—each individual—is taken to have significant views and feelings about life that are accessible to others who undertake to ask about them" (p. 23). They warn, however, that in postmodern culture, "the boundaries between, and respective roles, of interviewer and interviewee have become blurred as the traditional relationship between the two is no longer seen as natural" (p. 52). Nevertheless, you should not collaborate with the interviewee. You can be a good listener and ask good questions, but the line between interviewer and interviewee must be maintained. In other words, be flexible, but don't collaborate.

When it comes to other primary sources, you'll want original documents and artifacts, too, if possible. There is no substitute for the quality that results from the use of primary sources. As Tuchman (1994) observes, "finding and assessing primary historical data is an exercise in detective work. It involves logic, intuition, persistence, and common sense—the same logic, intuition, persistence, and common sense that one would use to locate contemporary data or information pertaining to one's daily life" (p. 319).

Primary sources are not always available; you may have to rely on *secondary sources*. Although of somewhat lesser quality, these secondary sources can be helpful. These may be individuals who were not actually present during an event or situation, but who were perhaps in the vicinity or who personally knew individuals who were there and can accurately tell you what those individuals said or did. Secondary documents are commonly used by researchers. These include faxes or photocopies of original documents. Perhaps an original document can be scanned into a computer file and transmitted to you via e-mail. Once in a while you can get your hands on an original document, but true copies of a document will serve you just as well. The situation with artifacts is more difficult to manage. It is highly unlikely that copies can be made of an object and sent to you for examination. For example, suppose you are studying advances in broadcast technology between 1940 and 1955 and would like to examine the old microphone used by CBS newsman Edward R. Murrow for some of his radio programs. If that piece of hardware exists, it may already be in a museum. Or it may be on a shelf in an old basement storage room at CBS. In any case, you may not get your hands on it. You may only be able to see it as you would any museum piece, on display in a glass case. You might be able to get a picture of the item, but a picture, or even viewing it in a museum, may not tell you much about the technology used in the microphone.

Are books and articles written by historians or other historical researchers considered primary or secondary sources? Good question. Some researchers feel that the distinction here is "fuzzy" (Tuchman, 1994, p. 318).

You have no way of determining how thorough and accurate those writers were in their historical research tasks. Most of the time, books and articles written by other historians or historical researchers are considered secondary sources and should be examined with a critical eye. Don't automatically accept what has been said or written about your topic by others.

If all else fails, you may have to resort to *tertiary sources*. These are third-level sources, and some historical researchers do not place much faith in the quality of data produced by individuals who probably were quite removed from an historical event or situation and who may have little to report except what they have heard from others. Word-of-mouth may be a good way to promote or advertise a product or service, but it is not a good way to gather quality data that you can use to answer your research questions. Some tertiary sources may be acceptable, but you will need to be very careful in using them.

Regardless of whether you use primary, secondary, or tertiary sources, you will need to consider some individual issues as you gather evidence. For example, what about a single statement? What if one of your sources made a statement that was particularly revealing, but no similar comment was made by any of the other primary individuals you interviewed? Can one statement be trusted as accurate? That depends on what else is known and whether that statement agrees with what is known. At best, most historians feel that a single statement has a low probability of being true. Still, in some situations, you may judge the statement to be accurate and include it as a piece of evidence. However, Shafer (1980) suggests you immediately discard "trivia, anecdotes, and jokes" (p. 43).

Additionally, a great deal of care should be taken in making causal connections. It is often difficult to assign one particular cause to an event; most events have multiple causes. You may be on thin ice if you make too many inferences that one person or event "caused" another person to act in some way or "caused" some event to take place. Causal connections may exist, but they are difficult to establish in today's complex, postmodern culture.

Here are a few more questions to consider. What about newspapers and magazines? Do they contain valid information? Are government documents to be trusted? Do business reports have useful information? These are important questions and each deserves an answer. Newspapers and magazines are filled with all sorts of material, including fiction, editorials, cartoons, features, and hard news. Hard news can be defined as reports about people and events that are fact-based and of current importance to an audience. Newspaper and magazine material can be used, but you should understand that these media are not error-free, even in their hard news stories. Some errors may be typographical; others may be the result of errors made by the individuals with whom the writers or reporters talked. Too, there are opportunities for writers to pass on their opinions as fact. Exercise careful judgment here.

Just because a document is produced by the government or some government-related organization does not mean that it is more (or less) reliable than a document produced elsewhere. Government documents are written by men and women who are subject to the same errors of fact and bias as the rest of us. Typographical errors often abound in government-produced publications. Don't reject these documents out-of-hand, but be cautious (Shafer, 1980, p. 85).

Business reports are often produced to create an impression, to enhance public relations, or to promote a product, service, or event. It is often difficult to find the "truth" in material of this sort, particularly in postmodern culture where discovering the "truth" of anything is a slippery enterprise. Nevertheless, business reports may be examined, facts may be checked, and individuals may be interviewed all with a view toward establishing what, if anything, can be used from a business report.

DEVELOPING A DETAILED PLAN

You are now ready to develop a plan that will help carry forward the research and, ultimately, address your research questions. As we have noted several times, there is no substitute for accurate and complete planning. Planning for an historical study is usually a little more difficult than planning for studies using other methods. For one thing, you will be dealing with issues from the past, and finding evidence about the past is often more difficult than, say, conducting a telephone survey. So much about the past is beyond the researcher's control. So much is unknown. Sometimes all one has is a series of questions and perhaps only a vague idea of who or what can answer those questions. Still, you should plan the project in as much detail as possible.

The following questions may be helpful in planning your historical project:

1. How will I gather the evidence that will enable me to answer the research questions?
2. With whom will I need to speak? Where are these individuals to be found? Will they be willing to assist my research effort?
3. What documents will I need to examine? Where are these documents located?
4. Will I need to examine artifacts (objects)? Where are these artifacts?
5. Will permissions be required before I can speak with individuals or examine documents or artifacts? How will I get the required permissions?
6. Will I have to travel to different parts of the country (or the world) to gather evidence?
7. How will I record the evidence I gather?
8. Will I need one or more research assistants?
9. What will this research project cost?

When you have answered as many of these questions as you can, you are ready to draw up a preliminary research plan. Shafer (1980) suggests the issue or subject you are studying should "have a beginning, a development, and a conclusion" (p. 43). You should identify the beginning point for your issue or subject and start there. Next, follow the natural progression of the development of that issue or subject to its conclusion. If you use this type of plan, you will find that the evidence you gather will make more sense, and you'll have less trouble near the end of the project sorting everything out. You might find it helpful to consider three separate but related plans. You may need a plan for talking with individuals, a plan for examining documents and/or artifacts, and a plan for handling the general logistics of the study. On the other hand, in order to conduct your study in a systematic fashion and to achieve a sort of unity among the evidence you gather, you may decide to develop just one overall plan.

Almost immediately you will need some way to organize the plans and keep the details of one separate from the details of the others (if you elect to use the three-plan approach). Jotting notes on yellow legal pads is often convenient, but numerous yellow sheets of paper can become mixed and one plan's details can be lost or misplaced among the details of another. There is no single, best way to organize and plan an historical study. Much depends on the personal preferences of the researcher. Perhaps the easiest way to develop your three plans is to use notebooks with different colored covers. For example, you could develop a plan for talking with individuals in a notebook with a red cover, for examining documents or artifacts in a notebook with a green cover, and the overall logistics plan could be developed in a blue-covered notebook. Spiral bound notebooks are widely available and generally inexpensive. If you want to be a bit more formal, you might use plain white or lined paper and place the completed sheets in three-ring binders (of different colors, of course).

Let's take a look at our red notebook, the one we are using to plan our interaction with individuals. Begin by writing the name of an individual at the top of the page. Each individual should have his/her own page. For each person, write what you already know about the person: address, phone number, place of residence, e-mail address. Include the name, address, or phone number of a person who knows the individual you need to contact. Is the individual well-known enough to have an entry in a reference book of some sort, such as *Current Biography*? What useful information did you find there? Then, on the back of the sheet, write the questions you wish to ask the individual. Finally, given the sorts of questions you have to ask the person, indicate whether you think the needed information can be gathered by letter, by phone, or by a face-to-face interview.

Use a similar process for each of the documents and/or artifacts you need to examine and record the information in the green notebook. Each document or artifact should have its own page and should contain the information you already know about the document or artifact as well as the sorts of information you hope to get from it. Do you need to know who wrote the document? Who received it? What it said? When it was written? If an artifact, when was it produced? Who had control over it or used it? For what purpose was it produced? Of course, you'll have many more questions than these, but you get the idea.

Using spiral-bound or three-ring notebooks for planning purposes requires the researcher to prepare plans by hand, that is, to write in the books, to actually use a pen and move one's hand to produce words on a page. For some, this may seem old-fashioned. After all, aren't we in the computer age? Don't we have all sorts of electronic gear designed to make writing easier? Isn't handwriting obsolete? Well, yes and no. We do not have to write everything by hand these days, but some researchers find it more satisfying (and often more convenient). Others believe using a laptop (ironically called a notebook) is the way to go. Planning could be somewhat easier on a computer. You could simply create three different text files, one each for individuals, documents/artifacts, and logistics. If you choose to use a computer for planning purposes, you should follow the same general process outlined earlier, that is, giving each individual or document a separate page and putting the appropriate information on that page.

However you choose to develop your plans, you should understand that a plan is almost always preliminary. As you talk with people and read documents, new questions will arise and new people with whom you need to speak will be identified. New documents may surface as you explore libraries, the personal records of those involved in your study, or the files of media organizations to which you have been given access.

LOGISTICS

Once you have done as much planning as you can in terms of the individuals with whom you need to make contact and the documents/artifacts you need to examine, you are ready to begin work planning the logistics, or specific details and arrangements, of your study. Open the blue notebook (or open a new computer text file) and, on the first page, prepare a tentative outline about what the logistics book needs to contain. You will need at least three main sections: individuals, documents/artifacts, and budget.

Open the red notebook (for individuals) and place it beside the blue one. Thumb through your notes on individuals and find the ones who can be contacted by letter or e-mail. Write the corresponding information in the logistics book. Decide which ones can be interviewed by phone and write the corresponding information in the logistics book. Finally, determine which individuals must be interviewed face-to-face and list those along with their critical information.

Look first at those you feel could be contacted by letter or e-mail. In the logistics book, draft a cover letter or e-mail introduction that will be sent along with a list of questions you would like to have answered. The cover letter should introduce the researcher, provide details about the project, and ask for the person's help. Spend some time writing and polishing this letter or e-mail introduction. A well-written, direct-to-the-point cover letter will often go a long way in getting the cooperation you need. You can find an example of a cover letter in Figure 7.1. You should modify the cover letter as needed to meet your specific needs and to meet the needs of an e-mail message. Remember to thank individuals for their help and

May 15, 2_____

Mr. John Q. Public
123 Main Street
Lansing, MI 11111

Dear Mr. Public:

My name is _____. I am an historical researcher working on a project about the development of radio news for my senior thesis at the University of _____. I need your help. My preliminary research indicates that you were a close friend and work colleague of the late John Doe who was a major figure in the development of radio news for ABC. I have found the answers to some of my questions by examining Mr. Doe's personal files (with the permission of his family). I still have several questions which you may be able to answer. I would very much appreciate your assistance in helping me understand the specific contributions Mr. Doe made to ABC radio news.

I have enclosed a separate sheet with a few questions that I hope you will be able to answer. I can keep your answers confidential or cite you as a source, whichever you prefer. I have also included a self-addressed stamped envelope. If it is more convenient, you can e-mail me your answers at historybuff22@xyz.edu.

I know you are busy and that there is considerable demand on your time, but I hope that you, as one of Mr. Doe's closest friends, will help me provide an accurate picture of Mr. Doe's accomplishments and his important contributions to radio news.

Feel free to contact my university advisor, Professor K. V. Baber, if you need information about me or my thesis project. His phone number is aaa-bbb-cccc. He can also be reached at historyprof@xyz.edu.

Thank you so much for your time and attention.

Sincerely,

Jane Smith
456 University Street
Chicago, IL 22222

Enclosure

FIGURE 7.1   Sample Cover Letter for Historical Research

enclose a self-addressed, stamped envelope so answers to questions can be easily returned. Returning answers by e-mail should pose no problem.

Next, use the cover letter as a basis for developing a script you can use to assist you in getting the cooperation of individuals you contact by phone. Don't read the script to the person whose help you are soliciting. Use the script to develop fluency in speaking with strangers whose help you need. Stammering or hesitating during the first few moments of a call may cause the individual to decline your offer to assist with the research study. At the very least, it will not motivate the listener to pay close attention to what you have to say. Be smooth, professional, knowledgeable, and caring on the phone. Remember, you need these people to help you. Treat them with respect. If they agree to help, get right to your questions. Don't waste their time, or yours. Thank them when the interview is completed. One additional suggestion about phone interviews: do not make the interview call on a cell phone. Cell phones are not always dependable. Calls are often dropped and reception can be spotty. Also, if the person you are calling has Caller ID (and who doesn't these days), he/she may not be inclined to answer if the ID shows your number and the word "wireless." Use a standard, old-fashioned landline for telephone research interviews.

You are now ready to consider what details must be handled for the face-to-face interviews. If this activity requires travel, it is often helpful to organize the interviews by geographical area. In this way, you may be able to minimize travel costs. You will need to contact these individuals, either by letter or phone, and ask for an appointment. Once the appointments are set, you can look at your schedule and determine whether two or more interviews can be done in proximity to each other. For example, if you need to interview someone in Washington, DC and someone in nearby Baltimore, MD, you can do both on one trip to that area. Why fly (or drive) to the DC area twice? Make one trip and complete both interviews. You can accomplish much if you avoid scheduling conflicts. Don't agree to meet someone in Washington at 10 a.m. and someone else in Baltimore at noon. You will not be physically able to keep both appointments. Spread them out a little in the day.

You next need to look at what documents/artifacts you wish to see and where they are located. Can some of these be examined during or near the time and place where you are conducting other research activities? Can copies be made of the documents? Who would make the copies? Are copying costs involved? Are some items you need likely to be of a sensitive nature? What precautions will you take to keep information confidential? Will you need to get permission from individuals or organizations in order to examine certain documents and/or artifacts? Will you need to make special appointments to see these items, or can you just walk in during normal business hours? Weekends? What about libraries you may need to visit? Where are they and what are their operating hours? Do you need special credentials to have access to some material in the library? How will you get these special credentials?

In other words, your logistical task is to think of and decide how to handle each little detail that comes with gathering information from individuals and organizations, and from examining important documents or artifacts. Spend some time considering each task and each aspect of each task. Consider the situation from all sides. Try to think of everything. Of course, you will not likely be able to think of everything, but you will almost surely think about almost everything. Unexpected situations do arise from time to time, especially once the project is underway. Expect the unexpected and be prepared to deal with it.

Your logistical planning is not complete. You must now consider the cost of conducting your research project, and this means developing a budget. Remember that a budget is simply a list of anticipated expenses. The cost of almost everything changes over time and you will not, as a rule, be able to determine the cost of your project to the penny. Still, having a general idea of what resources you will need to do the study is important.

Earlier in this text, we discussed budget preparation and noted that, for the most part, a budget can be prepared if costs are considered in four major categories: personnel, facilities/equipment, materials/supplies, and miscellaneous. Since historical research often requires travel, let's add at least one additional category to our budget: travel/lodging/meals.

If you are paying for the project yourself, you will most likely want to be frugal and avoid extra expenses whenever possible. If an outside organization is funding the research, you may have the flexibility to hire a research assistant. If you need an assistant and plan to hire one, make sure the individual knows how to do historical research. You can waste valuable time training an individual who has no idea how to do research of any kind, let alone historical research. In other words, hire a competent individual and pay him/her at a level commensurate with the person's skill and knowledge.

DATA GATHERING

You are now ready to start asking questions, interviewing individuals, visiting libraries, examining documents or artifacts, and gathering the evidence you will need to address your study's research questions. As you begin the study, remember that you must keep an accurate record of everything you do. Shafer (1980) thinks "adopting a standard method of recording things" is a good idea, particularly if the information you get involves names, dates, times, subjects discussed, and the like (p. 118). You can use spiral or looseleaf notebooks, computer text files, even note cards of various sizes.

Some historical researchers believe it is acceptable to abbreviate when taking notes. You are often interested in the "big picture" and abbreviating makes note taking somewhat easier. Others, however, believe that abbreviations are acceptable only when you are recording your observations about a document or artifact, but that when it comes to interviews, total accuracy is required. This means that answers to your questions must be kept in the exact words of the speaker. If you are conducting a face-to-face interview and you are fast, you may be able to write down the exact responses to your questions. However, more than likely you will want to audiotape the interview session, with the permission of the participant, of course. You can then go back later and transcribe or listen to the exact responses to your questions. If answers to your questions come by letter, you will have a ready-made copy of the data. If answers come by e-mail, you can simply print a hard copy.

When you have hard copies of any sort of data, it is a good idea to make multiple copies of each sheet and store the extras in a safe place. If you lose the originals, you'll have a backup copy or two. Lost data can severely damage any research project. Take steps to preserve the data. This includes making backup files if you are using a computer to record your data.

The documents you examine may vary somewhat in quality. Some will be well-preserved, and the writing on them will be legible. Others may be delicate or poorly preserved, and the writing may be hard to read. Document quality often is the result of how a document was stored and whether it was part of a public or private collection (Shafer, 1980, p. 80).

Must all historical data be qualitative, that is, words, phrases, statements, and the like from people and documents? No, some historical researchers gather quantitative data, that is, evidence that can be counted, calculated, or precisely measured (Shafer, 1980, p. 66). You should not be afraid of gathering quantitative data if such data have relevance to your project. Tuchman (1994) notes that although all data have problems, quantitative historical data may "contain all of the problems associated with contemporary qualitative data . . ." that is, they are often "collected and coded with particular questions in mind" (p. 320). This simply means that even quantitative data can contain biased or manipulated information.

What next? Do you begin conducting interviews with individuals or do you begin examining documents or artifacts? Can you mix the two activities? How you proceed largely depends on your particular preferences and the systematic plan you have developed for gathering data. Some researchers prefer to write to or talk with all the individuals in their planning book before going on to documents/artifacts. Others like to work with documents first, then individuals. Still others mix the two activities, particularly if a document and an individual are in the same geographical area to which one must travel. In short, there is no rule about how you should begin gathering evidence. Each researcher is different. You should proceed in a way that you are comfortable with but in a way that is logical and organized.

In whatever order you do the work, please remember to record your evidence carefully, either on audiotape, in handwritten notes, in a computer text file, or perhaps on videotape or in a photograph. Record date, time, place, individuals involved, documents examined, and the like. Do not rely on your memory to recall these details. A historical study often takes a lot of time. Even the best memories cannot always be trusted to remember precise details. Write everything down.

ANALYZING THE DATA

When you have gathered all the evidence you think you need to answer your research questions, you are ready to begin a careful examination and analysis of what you have found. It is not sufficient just to repeat or reproduce what you have discovered. As an historical researcher, you must examine the evidence for validity and organize it in some meaningful way.

First, examine the evidence *internally*. Ask this question: Is there consistency within the material I have gathered? For example, if several sources agree on a precise date for a particular event, you have consistency; you can be fairly sure the date is accurate. If there is inconsistency, you will need to examine each piece of evidence and decide why there is disagreement. In situations like these, you may be called upon to exercise your judgment and determine what the "truth" is, even though there may not be total agreement about some particular person, date, or event.

Next, examine the evidence *externally*. Ask this question: Is there consistency in the way my evidence relates to the known world? For example, suppose you know for a fact that CBS's Edward R. Murrow was in London, England, on a particular day during World War II. You have learned that Murrow saw and talked with more than two dozen individuals that day, eight of whom you have interviewed; you have copies of restaurant bills he signed that day. If you discover in your notes that one of the individuals you interviewed said he had lunch with Murrow that day at CBS headquarters in New York City, you would have reason to doubt that piece of evidence. In other words, some pieces of evidence may not match what we know to be true. That evidence can be discarded, but many researchers would likely reinterview the individual who got the date wrong and try to clarify the matter.

You should now begin to organize your evidence so that it may be used to answer the study's research questions. Shafer (1980) suggests four possible categories of evidence: interviewee responses to your questions (whether by letter, e-mail, or in person); comments from other historians as a result of your search of the literature; notes resulting from an examination of documents or artifacts; and other data you may have gathered during the research activity. Of course, if you see a more logical, more useful way to organize your data, you should use it. Gubrium and Holstein (2003) believe that "analysis takes the form of systematically grouping and summarizing . . . and providing a coherent organizing framework that . . . explains aspects of the social world that respondents portray" (p. 78). Remember that you will likely have some evidence that does not directly relate to or is irrelevant to your study. This evidence can be cast aside as "insignificant" (Shafer, p. 184).

Mainstream social science researchers, particularly those who gather quantitative data, are fond of saying that they are unbiased in drawing conclusions about their work because "the data speak for themselves." Do the data speak for themselves in historical research? Not usually. In historical research, the researcher "must become thinker and puzzle out meanings for him/herself" (Shafer, 1980, p. 187).

ADDRESSING THE RESEARCH QUESTIONS

As you examine the evidence you have collected, keep in mind that you are preparing to make judgments about the meaning and value of that evidence. Your judgments should be as sound as possible, backed by significant evidence. Historical researchers often call the judgments made as a result of an examination of the data *inferences*. In other words, you will draw conclusions. These conclusions result from a *synthesis* of the evidence, that is, a fitting together of all the things you have found into some form, or pattern, or picture that accurately describes the event, person, or situation you are studying.

The judgments you make about what you have found should enable you to address the study's research questions. The answer to a research question is usually more than a word or phrase. For example, suppose a research question asked this: What contributions did John Doe make to the development of ABC radio news? "He made many contributions" is not an acceptable answer. You must be specific in detailing his contributions. You should also indicate the significance of his contributions for his time and what those contributions mean to us today.

Take all the time you need to address (or answer) each of the study's research questions. You may be able to answer some completely, but may only be able to provide a partial answer to others. Answer all questions to the best of your ability and based on the evidence you collected.

EVALUATING THE STUDY

At this point you should take a critical look at the study you just completed. How successful was it in answering the questions you had about communication, media, people, or events in the past? What unusually delightful things did you discover? What disappointments did you face? Were the individuals with whom you dealt cooperative? Were you able to examine the necessary documents/artifacts? Was the study done within budget? What suggestions would you offer to future historical researchers interested in your subject? What new questions arose as a result of your research?

WRITING THE REPORT

The final step in your historical research project is the writing of the report. As you have seen in previous chapters, report writing is an important part of any research activity. The report writing process is covered in detail in Section III of this text.

THE CASE STUDY METHOD

A Brief Overview

As noted earlier, the case study method is popular among historical re-searchers. Please understand, however, that it is not limited to historical research. It can be used in connection with other research methods. As Stake (1994) notes, "We choose to study [a] case. We could study it in many ways." Regardless of what method we use in conjunction with a case study, the study should be focused around this question: "What can be learned from the single case?" (p. 236).

Researchers often choose the case study method when they want a "better understanding of [a] particular case," not because it represents other cases or "illustrates a particular trait or problem," but because the "case itself is of interest." In some situations, researchers study a number of cases jointly in order to inquire into [a] phenomenon, population, or general condition" (Stake, 1994, p. 237).

The Case Study Process

As you might expect, the first step in the case study method is to *select a case*. A case can be an "individual, institution, organization, event, issue, or some type of phenomenon" (Poindexter & McCombs, 2000, p. 289). You should be able to justify your selection, that is, explain why you selected the case.

Next, *pose a research question*. Stake (1994) has some suggested research questions that are general enough to meet the needs of most case studies:

- "What can be learned from [this] single case?"
- "What is common and what is particular about this case?"

You might elect, however, to pose a more specific research question relating directly to your case.

Assuming you have completed the basics of any research project, in-cluding a literature search and a consideration of the logistics required to conduct the study, you can begin *data gathering*. Your overall goal in gather-ing data is to collect enough information so that you understand everything about the case's historical background and its physical setting. You may wish to look at the case in other contexts, including economic, political, legal, and so forth. You will almost certainly want to identify people to interview and documents to examine. You already know something of these processes from information provided earlier in this chapter. However, as subjects are interviewed, you would do well to ask "who else would be relevant to talk to." This is called the *snowball method* of identifying subjects and is often used with case studies (Poindexter & McCombs, 2000, p. 209).

In rare cases, you may be able to directly observe an event or phenome-non. This does not, however, excuse you from the task of talking with others who know something about the case or from examining relevant documents about the case.

When you have exhausted all possible sources of data and feel that you have all the evidence available about the case, you should *summarize your findings* and *address the research question*. Your summary of the findings should be exactly that—a summary—not a listing of everything you found. You should get into the specifics of the study when you address the research question, providing names, dates, places, activities, and other precise information as you work to provide a complete picture of the case in the written report.

Finally, you should *explain the significance of the case for communication and media*. What can be learned from the case? Why was it worthy of study? What issue(s) does it raise for future consideration?

Remember that the case study method is often used in connection with other research methods. The information provided earlier, although brief, will give you some idea of how to proceed with a case study regardless of the method with which it is associated.

REVIEW QUESTIONS

1. Why is knowing about the past important in understanding the world today?
2. How does this chapter define *history*?
3. Why are postmodernists cautious about the study of history?
4. Why are primary historical sources preferred?
5. What are secondary and tertiary sources?
6. Why is planning so important for a historical study?
7. What is meant by *internal* and *external* analysis of historical data?
8. What specific problems often face a historical researcher?
9. Under what circumstances might one select the case study method for a research project?

SUGGESTED ACTIVITIES

1. Find examples of historical research in the scholarly communication journals. How did the researchers organize their study? What problems did they encounter?
2. Find a historical study that gathered quantitative data. Were qualitative data also gathered? Which type of data seemed to be more revealing, that is, which appeared to be more helpful in addressing the study's research questions?
3. Contact the Department of History at your university. Ask to speak with a professor or graduate student who is currently engaged in a research project. Inquire about the processes and procedures involved in that individual's research.
4. Find a professor or graduate student in your communication department who has used the case study method. Ask about the methods used to gather data for the study.

CHAPTER 8

Oral History

By KIM GOLOMBISKY

*History is the witness of the times, the torch of
truth, the life of memory, the teacher of life . . . .*

—CICERO

Oral history was reenergized in 2003 when public radio producer Dave Isay launched his StoryCorps project in New York City's Grand Central Station. Partnered with National Public Radio (NPR) and the Corporation for Public Broadcasting (CPB), StoryCorps records and preserves the spoken memories of ordinary people for posterity. To participate in Isay's brainchild, "narrators," as they're called in oral history, show up in pairs at any of StoryCorps' small permanent or mobile sound studios to interview each other with the help of a StoryCorps facilitator. Grown children interview their parents or grandparents. Brothers and sisters, husbands and wives, partners, or lovers reminisce. The oldest of friends trace their shared histories.

Narrators spend about 40 minutes in a StoryCorps booth and leave with a CD of their interview. Each interview costs about $200 to produce, but narrators are asked to pay only a $10 donation. "If you can't afford $10," Isay says, "you pay nothing" (Kniffel, 2005, p. 43). No one is turned away.

If the narrators grant their permission, StoryCorps sends a copy of the interview to the American Folklife Center at the Library of Congress, where the interview becomes part of a national digital archive of spoken American history. Anyone may contribute to Isay's vision of oral history as a people's history, and, thanks to technology, anyone can listen to this history at www.storycorps.net.

Isay says StoryCorps was inspired by the New Deal's Works Progress Administration (WPA) and the Federal Writers Project (FWP), which recorded average people's life histories during the Great Depression of the 1930s and early 1940s. Although the WPA recordings are considered an important moment in the evolution of oral history, oral history's roots begin much earlier. Orality, or spoken communication, was the only way to pass on knowledge until the advent of literacy, or written communication. In many places around the world, oral traditions continue to be an important means of preserving and sharing history.

In the lore of oral history's history, the Greek Thucydides is cited as the first oral historian because he interviewed people and included their statements in his *History of the Peloponnesian War* (Yow, 1994). The nineteenth century marked a watershed moment for U.S. oral history when historians began collecting interviews with early American settlers. Generally, however, oral history as a bona fide research method in the United States is credited to a Pulitzer Prize winning historian at Columbia University named Allan Nevins. Using large, awkward recording equipment, Nevins began documenting the testimony of historically significant men after World War II. He called his research "oral history."

In 1970, radio and print journalist Louis "Studs" Terkel popularized oral history with his book *Hard Times: An Oral History of the Great Depression*. Terkel began his career with the WPA Writers Project and has spent his life interviewing people to reveal the ways ordinary lives are extraordinary and extraordinary lives are ordinary. Ironically, because of his remarkable career, Terkel himself has become a historically significant figure and the subject of media interviews that future generations may track down one day.

This brief history of oral history demonstrates some important themes in oral history research. First, Terkel's status as a media icon, Isay's partnerships with NPR and the CPB, and Nevins' Pulitzer Prize illustrate a connection between oral history and journalism. They share many similarities, such as documenting what people say for the record. Second, like mass communications, oral history has a vested interest in communication technologies, from unwieldy early sound equipment, to film and video production, to digital and Web technologies. Third, and perhaps most important, what counts as history and who says it gets to count (much like what counts as news and who says it gets to count) is a moving target spanning everything from "great" men and women to the man or woman "on the street." The realization that definitions of history (and journalism) are not set in stone may be disconcerting. But it is also liberating. As StoryCorps demonstrates, you don't have to be a celebrity to contribute to historical knowledge, and you don't need a Ph.D. to become an oral historian.

A POSTMODERN PERSPECTIVE

Constantly questioning what history means is very much a part of using oral history as a research method. Questioning history also is very much in the tradition of postmodern thinking. So oral history becomes a good choice to consider for researchers working in the postmodern era.

For postmodernists, the issue isn't whether collecting and preserving history is a valuable endeavor. Instead, they would have us recognize that history itself is elusive. The way historians define it and practice it changes between individuals and over time. Even who may be called a historian can be debatable, which implicates power relationships. A postmodern perspective, then, also asks who or what is being included and excluded from the historical record, and why. Furthermore, both postmodern and communication perspectives remind us that how narrators intend their oral histories to be interpreted and how researchers and audiences actually interpret them are not necessarily in sync.

If there is no objective history out there simply waiting to be discovered without human interpretation, then a postmodern perspective also recognizes that changing technologies—as the means and media by which we collect and preserve what we decide to call history—also *mediate* our understandings of history. As Marshall McLuhan (1964) famously said, "The medium is the message." So, while we may be working communication technology, it also may be working on us, to stretch the ways we can know and experience the world.

In the end, good oral history research represents a delicate balance between fact and interpretation, and between science and art. We will be exploring these issues in greater detail.

DEFINITIONS AND USES

You already may have gathered that *oral history is a method of collecting and preserving the spoken word as a historical record.* You may also have surmised that oral history is about gathering people's "stories" and that oral history involves interviewing. Oral history is "a recounting of some experience, usually told to an interviewer, for historical purposes" (Stucky, 1995, p. 1). Uses for oral history in communication research are nearly unlimited. Oral history can be appropriate for documenting what it's like to work as an embedded journalist in a foreign war at the beginning of the twenty-first century. Oral history is also appropriate for preserving the history of an organization for organizational communication or public relations purposes. Before we talk about how to conduct oral history research, let's backtrack a bit to explore what oral history is and how you might find it helpful.

One online oral history course says, " 'Oral History' is a maddeningly imprecise term" (http://historymatters.gmu.edu/mse/oral/what.html).

Despite attempts to devise precise definitions for oral history, none seems to catch on, according to Yow (1994), one of the top contemporary experts on oral history research. Yow says a wide range of terminology appears synonymously with oral history, including: taped memoir, typewritten transcript, in-depth interviewing, life history, self-report, personal narrative, life story, oral biography, memoir, testament, recorded narrative, and life review. Yow (1994), however, suggests that oral history ought to refer to "the recorded in-depth interview" because it implies "that there is someone else involved who inspires the narrator to begin the act of remembering, jogs the memory, and records and presents the narrator's words" (p. 4). Of course, the "someone else involved" is the researcher actively looking to capture people's memories and stories before they are lost forever. We might extend Yow's definition of oral history by emphasizing the word "history." Not all in-depth interviewing is oral history. *History* distinguishes oral history from other kinds of in-depth interviews.

If "oral history" is a little muddy, "history" is a veritable quagmire. The problem is that most people tend to take the word "history" for granted. History means, well, *history*. But for researchers, understanding how we intend the word is important. *For our purposes, "history" means the practice of trying to document the past.*

In the postmodern era, we have come to understand that the people who write history unwittingly shape what we can know about the past. Historians only have limited access to all the facts of any historical moment. Historians also filter the historical facts they do have access to through their understanding of the present, which is any historian's only experience of reality. Furthermore, historians' ability to interpret evidence from the past is limited by who they are as people and what they are interested in. "Historically," Western historians have been white men. Thus, most of what we know about Western history today—our "received knowledge"—seems to lack any interest in recording other perspectives, such as the histories of women or people of color. Additionally, Western history tends to be preoccupied with "great men" and public events, excluding the possibility that we may learn something from studying ordinary peoples' lives, the private sphere of home and family, or low-status work and accomplishment in the public sphere. For example, oral historians may be interested in documenting how news professionals dealt with breaking the news of the September 11, 2001, terrorist attacks in New York and Washington DC. But it would be just as useful to document how "we the people" used mass media to make sense of the tragedy of September 11.

Furthermore, most histories everywhere in the world contain significant, though usually unintentional, national and cultural bias, according to contemporary historians. To return to our 9/11 examples, in addition to studying September 11 from a U.S. perspective, it would be equally useful to document how foreign news professionals handled the story as it unfolded, along with how citizens in other countries used mass media to make sense of it. "Historiography" critically examines the project of producing history by using particular philosophical perspectives. For example, feminist historiography examines our knowledge of history for the absence of and inaccuracies about women, while feminist and women's historians search for overlooked, unpublished historical information about women.

In sum, history is a human construction and always partial. This has important practical and ethical implications for conducting oral history research. Selecting whom and what to document implies "choice," and choice complicates impartiality. Yet, if historical researchers lament their inability to witness history as it happens, then it is easy to see the value of interviewing people who did witness history in the making. The catch, for oral historians, is to identify what kinds of history will interest future generations and then to locate and interview people who lived through that kind of history while they are still alive.

Not surprisingly, oral historians spend a lot of time debating whether it is preferable to conduct oral history "from the top down" or "from the bottom up." The "top down" approach prioritizes interviewing people who are famous, who have high status, who have been involved directly with important events, or who have large amounts of power to act and make decisions on behalf of large numbers of people. This is the "great" men and women form of history. The equivalent news values would be prominence and consequence. The assumption is that people become historically significant when they make a name for themselves. This is the most common kind of history, and it tends to focus on the highest echelons of people in arenas such as politics, government, economics, business and industry, science, and the fine and popular arts.

One benefit of doing top-down history is that public figures leave behind documentary evidence for oral historians to use as background and corroboration. Interestingly, the fact of prominence and the archival trail are due in large part to the news industry. In the top-down approach, historically significant people in many cases already have been newsworthy, whether locally, globally, or within particular professional, trade, or institutional communities. While unquestionably valuable, top-down history alone tends to result in rather elitist views of the past. In valuing high status people in the public sphere, top-down history tends to overlook the historical value of exploring what it is like to live "on the ground" through a particular era. Similar arguments occur within the journalism community. For example, business news in focusing on CEOs, profits, mergers, and scandals is often criticized for failing to cover labor—what it's like to be a worker along with the issues of concern to workers.

For journalism history, the problem becomes an even greater concern, according to Brennen (1996). "Traditional media historians have generally produced top-down press histories," she writes (p. 572). She criticizes media history for focusing on biographies of famous editors and publishers, on issues of media property and ownership, and on relationships between the press and centers of political power, such as journalists' relationships with U.S. presidents. She shows that "most media historians do not address fundamental questions of ideology, power, and domination, nor do they envision the media as vehicles of social or political power that may contribute to inequality within society" (p. 572). She argues that a more comprehensive media history would include "voices of the rank-and-file newsworkers" (p. 573) and that oral history is the method best suited to produce such history. "A labor perspective would address not only the work environment, conditions, expectations, responsibilities, and routines of newsworkers but also the effect of journalistic conventions and concepts such as professionalism, democracy, objectivity, and responsibility on their working lives" (Brennen, p. 579). Without detracting from the importance of top-down work, Brennen argues that also including "bottom up" historical perspectives improves our understanding of the media's roles in society.

The "bottom up" or "history from below" approach to oral history advocates giving "voice" to those who otherwise would never be heard. Lynd (1993), an advocate of this approach, writes, "We said there was needed a history of 'the inarticulate,' by which of course was meant, not persons who did not speak, but persons who did not write: persons who did not leave behind a trail of documents" (p. 1). As Lynd suggests, oral history becomes an especially valuable method for researching the lives of people who have not been famous enough to become news figures. Paradoxically, however, these people's anonymity makes it more difficult to identify them and do background research on them prior to interviewing.

Another bottom-up phrase is "people on the margins," meaning valuing the historical perspectives and knowledge of people who are not superstars, who are backstage rather than center stage, or who are marginalized from the centers of privilege and power. Feminist researchers find oral history a particularly useful method because it records women's own interpretations of their lives in their own voices. Such views can be dramatically different from common knowledge. Thus, like bottom-up oral history, women's oral history improves our understanding of the past.

But even projects designed to correct the historical record for women's absences may fail to recognize their top-down bias, says Brennen (1996). For example, the Washington Press Club Foundation's Women in Journalism oral history project, which ran 1987–1994, encompassed life histories across seven decades. But the project focused on 56 "notable" women journalists, such as Connie Chung, who were already high-profile people (Brennen). Burt (1998) urges mass communications historians to resist "the temptation to create heroes." She says the research question should not ask "why she was 'great'" (p. 18). Instead historians should ask "how her experience was typical of women journalists in her time, how she acted as a mentor to other women journalists, and how that experience would tell us more about the developing professionalization of women journalists" (Burt, 1998, p. 18).

Burt's advice to avoid "lionizing" subjects of historical research serves all oral historians well, whether they employ top-down or bottom-up strategies and regardless of the narrator's gender.

Clearly, on principle, most would agree that both top-down and bottom-up histories, and even histories in the middle, are important to a more comprehensive historical record. In practice, however, it's not that simple. First, as Brennen (1996) points out, many historians don't realize they are deploying top-down approaches or that there are other ways of thinking about history. Second, even though including both approaches is obviously a more thorough way to go about oral history research, "thorough" necessitates time and resources. Collecting even a few oral histories is a time-consuming process. Also, as noted, it's easier to identify prominent people than obscure people, and it's easier to conduct background research on prominent people than obscure people.

Third, for oral historians (and all researchers), fieldwork is a complex process of making difficult on-the-spot decisions after weighing the consequences. For example, your author once worked on an oral history project for an organization hoping to do public education about water conservation. The organization especially wanted to collect the memories of its founders who had been activists in the cause for water preservation. The author had to choose between interviewing the politically prominent older white men who literally formed the organization, or collecting oral histories from diverse women and men involved at all levels of the organization's early development. The second choice would have been preferable, but the age and health of the "founding fathers" became a priority. Indeed, shortly after tracking down the older men and collecting their oral histories, two of them passed away. Unfortunately, because the organization was formed in an era prior to the civil rights and women's movements, there were no people of color or women of equal professional status to the organization's literal "founders." So the resulting history was not only top down but also strictly about "great" white men. But, in this particular case, considering age was more important than considering race, ethnicity, and gender. *Age* necessitated a top-down approach. A more inclusive bottom-up history had to wait. For researchers, the lesson here is to be able to make informed reasoned decisions.

This brings up another point worth noting about oral history. As this chapter has hinted all along, one of the quirks of oral history is that it has a stronger relationship with the present than other kinds of historical research. To state the obvious, the human subjects oral history requires must be living. This can create some urgency in oral history. Other kinds of historians may feel pressure to locate and save precious documents before they disintegrate or are destroyed. But oral histories must always be collected *now*. Oral historians feel greater pressure both to recognize history in the making when they see it and to record the narratives of people living through what is yet to become history. Furthermore, by acting on their judgments, oral historians must take responsibility for defining what will become history. A recent resurgence in Studs Terkel's visibility in media interviews can be attributed to his age and health. Terkel had open-heart surgery at the age of 93, and this jolted people into recognizing that he is historically significant but cannot be with us forever. Unfortunately, we often don't recognize the importance of people's historical knowledge until the end of their careers or lives, which adds even greater urgency to the oral historian's work.

To review, perfect choices are rare for oral historians trying to document the past by collecting and preserving the spoken word. A pragmatic view suggests that neither top-down nor bottom-up history is intrinsically better. Both have their uses, and, for individual oral historians, it becomes a matter of asking the right research questions and then making the best possible decisions among available options.

The next step is to look at when and where oral history becomes an appropriate method for communication research. You might have guessed from Brennen's (1996) critique of top-down journalism history that oral history is an excellent method for documenting media history of all kinds. Given our discussion of oral history's immediacy, you might think about the kinds of media history in the making you currently are witnessing. Oral histories of people working in broadcast and print media already have a history, so to speak. What about Web, digital, and cross-platform media journalism? What is happening with cellular technologies? As Brennen argues, however, it is important to document more than just the histories of media stars, owners, and managers. Journalists and other news workers also represent important potential oral history narrators.

Beyond journalism and journalists, media histories also include histories of the music, film, entertainment, production, advertising, public relations, and telecommunications industries. Niches within these industries, such as sports marketing and public health campaigns, represent even more opportunities. Independent, ethnic, and minority media histories are vital as well. As you have learned, oral history is at its best representing diverse perspectives at all organizational, institutional, social, and cultural levels. Diverse perspectives also include accounting for gender, race, ethnicity, age, sexual orientation, disability, education, class, religion, and nationality. Furthermore, it is equally important to document histories of media consumers as well as producers.

Although history for history's sake is important, history is also useful. Using oral history in a public relations campaign to teach people about water conservation is useful. Imagine an AIDS prevention campaign employing oral histories of HIV-infected people. Public relations and social marketing are obvious ways to employ oral history methods.

Oral history is probably the most overlooked public relations tool, observes Conti (1995). Used externally, an organization's oral history can help communicate with publics. "Taking quotes from the oral history to use as a public relations, advertising, and marketing tool personalizes a company's products and services," says Conti (p. 52). "Companies also use oral history quotes for product displays, exhibits and even theater" (p. 52).

Used internally in such things as newsletters, oral history can link history, organizational mission, and organizational policy to make them all relevant for personnel (Conti, 1995). Willa K. Baum, one of the most respected U.S. oral historians, has worked on oral histories for companies such as the Levi Strauss Company. She has seen the value of oral history used internally in employee relations, organizational management, and strategic planning. Baum says, "The fact that a business thinks enough of a worker's contributions to record them and use them as a guide is a matter of pride for the workers and a matter of strength for the institution" (quoted in Conti, 1995, p. 52). Corporate oral histories, including oral histories of media and news corporations, become part of the organization's lore and culture. Organizational oral history also provides management with important resources for planning and making decisions, such as how the organization handled crisis or change in the past. In addition to teaching employees important lessons about their employer's past, Baum says corporate and organizational oral histories make good case histories for business students hoping to learn what has worked and why, or vice versa. The same goes for communications scholars, students, and practitioners.

Methodologically speaking, oral historians also learn what works or doesn't from their fellow oral historians. The next section, "Issues and Problems," covers some common issues and problems associated with conducting oral history research. Oral history is not a difficult research method, and usually it's great fun. But every oral historian has tales about missteps and mistakes in the field. Sometimes oral historians, including the author, learn painful lessons by ignoring good advice. So pay attention.

ISSUES AND PROBLEMS

In addition to problems associated with defining history, there are some other challenges in doing oral history research. Most of these fall into two categories: technical challenges and interpersonal challenges. *Technical challenges* refer to working with equipment and dealing with transcripts. *Interpersonal challenges* have to do with communicating with narrators and the researcher's responsibilities to narrators. A third challenge has to do with the nature of memory because, in the end, the oral historian collects memories. Like all collectors, memory collectors should know a little something about their specialty.

Technical challenges associated with equipment and transcripts in oral history research are fairly straightforward ones. In most cases the oral historian can deal efficiently with both by planning ahead. Oral history methods record peoples' narratives verbatim. First, and most obviously, this will require some recording equipment. Second, and less obvious to the novice, transcribing the spoken word into written language—into a written transcript—is tricky because spoken language and written language are dramatically different. While this fact challenges any researcher who must transcribe interviews, it is a particularly thorny issue for oral history because, in the strictest sense, transcription is tampering with a historical record.

To begin with equipment, the most important thing to remember is foresight. Like a good scout, be prepared. You would do well to remember the folk wisdom of "Murphy's Law": If something can go wrong, it probably will. Oral historians try to prepare for any eventuality, from equipment failure to no access to electricity. Packing things as simple as extension cords and extra batteries can save an interview. Test every piece of equipment ahead of time. This is worth repeating: Test *everything* ahead of time. Whenever possible, take duplicate equipment to interviews. Recording equipment, especially digital equipment, whether sound or video, is expensive. But losing an interview can be expensive, too. Once on-site, test the equipment again before you begin the interview. After you set up your recording equipment, do a sound check by walking around the room to establish the limits of your ability to pick up sound. Next, do checks with your own voice and also the narrator's, while both of you are sitting as you will be during the interview. Also check for extraneous sound to make sure it won't interfere with the recording. For video recording, in addition to checking for sound quality, check for picture quality, especially proper lighting on the narrator. During the interview, from time to time, check to make sure your equipment is still recording. Nothing is more heartbreaking than to get an excellent interview only to discover that the equipment quit 20 minutes into the proceedings.

While we're on the subject of technology, if a sound recording is a more dynamic representation of an oral history interview than a written transcript, then a video recording is even better. For centuries historians have relied on written accounts as historical documentation, but Sipe (1991) notes that film and video have become an even more valuable form of historical evidence: "Moving pictures also automatically document themselves, and they offer extraordinary evidence" (p. 78). Sipe points out that moving picture recordings better document not only the physical surroundings of the interview, but also the narrator's own idiosyncratic performance—from eye movement to head tilt to hand gesture. Nonverbal communication adds valuable information to the literal content of what is said. "The spoken word is embedded in a setting, a situation, a context. People speak with body language, expression, and tone. They respond to and refer to their settings and to objects" (Sipe, p. 79). Sipe makes an interesting point when he notes that oral history to some extent restores the primacy of orality to human communication. If this is so, then it is important also to point out that film and video restore the body to orality and the disembodied voice.

Long-term storage is another important technology issue. Make backup copies of everything, and don't keep originals and backups in the same location. It's best to let experts such as local historical societies or libraries archive your recordings along with accompanying documentation, including transcripts. If you are conducting proprietary research, that is, research that is paid for and belongs to a private concern, then your employer, client, or sponsor may wish to keep your work private. This mostly would be the case in situations where the information you collect may give the organization a competitive edge of some kind—a rarity when oral history is involved. Nonetheless, it is the researcher's responsibility to know in advance if this will be the case. Most organizations, including competitive commercial ones, find it flattering to know their oral history project is considered important enough to be housed in a library somewhere. When historical research is available and useful to everyone, it is called "public history." Most library systems have special collections experts who manage historical materials. In addition to public libraries and university libraries, many large organizations have their own librarians, archivists, or historians. You may wish to see if there is an oral history institute of some kind in your area. Last, don't forget about the World Wide Web. StoryCorps exemplifies the way the Web can make public history widely accessible.

Even though the original recording is always the primary historical document, written transcripts also still function to back up sound or video recordings. Transcripts also increase the ways people can study and use the information. Transcription is the painstaking process of typing a word-for-word written document of the recorded interview. Moving on to transcription challenges, then, the main difficulty for oral historians lies in "choices." For example, the oral historian will have to decide if it is appropriate to include the interviewer's questions in the transcript. Should off-topic discussions in the recording be included in the transcript? Generally, in both cases, the answer is "yes" because both questions and off-topic conversations remain part of the historical document. A good rule of thumb is to remind yourself that people in the future will want access to unadulterated historical evidence, not your edited version of it. However, there may be instances when the appropriate answer is "no." For example, an oral history interview used as part of a documentary for print, radio, television, or Web presentation might require focusing only on what the narrator said about the topic at hand.

Even editing out the interviewer's questions may not be as straightforward as you would guess. Often the speech of the narrator and interviewer overlap each other, as they finish each other's thoughts. Interruptions in which either the interviewer or the narrator interrupts the other are also quite common. Some kinds of interruptions are actually supportive ways to keep the talk flowing, such as "uh-huh," which tends to encourage the other speaker to continue speaking. Overlaps and interruptions are especially prevalent in "interactive interviews," which more closely resemble two-way conversations than straight interviews. Overlaps and interruptions are difficult not only to represent in a written transcript, but also to edit out without causing confusion in the stream of meaning.

On a finer level of decision-making during transcription, is it appropriate to correct for grammar? How does one punctuate incomplete or half-finished thoughts strewn throughout the interview? Sometimes a narrator won't have a direct answer to a question and instead will process her or his thoughts aloud for a while before settling on an answer. So what at first may seem like unfocused rambling actually may be important information to the trained ear. In these cases, the interviewer must be patient and listen carefully.

At the other end of the spectrum is something known as the "press release" response in life history interviewing (Wiersma, 1988). "Press releases" are answers that seem rote or rehearsed. If a rambling answer signals a question the narrator has never been asked to think about before, the press release may signal a question the narrator has answered many times before or heard others answer before. The problem with press release answers is that they can seem a little too pat, as if the narrator is parroting conventional wisdom rather than offering a personal interpretation or genuine insight. Here the interviewer's job is to probe ever so gently or to come back to the question later by wording it differently. The interviewer also must listen very carefully to press release answers within the context of the conversation for clues as to how the narrator may intend the meaning, even if the words used seem too familiar or cliché.

Perhaps, the most difficult choices are those involving "sub-vocals"— the "uhs" and "ums," and so forth, that people regularly pepper throughout their oral speech. Regional and cultural dialects, accents, and colloquialisms also may cause transcribing headaches. Novelists Mark Twain and Zora Neale Hurston are famous for their clever use of dialect in their writing to provide a sense of character, time, and place. For strictly academic use, transcription may do a greater historical service by including every syllable of dialect. Selective use of dialect, however, may improve readability for public history audiences. Usually the oral historian will have to choose some middle ground in order to make the transcript both historically viable and still legible.

Planning ahead and being consistent is the key for all these issues. After you have reviewed the recording of a completed interview, or set of interviews, establish a set of "rules" for how you will handle all these kinds of situations. Write down your rules so you have what amounts to a style guide to refer to. Remember that the goal always is to be as true as possible to the narrator's own meaning. Here your narrator is your best style guide. Let your narrators read, adjust, correct, and even footnote and append their own transcripts to be sure you have captured their intent. The narrator, after all, not the oral historian, is the expert on the content of the interview. Here is one instance where oral history methods depart from journalistic practice. In journalism, the reporter is most interested in capturing exactly what the subject *said*. In oral history, the oral historian is most interested in capturing what the narrator *meant*.

To save time, some oral historians pay to have their interviews transcribed. This is a costly though timesaving tactic. But most oral historians will tell you that they never know the real value of what they have collected until they do the meticulous work of transcribing. The simple process of listening and typing tunes us in to the content in ways the rush of interviewing does not. What is more, a stranger doing your transcription does not know you or the narrator and will never make exactly the same decisions that you would. Neither will voice recognition software, another timesaving option to manual transcription. Voice recognition software has become more accurate and affordable, and it may well represent the future of transcribing voice recordings. If you choose to use voice recognition software or to have someone else transcribe your interviews, you still will have to listen to the recording and read the transcript together to correct for accuracy and style issues. Then you pass the transcript on to the narrator for further corrections or editing.

Treating the narrator as a fellow researcher collaborating with the oral historian leads us to interpersonal challenges in oral history. It is most productive for oral historians to think of themselves as facilitators whose job is to create the circumstances in which the narrator may perform. To a great extent, that subordinates the oral historian to the narrator. Lynd (1993) offers this advice: "Interviewer and interviewee, historian and historical protagonist, meet as equals" (p. 2). However, of narrators, he cautions, "It is their story, not our story; they not we are those who do oral history" (p. 6). At the same time, the oral history interview, in essence, is about communication, and all communication is a response to the social context and the participants' interpretations of their relationship to each other. In sum, respect for narrators is critical, including respect for such things as age, race, ethnicity, socioeconomic background, and status, among others. A "generation gap," for instance, may cause communication difficulties if the oral historian is not sensitive or paying attention.

For example, the author had some difficulty establishing interactive rapport with one of the older "founding fathers" in the water conservation project discussed earlier. The narrator ignored, interrupted, and talked over the author's questions. The problem was due to age, status, and gender differences. The older male narrator assumed he had been asked to hold forth regarding his expertise because of his high status. A politically powerful man, he also was used to a certain amount of deference. Yow (1994) best explains the interaction: "A male narrator may tend to talk down to a female interviewer . . . we women may have to just tolerate the situation, seeing it more as a societal influence than individual arrogance" (p. 133). After the author recognized the water conservation narrator's style of communication, the interview proceeded without further trouble. In hindsight, it is clear that the narrator was trying to impress his younger female interviewer. The narrator was showing off a bit. But at the time, the author, as a woman of a different generation, at first misread the style as rude and even sexist, reactions the author had to suppress in her role as researcher and oral historian. The goal is to elicit and record the narrative, even at the expense of personal reactions, both positive and negative. It becomes easier to deal with these kinds of situations if the oral historian understands them as and attributes them to differences between communication styles.

In addition to communication issues, oral historians have ethical responsibilities to their narrators. Oral historians have an obligation to represent narrators' intent as accurately as possible. Oral historians also must be considerate of the process of remembering, which can be painful for narrators, as well as therapeutic. Simply being asked to participate in a history project may validate narrators and their lives. Likewise, simply having the opportunity to speak while someone else listens is an affirming experience. Yet the oral historian purposely or inadvertently may touch upon painful memories that narrators may have spent decades trying to forget. Oral historians also must think about the consequences of narrators speaking on the record because, once again, these historical figures are still living and must continue to get on in the world. The oral historian is obligated to make sure that narrators understand that they are speaking on the record, especially if narrators are participating in a public history project.

Last, there is the issue of remembering itself. Oral history has an uneasy relationship to social science, which values facts. As most people know, memory is not a particularly reliable source for facts. If, by the criteria of social science, oral history falls short on *science*, then it more than compensates for that lack when it comes to the *social* aspects of history. Oral historians recognize that the greatest value of oral history narratives is precisely their basis in people's memories. That is, we learn much about the way people do remember from oral history. We better understand and appreciate the ways people interpret, make sense of, recollect, and narrate into stories their personal accounts of things they have experienced, lived through, or witnessed.

After September 11 in 2001, and again after Hurricane Katrina in 2005, many Americans had difficulty processing and making sense of how such tragedy could happen in the United States. These events forced people to reinterpret their country, the world, and their day-to-day lives. It undoubtedly will be moving to hear the oral histories that emerge from these catastrophes. While other kinds of history focus on collecting material facts, oral history is most useful to future generations by showing how people attach *meaning* to the facts of a historical moment. Facts are facts, but people deal with facts by telling stories, and such stories are what transport us to other times and places. When narrators tell us what facts meant for them individually, we identify with and connect to our humanity. That is why people are so interested in this project called history in the first place.

Now that you know something about the vagaries of history, oral history, technology, language, communication, and memory, we can turn to oral history methods as a research process. The steps you take to design and execute an oral history project follow the flowchart you learned in Chapter 4. The overall three-part procedure is similar to conducting any research: design your project, execute your design, and analyze your results. For oral history research, the first phase, *design*, includes research and planning. The second phase, *execution*, involves going into the field to collect interviews. The third phase, *analysis*, includes organizing, analyzing, reporting, and archiving your interviews.

DESIGN

As with any research project, a new oral history project begins with a general problem or issue stated as a research question. For the sake of this demonstration, let's assume that you have a curiosity about Spanish-language media. To make things a little easier, let's also assume that you speak both English and Spanish fluently. You have noticed a Spanish-language newspaper called *El Periódico* in newsstands around your city. How long has this newspaper been around? Who started it, and why? What service does it provide? Who reads it? Who advertises in it? These are all excellent questions.

The next steps in the process are *discussing the problem and searching the literature*. In the case of *El Periódico*, you begin with a little local background research by telephoning the newspaper and then visiting the library. You glean some basic historical facts, such as: The paper has been publishing continuously since 1919. It began as a small advertising medium for the city's Cuban business community. The Diaz family has always owned and operated the paper. Arturo Diaz, the family patriarch, was a printer by trade and established the newspaper. Today his granddaughter Evelyn is the president. You also may gather some basic statistics on circulation and the like. As you learn more, you realize that *El Periódico* has been an economic, social, and cultural pillar of the city for a very long time. You also learn that Arturo Diaz has passed away, but his son, Arturo Jr., is still living, and is 95.

You realize that *El Periódico*, as part of the historical fabric of the city, has a rich history of its own that ought to be collected and saved. You also realize that, as an ethnic medium with longevity, the newspaper has historical value on a national level. A traditional history would be appropriate because the newspaper itself provides a written record of itself. In the local university library, you do find a master's thesis detailing how the newspaper survived during the Great Depression. But you decide that an oral history is a much more interesting and timely approach. Further library and Internet research turns up some:

- local and regional news clippings about *El Periódico* and the Diaz family
- books and articles on your city's Latin and Hispanic histories
- similar kinds of oral histories conducted in other cities
- Web sites providing guidance on researching U.S. Latin and Hispanic history.

All of these resources provide you with helpful background knowledge, and some of this knowledge may become part of your project's final report.

Now you can *refine your research question*. You could take any number of different avenues at this point. You might be interested in a particular historical period, such as the master's thesis about *El Periódico*'s Depression years. Or you might be interested in a top-down genealogy of the Diaz family's leadership at the paper. Or maybe you are interested in the ways the paper has competed with its other advertising competition in the city. Ultimately, the choice is yours. Let's assume your refined question is, "How do the oldest living people who worked at *El Periódico* view the role of a Spanish-language press in this city?" The next steps are to *develop a detailed plan for your project and handle the logistics*.

First, you need to compile a list of people to interview. Baum says, "You start with who's alive and has a good memory, and then you expand out" (quoted in Conti, 1995, p. 52). You query each new contact, called an "informant," for the names of additional informants. Then you prioritize their importance to your research question. Obviously, because of his age, Arturo Diaz Jr. is an important narrator. But let's assume that you also decide to interview a variety of people including other Diaz family members, as well as reporters, editors, advertising sales people, those who worked in the business office, and production and press people who have worked for the paper. You also hope to interview some long-time subscribers, advertisers, and even some political leaders from both the local Latin/Hispanic community and the city. You want a variety of perspectives and views, and collecting oral histories from people in different roles at the paper will allow you make some comparisons. You might find different kinds of answers to your refined question about the role of the Spanish-language press. Before you can begin scheduling interviews, however, you have some work to do.

Next, you must develop a general questionnaire so that you ask the same kinds of questions of each narrator, although you understand that each narrator is unique and that the narrator's particular job at the paper will necessitate some narrator-specific questions. The kinds of questions you ask are open-ended to encourage the narrators to speak on the topic as long as possible. You think about the kinds of probing questions you might use to follow up your questions. You realize you probably will need two versions of your questionnaire, one in Spanish and one in English. You also realize with a sinking feeling that you will have to do double transcriptions of interviews so that you can make them available to both English-only and Spanish-only audiences. Now it's getting complicated.

Before you finish your questionnaire, you also establish a "boilerplate" that goes at the beginning of each interview. The boilerplate includes the name of the project, the interviewer's name, the narrator's name, and the date and place of the interview. You will read this boilerplate as a script at the beginning of each recorded interview to identify the recording. You also decide to begin each interview by collecting general demographic and background information from each narrator, including date and place of birth. This will serve two purposes. First, it will relax the narrator with easy questions, and second, it will record important information between the boilerplate and the actual interview. Before finishing the questionnaire, you decide upon a formal script for ending each recording: "That concludes this interview. Thank you for participating."

While you're sitting in front of the computer, there are a few other forms you will need. You will need an interview log form so that you can keep track of each interview's progress from interview appointment to the narrator's final signoff on the transcript. You also will need a narrator release form. You will ask each narrator to sign a release before you begin recording the interview. Again you realize you will need both English and Spanish versions of your release form. At the bottom of your release form, you include a line for "restrictions" because sometimes narrators choose to restrict the use of their interviews. For example, a narrator who still works at the paper may choose to release only the proofed and edited transcript but not the recording. A sample release form is provided in Figure 8.1, but you may need to customize some of its features.

Name of Oral History Project

RELEASE FORM

I, _____ (insert narrator's full name) hereby release my recorded interview and accompanying transcript(s), which are the result of my voluntary participation, for use as part of the _____ (insert name of project). I grant _____ (insert name of project) the right to use this gift for historical and education purposes. The recorded interview represents the primary documentation of my spoken word. Any transcription of my interview represents an edited version, as the spoken word is necessarily difficult to represent in written form.

Narrator: _____ (signature)

Date: _____

Address: _____

Interviewer: _____ (name and signature)

Date: _____

Address: _____

Restrictions: _____

_____

FIGURE 8.1 Oral History Release Form

The interview log form is for your use only. It should include the narrator's name and contact information. The form also keeps track of telephone and written correspondence with the narrator, along with a list of written documents collected to go with the oral history, such as letters, a résumé, photographs, and copies of periodical clippings, and so forth. Last, the log should include a way to keep track of the various stages of the narrator's oral history, beginning with the signed release and recorded interview and ending with the archived final recording and accompanying written documents. Also include a space to note the date when the narrator approved the finalized transcript. The important thing to remember is that you simultaneously are preserving a historical record and participating in that record. Be diligent in documenting everything, even the mundane and seemingly trivial.

Another form, called a "deed of gift," may come in handy, as well (Yow, 1994). If narrators wish to turn over one-of-a-kind documents or artifacts to be archived with their oral history narratives, you will want to have their owners sign off on such items as gifts to the oral history project. This is especially important for gifts that are valuable due to either their rarity or their monetary value—or both. Such a form states the donor's name, describes the item(s), specifies the item(s) as a gift for the project, and provides spaces for signatures and the date. Take a few of this form with you when interviewing.

After you have completed your paperwork, you can begin to contact narrators. You introduce yourself, explain the project, invite them to participate, and begin scheduling interviews. But you still aren't ready to interview your narrators yet. Between the time narrators agree to be interviewed and the date of the actual interview, you do background research on each narrator to learn as much as you can about each one. This may involve library research, preliminary interviews with narrators and other informants, requesting a copy of the narrator's résumé, and so forth. You must be something of a detective here, especially if the narrator has not been a public figure leaving a paper trail. When mass communications professor Gary Rice teaches his students how to do oral history research, he says, "Students learn a basic rule about interviewing: The more you know, the better your interview will be" (Rice, 2000, 612).

Before you hit the field, you also need to project a budget, gather equipment, and determine interview locations. Other than your time and the equipment you need, you can conduct oral history on a shoestring budget. But you still need to think about and plan for your expenses. For example, costs associated with printer paper and ink/toner, along with making copies of documents and transcripts can add up. Do you need to budget for gas money? Or can you use public transportation? How much will that cost? How much postage will you need? Is the project going to inflate your telephone bill? Do you plan to hire someone to do your transcribing? Will you buy special software? If you can't transfer files to be archived electronically, how much will CDs or portable memory drives cost? All these seemingly incidental costs quickly can tally a dent in your checking account, so planning is essential.

About equipment, unless you plan to make this your life's work, you might consider borrowing or renting equipment before you run out to spend your savings on the latest high-tech devices. Perhaps your school or employer has equipment you can check out. If you're lucky, family or friends will have video or sound recording equipment you can borrow. Don't forget the accompanying accoutrements, such as batteries and extension cords, which also may impact your budget.

In a project involving an institutional or commercial concern, such as *El Periódico*, perhaps the organization will be amenable either to supply equipment or to fund your costs. It never hurts to ask. You realize, however, that if you take anything of value from the organization, such as payment for your services or equipment, then, to some degree, you have compromised your independence. It may not be a problem, but you need to proceed with caution. Partnerships in the field can be productive, but you will want to establish your prerogative, as politely but firmly as possible, to make decisions about the project. Dave Isay's expensive StoryCorps project became a reality with the help of NPR and CPB. The Saturn car company is also a StoryCorps sponsor. StoryCorps probably has contractual agreements with its financial underwriters. But most oral history projects exist on a much smaller scale, requiring friendly agreements rather than legal ones.

There also remain some logistics to work out regarding interview sites. Where to interview narrators may or may not be a factor in your oral history project. But it is worth thinking about. Some elderly narrators may be confined to their homes, whether a private residence or a nursing facility. This may not be a bad thing because people usually feel most comfortable in their own spaces, which, in turn, will lead to better interviews. But interviewing people at the sites relevant to the topic of the oral history project can be helpful in evoking memories, too. To return to the *El Periódico* oral history project, interviewing narrators at the newspaper offices or printing plant would be sensible. Places, objects, sounds, and smells elicit emotions and memories. If you plan to interview at a place of business, you obviously must get permission and coordinate scheduling with not only your narrator but also the business. Interviewing indoors, either at a residence or a business, provides creature comforts such as electricity, water and beverages for parched throats, restrooms, heat and air conditioning, and shelter against inclement weather, not to mention comfortable seating and writing surfaces. Don't rule out the possibility of interviewing outdoors, though, if the site is pertinent to the topic or project. Outdoor locations may have powerful emotional associations, too. Outdoor locations also may provide potent visual cues, especially if you are recording video. Of course, interviewing outdoors creates logistical problems, so, again, be prepared and plan ahead. Scout your interview locations in advance.

Having refined your research question, completed your background research, scheduled your interviews, planned a budget, identified your interview sites, and packed your paperwork and equipment, you now are ready to begin interviewing.

EXECUTION

Oral history interviewing is exciting. You meet interesting people and listen to the fascinating stories they tell. After all your preparation, your curiosity about your research question has increased. You are anxious to begin getting some answers. *Executing the project* is actually fairly straightforward at this point, but it can be exhausting for both you and your narrators. Consideration for narrators' stamina and comfort is important, especially if narrators are older.

Interview etiquette may seem like a "no-brainer," but it bears mentioning. Your job is to put the narrator at ease. Be a gracious host. Be friendly and relaxed. Greet your narrators, and thank them for their participation. Explain the process and the steps you will be going through from the sound check and boilerplate recording to the wrap up. Make sure your narrator knows when you are recording and not recording. It is not against the rules to share the kinds of questions you'll ask ahead of time. You even may provide your narrator an advance copy of the questionnaire. This is not a surprise attack. You are an oral historian, not an investigative journalist on the hunt. You want to record the best oral history possible so blindsiding your narrators probably is not the best plan.

During the recorded interview, you need to be patient during long pauses. Don't rush to fill a silence. Wait for the narrator to resume speaking. If things get emotional, be sympathetic. Sometimes a narrator may ask you to stop recording, either to gain composure or to say something off the record. You are obligated to comply with the narrator's wishes. There even may be occasions when you decide to stop recording because the narrator is revealing too much sensitive personal information. This is a matter of using good judgment and being respectful of your narrator. The oral historian must balance the goal of collecting useful historical testimony with invading narrators' privacy. Sometimes you need to step in to protect a narrator if the narrator is a little too enthusiastic and forthcoming with private details. Remember that unlike human subjects participating in other kinds of research methods, oral history narrators don't have the luxury of anonymity.

The length of an interview depends on the narrator. Generally, both narrator and interviewer are productive for only about an hour, or two at the most. If you need more time with a narrator, schedule additional interviews. At the end of the interview, thank the narrator, offer some words of encouragement on a job well done, and say you will be in touch when it's time to proof the transcript.

A final word about conducting group interviews is in order. Generally, oral history interviews are one-on-one between an interviewer and a narrator. There may be extenuating circumstances for breaking this rule, but you will need a good reason to do so. *Never* interview a husband and wife together, says Yow (1994). One or the other will dominate the interview. Your author admits she has broken this rule more than once. The first time it happened, your author interviewed a husband and wife together out of a perverse curiosity about Yow's admonition against it. Suffice to say that Yow is an expert for a reason. Another time, the author broke the rule because the narrator was ill and needed his wife as his caregiver present to attend to him. In the second case, breaking the rule was a reasonable accommodation in order to get the interview, and the wife was not participating in the interview.

If you are collecting a series of oral history interviews, you may be in the field for weeks or months. A large project may require a year or more to complete. For long projects, the implementation phase of interviewing may overlap with the analysis phase. You may continue to schedule interviews while you have begun transcribing. For one thing, it's better to transcribe interviews sooner rather than later. Your memory will be fresher, and you may learn things to improve your next interviews. And don't forget that your narrators are waiting to hear from you to proof their transcripts. Overlapping phases can get complicated, which is why you will want to be systematic about updating and maintaining your interview log sheets.

ANALYSIS

As its name implies, the analysis phase involves more than transcription and archiving. Analysis requires *organizing and making sense of the information* you have collected and then drawing some conclusions from it. How you write up and present your conclusions depends on the purpose and circumstances of the project. Before discussing analysis further, though, let's return briefly to the process of transcription.

We already covered some of the challenges in transcribing your interview recordings. As a word of caution, in addition to making backup copies of your recordings, don't forget to make backup copies of your transcripts, both electronic and hard copies. Computers crash, hard drives and memory drives fail, and CDs are not always reliable. Also, because transcripts go through various stages of proofing and editing, be sure to date, label, and log each version to avoid confusing yourself. When you pass a proofing transcript on to a narrator, be explicit that you are asking the narrator to correct both your errors as well as instances where the narrator may have misspoken. In cases where narrators wish to correct or change their statements, you obviously cannot change the recording. But you can insert footnotes on the transcript. Don't forget to get the narrator to sign off on the transcript.

Ask the narrator when you may pick up the corrected transcript. If you want the narrator to mail the corrected transcript to you, you will have to provide an envelope with prepaid postage. Some narrators may wish to exchange the transcript electronically. In sum, you and your narrators have worked very hard to record interviews and prepare transcripts, so take the necessary precautions to protect your work.

As each transcript is completed, you will be preparing it for archiving. Attach hard copies of any accompanying documents, as discussed earlier. Also attach a copy of the narrator's release form. Don't forget to attach the deed of gift form if you are including donated items in the package to be archived. Last, write and attach a brief preface or introduction to the transcript. This is the place to describe the significance of the narrator, summarize the content of the interview, and offer your personal insights regarding the interview. Use the introduction to remind readers that the transcript is a secondary document and refer them to the recorded version as the primary document. Put your name on the introduction as further documentation.

Once you have completed all the transcripts, you are ready to analyze your findings and *evaluate the study*. Analysis can be as simple as answering your own question if the project is merely a hobby. Or it can be as complicated as writing a book or producing a documentary. Somewhere between these two extremes, most oral historians find themselves *writing a report* of some kind, whether for academic or public history purposes. Oral history research reports look like other kinds of research reports in that they include:

1. an introduction that states the research question and answer
2. a background information section to contextualize the project
3. a literature review
4. a detailed summary of the research method employed
5. a concise report of the findings
6. your own analysis of what the findings mean
7. a conclusion that reports the study's limitations and suggests areas of further research
8. a complete list of reference materials cited in the report
9. any appendices, exhibits, pictures, charts, graphs, or figures used for illustration purposes.

In the case of the *El Periódico* project, the final report will need to be in English and Spanish. Whatever its final format, the point of analysis is to isolate the answer or answers to your refined research question. Be careful to limit your conclusions to your own project. Oral history research cannot be generalized.

The very last step in the project is archiving. First, pass on a complete set of the interview documents, both recorded and written—as they will be archived—to each of your narrators so they have personal copies to keep. If you have an organizational sponsor, such as the Spanish-language newspaper, offer your organizational contact person a complete set of the final project including documents and recordings. Second, find a suitable home for the project, whether it's a library, historical society, museum, or oral history institute. Most of these kinds of institutions are equipped to handle historical materials and would be thrilled to receive your thorough and interesting work. Additionally, there may be other kinds of organizations that have a stake in preserving your project. For example, in the case of *El Periódico*, perhaps there is a Hispanic or Latin chamber of commerce, fraternal organization, or social club that may wish to archive this kind of oral history. Beyond the local level, there may be national organizations or associations with some vested interest in your topic. This also is worth exploring. The best places to archive oral history are those that offer experts in archiving and make the work available to the public. Don't forget to keep a set of everything for yourself if you want easy access to it and don't mind housing it.

In the end, the purpose of oral history is to share it. Despite the challenges associated doing historical research, oral history is worthwhile and rewarding work. If oral history makes sense as a method for your research, you will discover what oral historians already know: There is something gratifying about connecting with people, listening to their stories, and preserving them to share with future generations.

REVIEW QUESTIONS

1. Why do you think the human subjects of oral history are called "narrators"?
2. How is oral history defined?
3. What distinguishes oral history from other kinds of historical and interviewing research methods?
4. What are some of the reasons why "history is a human construction and always partial"?
5. Why is it important for oral historians to recognize the difference between top-down and bottom-up approaches to history?
6. When does oral history become an appropriate or useful research method in communication?
7. What are some technical challenges that oral historians deal with?
8. What are some challenges and issues involved with transcribing oral history interviews from audio or video formats to written text? What are some interpersonal challenges that oral historians deal with?
9. What are the steps involved in the planning process of an oral history project?
10. What kinds of documentation forms does an oral historian need for doing oral history?
11. What are the steps involved in executing an oral history project?
12. What kinds of ethical obligations does the oral historian have toward narrators?
13. What is the significance of the fact that, "unlike human subjects participating in other kinds of research methods, oral history narrators don't have the luxury of anonymity"?
14. What are the steps involved in the analysis phase of an oral history project?
15. What are some options for archiving an oral history project?

SUGGESTED ACTIVITIES

1. Visit the StoryCorps Web site at www.storycorps.net. Listen to some digital stories available there. Use the site's links to explore whether participating in the StoryCorps project is feasible for you or your class.
2. Locate and read an oral history housed in your library. Is it a top-down or bottom-up history? How do you know?

3. Research whether your campus library has a special collections historical section. Ask whether you or your class can schedule a visit to learn more about it.

4. Track down a local historical society or oral history group. Ask for an invitation to attend its next meeting or visit its offices. Invite a representative to speak to your class.

5. Practice your new skills by collecting the oral history of a classmate or friend. Afterwards, talk with your narrator about how each of you experienced the process.

6. Record the oral history of your family from your oldest living relative. Share it with family members.

CHAPTER 9

Text Analysis

*No fine work can be done without concentration
and self-sacrifice and toil and doubt.*

—MAX BEERBOHM

Text messaging is popular these days with cell phone users. Abbreviations, some of them unique, are often used to facilitate rapid typing on the phone keypad. For example, instead of "see you later," a text messenger might send "CUL8R." A person with little experience in text messaging might find some messages difficult to understand. Communication researchers are also interested in texts and messages, but in a significantly different way.

In Chapter 2, we noted that communication of any sort, particularly media communication, follows a four-step process: originator, message, medium, and receiver. We also noted that most research activities can be tied directly to one or more of these steps. Survey research, for example, is usually linked to the receiver of a communication, but it can also be linked to any of the other steps. Many communication researchers acknowledge the importance of both originator and receiver, but feel that one of the most important steps in the communication process is the message. *A message may be defined as that which is transmitted* (O'Sullivan, Hartley, Saunders, & Fiske, 1983).

Communication researchers have developed several ways to analyze communication messages. If we understand a message, that is, what a communication says or means, we can get a better idea of what impact it might have on a receiver. To get a clearer understanding of a communication message and what it might mean, communication researchers often use a research method called *content analysis*. Another popular method is called *framing*. Both these methods attempt to find out *what* messages are being presented as well as *how* they are being presented. Usually no attempt is made to directly link a message to a receiver response, but such links are commonly implied.

This chapter is a little different from others in this book. In this chapter, you will find three different methods of text analysis: content analysis, reader-response, and deconstruction.

"A text usually refers to a message that has a physical existence of its own, independent of its sender or receiver" (O'Sullivan et al., 1983, p. 238). A *text* is not the same as a *message*, although the two terms are often used interchangeably. Message deals with the meaning of a communication; text is the physical component that contains the message. For example, if your best friend sends you a birthday card, the card itself would contain the text—usually some sort of poem or sentiment—but the message (or meaning) you'd get from it is that your friend is offering his/her congratulations and best wishes on your special day.

A text does not usually have only one meaning. To continue with our birthday card example, suppose you are turning 30 years of age, and the card your friend sends has this message: *Happy 30th Birthday; the best years of your life are over!* Well, it isn't a very clever message, to be sure, but greeting cards are not known for their creative and expressive language. Still, you could get more than one message from this text. You could take it all in good fun, realizing that your friend is poking fun at your having reached the ripe old age of 30! Or you could be offended and, perhaps, a little depressed, feeling that what the card says might actually be true. In short, a text is the physical vehicle or structure that contains a message sent to a receiver. A text can take a variety of forms, including writing, film, television or radio programs, Internet communications, and even speech.

PART I—CONTENT ANALYSIS

by Timothy E. Bajkiewicz

HISTORICAL DEVELOPMENT AND METHOD IMPORTANCE

Communication researchers consider content analysis one of their most basic, bread-and-butter methods because it makes intuitive sense: communication creates content which we then gather, categorize in some way, and study. It has a long history and stands as one of the original investigative techniques included in the 1940 memorandum that helped launch mass communication research (Czitrom, 1982). Content analysis is also a very popular social science research method, employed in 30% of all the communication studies published in major academic journals from 1980 to 1999, second only to survey research (Kamhawi & Weaver, 2003).

Butler (2002) says that, for postmodernists, "we live in a *society of the image*. . . . Information, by now, is just something that we buy" (p. 111). Content analysis is about examining those images and information. In Chapter 6 of this book, research is compared to dipping a spoon into a pot of soup and seeing what we find. Given today's media world, imagine instead an ocean of soup. The abundance of media outlets—legacy broadcast stations and networks, cable networks, Internet sites, magazines, and newspapers, just to name a few—gives a content analysis researcher plenty to do and examine. In fact, there are always too many and too many different kinds of communication content to analyze, which is an old challenge for this research method. There are other challenges, too, including how to choose content and study it in a systematic fashion. Historically, content analysis has appealed to researchers because, unlike other methods, they could involve nonacademic people in much of the process, especially data collection. This makes communication research more accessible and less of an "ivory tower" exercise. And often you do not need a college degree to understand (and maybe even appreciate) the general findings from a media content analysis, like teen magazine covers were more sensational in 2004–2005 than in 1994–1995 (Nice, 2007).

With its grounding in what many traditional researchers would label "facts" and "truth," content analysis is also one of the more difficult research methods to reconcile with a postmodern perspective. In any case, after you learn about content analysis, it becomes a bit contagious: you read a newspaper article or watch a TV show, begin to consider various possibilities of trends in the content (laudatory or disturbing), and then wonder, "What if I did a study where I gathered all the shows from. . . ."

DEFINITION AND USES

The beginnings of content analysis can be traced back to colonial times and an analysis of anti-federalist essays in 1787 (Berelson, 1952). At the turn of the century scholars also used it to study English poetry and prose, and in the 1920s journalism students used the method to study newspapers. But it was World War II that firmly established content analysis as a communication research method. As the war approached, Harold D. Lasswell—one of the founders of communication research—studied the rise of new media propaganda techniques during the 1930s. During the war he ran a government program that studied media around the world, especially in Europe and Japan, where newspaper stories and radio transmissions gave clues about troop movements and enemy plans. On the home front, the U.S. government analyzed messages from what it considered suspicious organizations to use as evidence against them. (A situation that enraged civil liberty advocates and resulted in sharp criticism of the policy.) With the post–World War II baby boom and corresponding explosion of media content in the United States, content analysis quickly became a primary tool to help scholars understand communication in a modern world.

One of those scholars was Bernard Berelson, who analyzed German opinion and morale for the U.S. Office of War Information. His 1952 book outlining basic content analysis methods is still considered a classic in the field, and all subsequent discussion about the method is based on his original definition: "Content analysis is a research technique for the *objective, systematic*, and *quantitative* description of the *manifest content* of communication" (p. 18, emphasis added). Berelson explained each part of his definition. *Objective* means that different analysts should be able to apply well-defined categories and achieve the same results. *Systematic* means two things: first, a full analysis of all relevant content instead of only a partial analysis of only some relevant content; and second, that the information gathered be applied to a scientific problem and have general application. Berelson said content analysis is *quantitative*, which he called "perhaps the most distinctive feature of content analysis" (p. 17). This means understanding how often content occurs based on its presence or absence, which may or may not include actual quantification with numbers (although it most often does).

Berelson's (1952) definition also included the term *manifest content*, which means the observable components of a message, like sentences in a newspaper article or images and sound in a TV broadcast. This is in contrast to *latent content*, or parts of a message with some meaning that is not directly observable, such as the intent of the content's author or producer. This gets to a core debate for content analysis: How should you consider and practically handle manifest and latent content? We can see, for example, the words of a newspaper article in front of us, but can we really know the intent of its author? Berelson says content analysts should assume that you can draw inference between intent and content, and that similar meaning is shared by the communicator, audience, and analyst. However, he cautions that this is true only for materials "where understanding is simple and direct" (p. 20), like a news story as opposed to a poem, and that content analysis is only appropriate for the former and not the latter.

Klaus Krippendorff was another scholar who helped refine and expand early conversations about content analysis. He agreed that the method is focused on analyzing manifest content, and wrote that while "content analysts are rarely interested in what messages are *intended* to mean" (Krippendorff, 1969, p. 5, emphasis in original), the method is used in "justifying particular content inferences from the text" (p. 12). Krippendorff's (2004) contemporary definition says, "Content analysis is a research technique for making *replicable* and *valid* inferences from *texts* (or other meaningful matter) to the contexts of their use" (p. 18, emphasis added). Two research terms that appear in his definition are discussed in more detail in Chapter 3 of this text: *replicable* (tied to reliability) and *valid* (i.e., validity). *Replicable*, for Krippendorff, means that researchers at any point in time, and even using different methods, should draw the same conclusions from the same material. *Valid* means that any conclusions can be supported by evidence. A third term, *text*, is used by various postmodern and critical researchers to indicate their focus of interest. It can refer to words on a page, but it is used broadly to mean any communication creation, including audio/visual media.

Krippendorff (2004) talks about three traditions of considering content analysis. In the first, content is in a container: it is inherent in a text and just waiting to be discovered. (He puts Berelson's classic definition in this category.) In the second, researchers make inferences about the content source, which should include contact with that source; this type does not take into account analyzer bias or perspective. Krippendorff says his own definition is part of the third tradition—what he calls ethnographic content analysis— where content "emerges" from the text in context. Borrowing some terms from anthropology, he calls this process *emic* (from the insider's perspective) rather than *etic* (from the outsider's perspective) as "it attempts to rely on indigenous conceptions rather than on analysts' theory-imposed conceptions" (p. 21).

This research method has many different applications and uses for communication scholars, including describing communication content, testing hypotheses about messages, comparing how communication content reflects what happens in the world, examining how media portray certain groups in society, and whether communication has a direct or indirect effect on human behavior (Wimmer & Dominick, 2006). The last focus, known as *effects research*, intensified near the end of twentieth century to address media's growing influence (Riffe, Lacy, & Fico, 2005). Scholars used content analysis to study gender representation in online reviews of video games (Ivory, 2006), how different magazines discussed heart disease (Clarke & Binns, 2006), and how democratic movements in southern Africa used radio to communicate their political views (Kivikuru, 2006).

A POSTMODERN PERSPECTIVE

Krippendorff's (2004) third tradition of content analysis—one that places the analyzed text within the context of who produced it—is a marked departure from how most scholars have traditionally positioned content analysis as firmly part of the mechanical world paradigm (discussed in Chapter 2). In that perspective, studying the individual parts tells us about the whole. In terms of content analysis within that paradigm, analyzing many individual pieces of communication content should provide an idea about how common or unique that content is in *all* communication. As you have read repeatedly in this book, postmodernism rejects such sweeping generalizations. Likewise, in first defining content analysis Berelson (1952) says similar message meaning is shared by everyone. Postmodernism suggests that we have unique perspectives, and therefore each would interpret the same message differently. However, one cannot reject the power of content analysis as a research method and its potential to demonstrate, by example, how media, communication, and culture are interrelated and interdependent.

At this point you may be wondering whether content analysis can really function within a postmodern perspective—something many communication researchers wonder, as well. The combination does present a conflict between rationalism and empiricism (discussed in Chapter 2), between postmodern reasoning regarding modern culture and society, and how to best gather, catalog, and study what we create and communicate. Postmodern content analysis really supports what has been labeled the pragmatic approach, which recognizes that although research models are inherently inadequate, we need their structure and intellectual contributions to broaden our understanding of the world. The postmodern researcher using content analysis is betwixt and between rationalism and empiricism, utilizing both perspectives but staying in neither.

In one of the few scholarly articles that discusses content analysis within a postmodernist framework, Thomas (1994) said the method focuses on examining what are essentially cultural artifacts, or unique creations that have special significance to certain people. Studying artifacts in this way began with the heralded anthropologist Margaret Mead and her classic studies of South Pacific island cultures in the 1920s. To her, studying a culture's media and art could substitute for directly studying the people and their behavior, although she considered this a poor replacement. Thomas argues that any data gathering method helps our understanding. For him, organizing data into categories and using statistics to help explain relationships is no different from how people categorize their daily lives and use language to describe and share meaning. He also criticized postmodern researchers for often making wild, unsupported conclusions based on methods that do not provide the kind of evidence supplied by content analysis.

The postmodern content analyst should realize that all communications are social constructions and part of a very long chain of events influenced by countless perspectives. Most researchers point to only content creators and those who directly influence them, but it is never that simple. For a newspaper, this chain may begin with a reporter, but also includes the copy editor who proofed the story for structure and errors, the photographer who took an accompanying picture, the reporter's editor who helped shape the story, the managing editor who set policy for the editor, and the executive editor who implements a vision for the paper. Likewise, for a local TV news broadcast this includes reporters, video photojournalists, video editors, show producers, and the newsroom management. Ill-defined visual and production elements, often overlooked by content analysis researchers, can be just as influential in the communication message (Zettl, 1998). So, in considering who potentially influenced content, we must add newspaper page designers, printing press workers, TV studio crew members and control room staff like directors, and even transmitter engineers who control and tweak the signal that ultimately ends up on our living room TVs. Modern culture consists of many collaborative, creative efforts, but the daily creation and production of communication messages is among the most complex and, when you consider it all, pretty amazing.

ADVANTAGES AND DISADVANTAGES

In a broad sense, the biggest advantage of content analysis is the data gathered from a communication message (often a media message) which act as evidence in support of responding to research inquiries. What better way to answer questions about communication than by collecting and studying it? In this way content analysis is much like historical research or textual analysis: you begin with something created by someone, a primary source.

Gathering data for content analysis is usually not as dependent on involving people as other research methods, which can be a huge advantage. Of course, surveys and focus groups require participants other than the researchers, and, as you have read elsewhere in this book, we must handle research participants with the utmost care. This includes scheduling and logistical issues to secure their involvement, not to mention potential institutional review board (IRB) review within your school or university for any research involving humans. Content analysis researchers could have gathered all the necessary communication texts themselves. But just because you are looking at communication messages rather than talking to people does not mean data gathering for content analysis is easy or inexpensive. In fact, a major disadvantage of the method lies with whether you have access to the materials you want to study. Many content analysis researchers are forced to alter their original research plans based on access issues. For example, you can access original copies of every Irish newspaper ever written through the free, online archives at Trinity College Dublin, but if you want to look at seventeenth century British newspapers you would physically need to go to The British Library in London. Likewise, to visually study network news broadcasts you might use the television news archives at Vanderbilt University in Nashville, Tennessee. You could pay to spend a few days there, but that would probably not be enough time to examine everything in detail. You could also pay the fees to obtain copies of broadcasts, but to study just one 30-minute show each week for a year would cost several thousand dollars in duplication costs.

Some of the other qualities of content analysis that some may consider advantages could also be viewed as disadvantages in a postmodern context. Remember that Berelson's (1952) definition said content analysis is the "objective, systematic, and quantitative description of the manifest content" (p. 18). First, Wimmer and Dominick (2006) discuss each, and for them "objective" means that everything is done to remove researcher bias from the study. This begins with solid operational definitions and categories for classifying content so that anyone at any time could replicate the study and organize the content in similar ways. In a postmodern world, objectivity does not exist, since this suggests a singular, correct viewpoint from which to observe reality; instead, postmodernism posits multiple individual, relativistic viewpoints. A postmodernist accepts that true replication of a study is impossible because it occurred within a particular and unique temporal and cultural context. Research objectivity is most likely another metanarrative in ultimately suggesting that "all knowledge has a secret unity" (Butler, 2002, p. 13).

Second, "systematic" relates to researchers consistently applying explicit guidelines and content classifications, in part to assist in future replicability. Thinking postmodernly, nothing is ever truly consistent, but guidelines provide needed structure to our approach. Finally, Wimmer and Dominick (2006) discuss how the "quantitative" aspect of content analysis is crucial in accurately representing content and allows for statistical tools to help answer research questions. Holsti (1969) warned that the quantification in content analysis would attract researchers who may then do trivial research because they get caught up in counting. While everyone recognizes the importance of numbers and mathematics, statistics is part of the postpositivist paradigm that deifies science and says Truth exists, but that we can only know it imperfectly. Instead, postmodernism recognizes and celebrates diverse, holistic perspectives for evaluating content and determining impact beyond mere counting.

BASICS

For a media content analysis we can just gather up some TV shows or magazines, take a look, and describe what we see, right? Not quite. Many of us already do that informally with friends and family. Instead, content analysis is a methodical and structured examination that requires a detailed plan. But first, it requires solid research questions, as discussed in Chapter 4. If using content analysis, these questions should focus on issues related to *manifest* content, or that which is observable and measurable in some way. A postmodern research perspective suggests that *latent* content, or unobservable content like the author's intent, is really unknowable and essentially speculation. To discuss how to do a content analysis we will use Krippendorff 's (2004) framework that is specific to content analysis: (1) unitizing, (2) sampling, (3) recording/coding, and (4) analysis.

Unitizing

Krippendorff (2004) calls the first steps "data making" (p. 83) because during those steps we move from actual content to a more abstract level of data that we create to represent that content. In the first step, unitizing, we choose the specific content to analyze, which is also called defining the universe for the study (Wimmer & Dominick, 2006). Ask yourself: What content would best address my research focus and questions? It may be obvious—if you want to know how broadcast network newscasts discussed a particular issue, then you would probably want to study complete newscasts, at least at first. Subsequent research could content analyze only transcripts with no images, or only images without any reporter narration. Successful researchers must think creatively about what content they study and how they obtain it.

Note that content is not limited to only the final, finished communication product, like a newspaper front page, an Internet Web page, or a speech. These are most often studied because they are what the public sees (or hears) and, therefore, are more easily accessible. Generally, the more difficult the content is to obtain, the higher likelihood scholars will consider research studying it as a unique and useful contribution to our understanding of it. A "behind the scenes" version of a communication message might also be worth studying, in other words, how the message was conceptualized, developed, and modified before it was presented.

Unitizing also addresses *when* the content was created, or more specifically, during what time period. For the postmodern researcher content is created within countless contexts—cultural, ethnic, and economic—and arguably all are affected in some way by time. Krippendorff (1969) wrote that "Content evolves in the process of analyzing messages in a particular *situation* and for a particular investigative *purpose* from which it cannot easily be separated" (p. 5, emphasis in original). Focusing your content analysis in terms of time serves several purposes. Say you are interested in old radio shows like *The Lone Ranger*, which aired on Detroit's WXYZ from 1933 to 1956 (The Museum of Broadcast Communications, 2005). That is 23 years and more than 1,000 shows worth of "Hi-Ho, Silver!" Studying all that content would take a superhero! If your research question asked, "How was race discussed in *The Lone Ranger* radio show?" then you may be interested in getting a sense of the show's entire run. You would use sampling techniques to choose a manageable number (discussed in the next step). But maybe you are only interested in the pre–World War II years until 1941, which would be fewer shows. In any case, limiting the time you study content provides boundaries that focus your research, create manageable work loads, and situate that content and your findings within recognized historical and cultural time periods.

The ultimate goal of unitizing is selecting a *unit of analysis*. This is the smallest unit of information handled by the researchers to address a particular research goal, and so is the real "in the trenches" content measured. For example, in studying newspaper sports sections the unit of analysis may be paragraphs, sentences, headlines, or even photos. If you are studying a political speech, the unit of analysis might be the words, phrases, or sentences used by the speaker, or perhaps his/her gestures and body movement, maybe even the reactions of the audience. What you choose depends on the kind of evidence you need to respond to your research questions. Create clear operational definitions of your units of analysis for yourself and your content coders. It is a good idea to consider this early, but then revisit your unit of analysis after some preliminary coding. The postmodern researcher values perspectives and contributions from fellow researchers and coders and may want to come to some consensus about a given unit of analysis before the full coding effort begins.

A study may have several units of analysis, which can quickly get complicated and confusing. For any data collection effort it is often a good idea to gather as much information as possible because this is when you are closest to the content and best able to recognize its worth. Many researchers gather different kinds of content simultaneously, all for the same research topic, and then parse out the discussion and findings over several research publications. However, while considering units of analysis remember Holsti's (1969) warning about counting for counting's sake, something every researcher has done at some point. Designing and executing a research study can become a bit intoxicating, and rapidly overwhelming, when you start to consider just how much data you could collect. Continually use your research questions to focus your efforts and stay on a productive path.

Sampling

If your study's focus is narrowly defined, you may be able to gather all the possible content, called a *census*. However, most studies initially have too much potential content to study (e.g., all the newspapers in the United States), so we select only a portion of that universe, called a *sample*. While the universe is all the possible content, the *population* refers to the specific content addressed by the research (Riffe et al., 2005). The *sampling frame* is the list used to choose a sample. If the entire population of content is available to the researcher, then the population and the sampling frame are identical. This was not the case in a content analysis of 89 news Web sites on the morning of 9/11 (Randle, Davenport, & Bossen, 2003). The researchers began with a list of Web sites from the Newspaper Association of America (the population), but overwhelming Internet use made some Web sites unavailable. Thus, those sites were dropped from the sampling frame.

Choosing a sample from a sampling frame for content analysis is essentially like sampling for surveys (see Chapter 6). You could perform a *simple random sample* so that each member of the sampling frame has an equal chance of being chosen, or a *systematic random sample*, where you begin with a randomly chosen piece of content then include every *n*th one. Instead, most content analyses use some kind of *multistage sampling*. For example, a study interested in a sample of newspapers from around the country may first organize papers by market size and publication figures, then organize them by region, and then select so many of each market size from each region. Most researchers would then use random selection once the sampling frame is categorized by stage.

Samples must also be sensitive regarding time, since most media are created on a schedule. You could create a *composite* of the time that includes samples of content. For media created every day, you might create a *composite week* that reflects a sense of that publication. Let us suppose that for a year's worth of newspapers you only want to examine eight weeks; you could randomly choose eight Mondays, eight Tuesdays, and so on until you have eight weeks worth of content. Be aware that the cyclical nature of media coverage can *confound*, or create confusion with, the results if not planned for in the sampling stage. In studying advertising in November and December you would be foolish not taking into account the holidays, or not connecting the June spike in weather stories on Florida newspaper front pages with the beginning of hurricane season.

Instead of letting chance select your content you could use a *purposive* sample and select content based on an expressed rationale. Dibean and Garrison (2001) chose which online newspapers to study based on a purposive combination of market size, national scope, and online history. Almost 70% of the 486 content analyses in journalism's top scholarly journal from 1971 to 1995 used purposive samples, as opposed to around 20% using census or representative samples (Riffe & Freitag, 1997). The other roughly 10% used a *convenience* sample, which, as the name suggests, is easy to obtain for whatever reason. Correctly labeling your sampling methods helps other researchers understand how you approached the content and collected data.

As discussed elsewhere in this book, sampling is an essential part of the mechanical world paradigm that suggests that knowing a little bit about something, if the bits are evenly distributed so as to be "representative," privileges you to make grand, sweeping statements about the whole. A postmodern research perspective does not reject a systematic approach to considering how to collect content; however, that view contends that any research findings could not be generalized to the entire population. Instead, the postmodern content analyzer realizes the limitation that a study's findings do not apply beyond the content selected.

Recording/Coding

Many definitions of content analysis, especially early ones, equate the method with coding (Krippendorff, 2004), which is without a doubt the most thought- and time-intensive step. Recording and coding essentially create what Krippendorff calls a special "data language" (p. 150) that connects real information, like sentences on a page, to numbers or notations representing that information; for example, you see a headline about your topic, so you make a mark on a sheet. *Recording* is the act of interpreting chosen units of analysis and creating data to analyze later, whereas *coding* is this interpretation by a set of rules. The remainder of this section will use only the term *coding* for both concepts. You create these rules as part of a *codebook* that demonstrates, defines, and displays how you will categorize your units of analysis. It literally is the translation of the data language between reality and research, so take care that it is clear and understandable to everyone involved. During coding and analysis, the codebook becomes your go-to reference about handling and categorizing your content.

Content categories should meet three criteria. First, they must be *exhaustive*, meaning there must be a category for all content. There are two approaches to creating content categories. In the first approach, *a priori coding*, you create categories before coding, usually in line with previous research or a theoretical framework. For example, the author of this section and a colleague content analyzed breaking news e-mail alerts from network news organizations according to categories established in several repeated national studies of news content (Bajkiewicz & Smith, 2007). This approach risks being inflexible if (usually when) coders find content that does not properly match any of the categories provided. In the second approach, *emergent coding*, you create categories only after first examining some of the content. This is in line with postmodern rationales that recognize more value in indigenous categorization rather than imposed models. It is similar to the qualitative research method called *grounded theory*, which builds theory based on "grounded" ideas from the data (Creswell, 2007).

Second, content categories must be *mutually exclusive*, meaning the same content cannot be in two categories simultaneously. For example, in coding for a content analysis about sexual health messages in media, it seems simple to indicate if the source was a TV show, movie, magazine, or music artist (Hust, Brown, & L'Engle, 2007). However, it becomes potentially more difficult when deciding if a particular sexual scene should be coded as, for example, "pregnancy" or "condoms and contraception." Clear, unambiguous operational definitions for every concept and category relevant to your study not only focuses your research, but also helps your coders to be more efficient.

Third, content categories should be *reliable*, meaning that different coders using your coding scheme should categorize content in similar ways. It becomes difficult during coding when a coder finds a unit of analysis "in between" two categories, or wants to reject part of the coding scheme entirely. This part of content analysis research is powered by human interpretation, which leaves coding and its results wide open for debate. A postmodern approach only makes the situation more complicated since, as discussed by Thomas (1994), postmodernists claim that "interpretational variability" (p. 687) happens constantly. While postmodernism frames social perception as relativistic, reliability in this sense should be considered as providing stable "rules of evidence" (p. 695) for your research. *Intercoder reliability* provides "the extent to which independent coders evaluate a characteristic of a message or artifact and reach the same conclusion" (Lombard, Snyder-Duch, & Bracken, 2005, n.p.). By comparing each coder's choice, we see how they agreed about placing content into the defined categories. Dozens of indices exist for rating intercoder reliability, but the most often used in communication research are percentage agreement, Holsti's method, Scott's pi, Cohen's kappa, and Krippendorff's alpha. Refer to Lombard et al. (2005) for more information.

Choose coders carefully and reward them kindly, since this can be time-consuming and mind-numbing work. While postmodernism recognizes that coders approach the task with biases and preconceptions, coders should be fair and willing to follow the codebook. "Even very strict instructions need to be read, understood, and followed by humans, and coders are humans even when they are asked to act like computers" (Krippendorff, 2004, p. 126–127). If possible, whoever creates the codebook should not also code content—an often violated and somewhat unrealistic provision given that most studies are done on a shoestring budget. Performing a *pilot study*, an initial study that usually examines a smaller amount of data than the full study, helps identify a multitude of potential problems, from content categories to coder choices, and should include a check of intercoder reliability.

Coding Instructions for News Web Pages for Columbia Space Shuttle Disaster

There are 21 categories of online items (most are links). Seven of those 21 also require description by type, if present. Code a zero (0) if the category is not present (if category is not present, code 0 for type, if applicable). If an item is present, code the number of items of that category in that cell of the Microsoft Excel® spreadsheet. For example, if I code five links to other publications, I would place a 5 in the appropriate cell. (During the training session I had mentioned using only 1s and 0s, but coding a number of 0, or whatever it is, provides more information.)

There will be an Microsoft Excel® spreadsheet (file) for each of the four papers/Web sites you will code. Look at the bottom tabs for the correct day and if that tab is for a top page (T) or a special section (S). For example, the special section tab for 2/3 is marked "2_3 S". There will be 13 total bottom tabs (2/1 had no special sections, with two per day for six days 2/2–2/7). 13 × 4 = 52 total pages.

Categories and type will be in this order in the Microsoft Excel® spreadsheets. Clarifications are in parentheses. Descriptions of item types follow. For all coding, code *only* that content relevant to Columbia (e.g., a picture of a snowstorm should not be coded).

Categories of online items
1. Code a "1" if you had to "noticeably scroll" to find content (if on bottom edge of screen code "0"; if a page or two down code "1")
2. Special Columbia graphic
3. "Complete Coverage/Full Report" link
4. # Still photos (still on page, not a gallery)
5. Type still photos
6. # Photo gallery links (labeled as a gallery, not an interactive graphic)
7. Type photo gallery. . .

Remember, if the category is not present, code a "0" in this cell.
1. Shuttle Columbia accident (event)
2. Debris recovery effort
3. Cause/accident investigation
4. Shuttle Columbia mission/history
5. Crew related (mission or non-mission, like history)
6. Crew family reaction
7. Public reaction
8. International reaction
9. Official reaction (not NASA)
10. NASA reaction. . . .

FIGURE 9.1   Sample Coding Instruction Sheet (Partial)

Coders require training on the type of content, units of analysis, and content categories. They should have a *coding instruction sheet* (see Figure 9.1 and a *coding sheet* (see Figure 9.2) to enter their choices for later data analysis. Typically, the coding sheet is a physical piece of paper with category choices. This preserves the data in print form, but its information must be carefully and correctly entered into analysis software. Coders can also enter data directly into a spreadsheet or analysis database, which removes the potential for data entry errors going from sheet to software. However coding is accomplished, use good data management techniques to keep your data safe; for example, make multiple computer file backups and

---

This coding sheet was set up as a Microsoft Excel® spreadsheet and corresponds with the categories discussed in Figure 09-1. Coders directly entered coding data into the spreadsheet, which was then transferred to SPSS software for data analysis. Each category in the following represents a data cell in the spreadsheet, with coding information entered into the adjacent cell. (For this example categories are listed vertically down the page; however, to facilitate entry of each case into SPSS, categories act as row headers that are arranged horizontally across the page.)

Scroll	
Col graphic	
Comp coverage	
# Still photos	
Type still photos	
# Photo gallery	
Type photo gallery	
# Story links	
Type story	
# AP	
# Video	
Type video	
# Int graph	
Type int graph	
# Audio	
Type Audio	
# Sp text	
Type Sp text	
# Diss	
# News Web	
# Other Web	

FIGURE 9.2 Sample Coding Sheet

copies of completed coding sheets, and store in different places. Coded data may represent literally hundreds of hours of work and research dollars, so treat it with care.

Analysis

Scholars usually enjoy this aspect of a study because they finally see the fruits of their research efforts. In this final step you process the data collected by the coders and consider the results in order to respond to your research questions. It is not enough to only report quantities found—in addition to answering your own research questions, good research always addresses two others: So what? Who cares? Refer to Section III of this book for guidance on writing the research report, including writing style, grammar, and report format.

This section includes three aspects of Krippendorff's (2004) content analysis framework. First is using established statistical techniques for "reducing data to manageable representations" (p. 83), the last of his "data making" steps. Depending on the type and level of data (i.e., nominal, ordinal, interval, or ratio) such techniques may include measures of central tendency (e.g., mean, median, mode), parametric statistics (e.g., t-test, ANOVA) or nonparametric statistics (e.g., chi-square, Mann-Whitney U test). These procedures summarize vast amounts of information to make analysis possible; otherwise, we have literally countless marks on pages with no idea what any of them mean. Postmodern content analysis does not preclude using statistics to explain data and relationships; quite to the contrary, numbers can provide evidence to support or refute otherwise unsupported claims (Thomas, 1994). However, the basis of statistics is rooted in the mechanical world paradigm of sampling part to understand the whole, which postmodernism rejects.

The other two aspects of Krippendorff's (2004) framework for analysis are creating inferences from the text (used broadly here to mean any content) and responding to the research questions. He stresses constructing *analytical constructs* that act as a "model of the relationships" (p.172) between concepts represented in the original text and the analysis of those concepts. For example, Kiernan (2003) searched for mentions of scientific journal articles, while his research question asked "What is the relative effect of coverage by the *New York Times*, other daily newspapers, and national network television on citation rates of published research?" (p. 5). To explore the "relative effect" the researcher had to abstract from the concrete data collected. Overall, Krippendorff (2004) suggests that the analysis phase include summarizing inferences for easier understanding, discovering patterns, and comparing findings to other similar studies (p. 91). Hopefully, these studies were covered as previous research in the report's literature review. Mentioning them again in the report's final sections provide a wonderful circular notion to the research process by placing your study's findings within the context of the broader body of knowledge about your topic.

Conclusion

In the postmodern tradition I will step out as "author" of this section for some final remarks, something you are encouraged to do with your own study. Like much research, conducting a content analysis often begins with one feeling intrigued and ends with one being somewhat obsessed. It is fantastic to be first "down in the data" and then "up in the clouds" considering your findings. But be prepared: content analysis is a lot of work. You will stretch your notions of content as you begin to gather whatever you will study, and more than likely you will end up owing friends and colleagues for their coding assistance. For this method, the devil really is in the details, and there are plenty of details. Besides postmodern-rejected ideas of reliability or replicability, I hope you do good research out of personal pride. Completing a study is a great feeling, especially when you know you have done it correctly and done your best.

PART II—READER-RESPONSE

The reader-response approach to a text has a long history in the world of literary criticism. Applied to literature, it "encompasses various approaches . . . that explore and seek to explain the diversity (and often divergence) of readers' responses to literary works" (VirtuaLit Critical Approaches). The notion probably dates back to Plato and Aristotle, both of whom "were aware of the effects of works of literature. Plato, in fact, worried that poets would stir up the emotions of the audience" (Approaches to Reading and Interpretation).

The reader-response approach to literature can be easily adapted to fit communication research needs. It's actually quite simple. For example, instead of the text being a piece of literature or a poem, the text we propose to examine could be a speech by a public official, a communication document of some sort, the transcript of a dialogue between two people, or it could be a media text, that is, a television or radio program, a film, an advertisement, a newspaper or magazine article, and so forth. This part of the chapter will focus on the reader (receiver) of media messages rather than on the originator. For our purposes, the reader-response method is based on three general principles:

1. "Reading is believed to be dynamic and interactive;
2. Meaning emerges from a transaction between readers and texts;"
3. Responses to texts do not equal interpretation of texts (Background of reader response theory, 2008).

By now it should be obvious that when we speak of "reading" a text, we also speak of "viewing" a text or "listening" to a text since we are applying the reader-response method to all communications.

READER-RESPONSE ASSUMPTIONS

In order to make a reader-response approach to communication research work, we must accept several assumptions. Let's use media communication as an example.

- Media consumers are active, not passive, in their responses to media texts.
- A media text can be any media product that has content, that is, a message, and is presented to an audience.
- A media text has no single, "correct" meaning or interpretation.
- Meaning is created by the interaction of media consumer and media text.
- There can be several interpretations of meanings of a text.
- Media consumers are encouraged to have their own personal reactions to media texts.

One can easily apply these assumptions to forms of communication other than media by simply removing the word *media* from each. For example, the first assumption would read as follows: Consumers are active, not passive, in their responses to texts. The second assumption would become "A text can be any product that has content, that is, a message presented to an audience," and so on.

READER-RESPONSE APPROACHES

There are at least four different ways to use the reader-response approach. A *rhetorical approach* analyzes a text in terms of the rhetorical strategies used to influence readers. A *structuralist approach* describes the codes readers acquire and use to determine the meaning of a text. A *phenomenologist approach* studies how the mind processes texts. Finally, a *subjective approach* focuses on individual readers and reveals their response to a text. While all these approaches have merit, three are beyond the scope of this textbook. Our approach here will be the subjective one.

THE READER-RESPONSE PROCESS

Using a reader-response approach will require you to modify, to some degree, the process suggested by the research flowchart presented in Chapter 4. Many of the basic research activities will remain the same. You should state the problem or issue you wish to study and discuss the problem with other interested parties. You should probably conduct a literature search, although you may not find a lot of information about your problem if you are looking for work that has been done using reader-response in communication. Reader-response has a rich history in the interpretation of literature, so some information may be available in literary journals. There may be information about your topic available from research by individuals using other methods. This information may or may not be useful, but it is worth examining. These basic steps should result in a general research question relating to your topic. For example, suppose you are interested in viewer response to the popular television show *American Idol*. Your general research question might be this one: How do viewers respond to the popular television show *American Idol*? Other methods might require multiple research questions, but one general question fits reader-response nicely. More specific questions will come later.

Your research design can make use of some of the elements of survey research. You will need to contact individuals and ask them questions about their responses to *American Idol*. You need not develop a questionnaire of the sort used in survey research. Your list of questions will be much shorter and all of them will be open-ended, that is, no set of responses will be offered from which the participant will be required to select one. In other words, you will be gathering qualitative data resulting from in-depth interviews. Interviews should probably be done in person rather than on the phone. Neither is it recommended that you have participants write down their responses. Written responses are often brief and unrevealing. Phone interviews can be difficult because you will need to record everything a participant says. This may involve audiotaping the phone conversation, a practice that makes many people uncomfortable. You will get the best data from one-on-one interviews where you record what the person being interviewed says and where you can give the person plenty of time to explain his/her responses. You can write down the responses or tape record them. By this time, you should be well aware of how to record and preserve research data. Several chapters in this book have tips on proper data recording, but at this point in your study of research methods, you should have little trouble deciding how to record interviewee responses.

There are many other decisions to make. How many people will you need to interview? Will you conduct all the interviews or will you use an assistant? Will the assistant need any sort of training? Where will you conduct the interviews? How long do you anticipate an interview will take? In other words, the logistics of this research method are just as important as those for any other research method. You will likely need to develop a budget for the project. You will be conducting in-depth interviews with your study participants. You should consider the logistics required to successfully complete your project.

In general, the reader-response process follows these steps:

- identify and contact participants;
- arrange an appropriate time and place for an interview;
- explain the general nature of the project and ask for permission to tape record the interview;
- ask the reader-response questions you have developed; and
- conclude the interview and thank participants.

Identifying and contacting participants for your reader-response project may not be all that difficult. The first decision you will have to make is whether to contact complete strangers or people you know. Some researchers would suggest that contacting people you know (and who know you) might introduce bias. Possibly, but remember that in postmodern culture, achieving objectivity is almost impossible. This does not mean that you should just give up trying to be objective. If you decide to use people you know, you should probably avoid close friends, but you might get some useful data from mere acquaintances.

Contacting complete strangers is usually no problem if you are doing telephone survey research. However, given the nature of the culture these days, especially crime rates, scams of all sorts, and the loss of personal privacy, many people may be hesitant to agree to an interview. Almost no one goes door-to-door anymore, except perhaps politicians seeking election, so asking a stranger to let you come for an in-depth interview may not result in many takers. It might be safer and more efficient to contact people with whom you have some connection. How many participants will you need? That depends on the time and resources you have to give to the project. In keeping with our general modification of traditional social science procedures, you will not draw a random sample of any sort and will not generalize your findings to a larger audience. The number of participants is not irrelevant, but you really don't have to have a large number. You might try to interview about 8 to 10 individuals for your first reader-response research activity. This will generate a lot of data. And it may take you some time to complete the interviews. Still, if you are interested in a range of responses to a communication text, you will almost certainly need to do more than 3 or 4 interviews.

You might ask this question: Should I pay attention to demographics, that is, gender, age, education level, annual income, and the like, when I select participants? That depends. You may have to use those who agree to participate, regardless of their demographic characteristics. On the other hand, if the text you are asking participants to respond to is one that is designed for a particular audience, you may need to select participants carefully. For example, if you are interested in responses to a special concert on Music Television (MTV), you would probably do well to ask the types of people who might have seen the concert. It is doubtful many people in their 50s and 60s saw the program. You might want to contact individuals who were more likely to have seen the program, perhaps individuals in their teens or 20s.

Next, you will need to work on *arranging a time and place for the interview.* There are a couple of ways to arrange a meeting in a place offering minimum risk to both you and the participant. Bookstores are popular meeting places. Most national bookstore chains have a café area where coffee and pastries are available and where tables may be used by customers. Bookstores are public areas and are often busy and noisy. Still, you could meet a participant at a local bookstore and conduct the in-depth interview. This type of meeting might work well if the participant can clearly recall the text, that is, the television or radio program, the magazine or newspaper, the speech, or whatever, you are studying. If you think the participant may not clearly recall the text, you may wish to reacquaint him/her with the text. This is no problem if the text is printed material, but may be a problem if the text is a broadcast or some other electronic text that cannot pass from your hand to the participant's hand. You may wish to arrange for a special room of some sort where audiovisual materials may be presented. This sort of thing probably rules out bookstores, but libraries often have a "community room" that you might be able to use. Libraries are accessible public places so safety concerns may be eased. If you are a college student, you might be able to arrange a place on campus for the interview. The campus library may have study rooms or a classroom building may have a seminar room you can use. You will need permission from campus officials, of course, to use these rooms. Still, arranging meeting places is important and part of the logistics task of any research project.

Arranging a time to meet may be a little problematic. Many people are very busy (or think they are) and may have schedules so full of activities and responsibilities that they can't find time to meet you for an interview. This will call for some flexibility on your part. Most people like to consider weekends a time to relax and refresh for the coming workweek. Suppose, for example, that you contact an individual who agrees to participate, but can only meet you at 5 p.m. on Sunday afternoon. You would prefer meeting the person on a weekday, of course, but your participant says it is Sunday afternoon or nothing. What do you do? You really have no choice. Good researchers never pass up an opportunity to gather quality data, even if it disrupts their lives a little. You will, of course, agree enthusiastically to that Sunday afternoon meeting. You will conduct the interview at the appointed place with the same positive attitude and research approach that you've used for other interviews.

Upon meeting a participant, you should introduce yourself and briefly *explain the nature of the project* without giving away anything about the sort of response you expect from him/her. Ask for permission to audiotape the session and stress that the person's comments will be held in strict confidence and that the participant's name will not be associated with his/her responses. If the participant does not agree to the audio taping, you will have to write down exactly what the participant says in response to your questions. This will be a difficult task, but one you must accomplish. You should also collect some basic demographic information: gender, age, education, annual income, and the like. These variables may help you place the participant's comments in some larger context.

You are now ready to *ask the reader-response questions*. These questions were, of course, prepared in advance and designed to elicit information from the participant about his/her response to a text. The following general questions, adapted from those developed by Hall (2002) may be of some help when you prepare your list of questions for your participants:

1. "What is the predominant effect of the text on you? Confusion, suspense, identification with characters, interest, boredom, amusement, terror, etc. Expand as much as possible."
2. "Why do you think the text had that effect? Was it the subject matter, language, organization, characters, themes, gaps, or blanks in the structure?"
3. "Did you have prior knowledge or expectations about the text or the medium through which it was delivered? Why did you have those expectations?"
4. "What does your response tell you about yourself?" About your habits, your values, your assumptions about communication, your notion of what is normal or conventional? (pp. 1–2).

You will not, of course, ask exactly these questions. They are presented here to get you thinking about the questions you will want to ask about the text you are studying. There is no minimum or maximum number of questions you may ask. Since you will be conducting an in-depth interview, you will want to offer participants the opportunity to fully expand or explain their answers to your questions.

When the participant has answered all your questions to the best of his/her ability, you should *conclude the interview*. This includes thanking the individual for his/her participation and assuring the person that his/her responses will remain confidential.

DATA ORGANIZATION AND ANALYSIS

All the interviews have been completed. You have audiotapes of all the sessions. What next? As you may recall from Chapter 8, you will need to turn these audio recordings into transcripts. Remember to preserve the audiotapes (you may have to refer to them later) and to make multiple copies of each transcript. Each transcript may be given an identification number, a number that will tell you—and no one else—whose responses those are.

There are several ways to organize and analyze reader-response data. You could handle each interview as a mini case study. Babbie (2002) defines a case study as "the in-depth examination of a single instance of some social phenomenon" (p. 440). Obviously in this case, the social phenomenon being examined in depth is an individual's response to a text. If you use each interview as a case study, you will be presenting a detailed report of a participant's response and may be able to place that response in some personal, individual context relating to the participant. You will have as many case studies as you had participants.

You could decide to look at all participant responses at the same time and find similarities and differences. You would then summarize your findings and note especially responses that were particularly revealing: use of language, raising or lowering of voice, display of emotion, and the like. Some researchers believe many people respond to a text in essentially the same way. Similar responses to a text can be said to form a sort of interpretative community, that is, a group of individuals who share the same reaction(s) to a text. If your search of the literature revealed other studies that report reader responses to the text you are studying, you should probably compare those findings to yours.

As with focus groups, and regardless of how you organize and analyze the data, it is a good idea to include as many of the actual participant interview statements as practical. You can summarize and comment on what participants said, of course, but nothing strengthens a piece of research more than presenting the actual data in the written report.

ADDRESSING THE RESEARCH QUESTION

You are now ready to address your research question. There will probably be more than one answer to the question. Remember you asked participants for their personal responses to a text. You could have as many different answers to your research question as you had participants. However, you will more likely have fewer answers than the total number of participants because some participants may have had the same or similar responses to the text. Again, if some participant statements can serve the answering function, be sure to include them, word-for-word.

EVALUATING THE STUDY

How successful was your reader-response research project? What problems did you encounter and how did you solve them? Did the unexpected happen? What surprised you most about participant responses? What disappointed you? Did the study serve to provide at least a temporary answer or two to the research question? What advice would you give others who are interested in doing reader-response research?

WRITING THE REPORT

Remember, a project is not complete until it has been written and made available to other researchers. Your reader-response report will look much like other research reports in terms of format: introduction, problem statement, literature search, methodology, results, and conclusion. There may be some slight variation of this to accommodate your unique project, particularly if you report results using the case study approach. Still, one of the reasons for writing the report is to communicate what you did, when, how, and why to other researchers. For more tips on writing the report, see Section III of this book.

PART III—DECONSTRUCTION

Let us now consider a text analysis method that is uniquely postmodern: *deconstruction*. There is nothing like this method in mainstream communication research. It will be a challenging method to understand and use, but it illustrates some of the points postmodernists are making about reality, culture, communication, and media.

WHAT IS DECONSTRUCTION?

"Deconstruction is a movement of thought, growing out of the work of the contemporary French philosopher and critic Jacques Derrida, which calls into question the possibility of securely establishing the meaning of any human construction, including any text" (Smith, 1989, p. 21). Derrida was quite popular in his time. Hundreds of people came to hear him speak, and films and television programs were devoted to him and his work. Scholars wrote countless books and articles devoted to his thinking (www. plato.stanford.edu/entries/derrida/, 2006, para.1).

Although Powell (1998) believes "defining deconstruction is an activity that goes against the whole thrust of Derrida's thought" (p. 100), we are nevertheless going to do it. Furthermore, it challenges a researcher's desire "to secure a fully centered human subject comfortably situated in a world of roles, statuses, norms, values, and structured social systems" (Denzin, 1994, p. 185). It short, deconstruction questions some of the most important things mainstream social science (and communication) researchers take for granted.

Norris (1996) notes that *deconstruction* has become "something of a buzzword among commentators on the postmodern cultural scene." The term is regularly used by all sorts of individuals, including novelists, politicians, newspaper columnists, and media pundits (p. 136). Most of them use it incorrectly. They might have a vague idea of what it means— questioning truths and assumptions that everyone else takes for granted— but their use of the term does "not reflect a specialized, critical grasp of the concept" (p. 136).

When the term *deconstruction* is applied to something, it is often with "a strongly negative connotation; thus 'deconstruct' = 'take things apart', such as literary texts, philosophical arguments, historical narratives" and the like (Norris, p. 137). This, too, shows a misunderstanding of the fundamental nature of the term. Simply put, what deconstruction does is this: It "requires that traditional concepts, theory, and understanding surrounding a text be unraveled, including the assumptions that an author's intentions and meanings can be easily determined" (Denzin, 1994, p. 185). Thus, written words ≠ spoken words, spoken words ≠ mental experience, and voice ≠ mind. Meaning is indeterminate, so the best we can do is look for possible meanings and examine the differences among them (p. 185).

CAN DECONSTRUCTION BE A RESEARCH METHOD?

No, says postmodern scholar Christopher Norris (1996). "To present 'deconstruction' as if it were a method, a system or settled body of ideas, would be to falsify its nature and lay oneself open to charges of reductive misunderstanding" (p. 1). Yes, says postmodern scholar Norman Denzin (1994). Deconstruction "may be employed as a postmodern research strategy for the interpretative study of contemporary society" (p. 182). No, says Derrida himself. In his "Letter to a Japanese Friend" Derrida flatly declares: "Deconstruction is not a method and cannot be transformed into one" (Royle, 2000, p. 4). If you have a method, you have already determined how to proceed and this creates a sort of bias or limitation because any method is systematic and closed. A method is a procedure of some sort and by its very nature is not open to new ideas or approaches beyond what the method allows (pp. 4–5). Well, that would seem to be the end of it. If the originator of the term believes it cannot be used in a certain way, we must take his word for it, right? Not necessarily. Read on.

DECONSTRUCTION AS RESEARCH METHOD

Deconstruction has its roots in an analytical method called *hermeneutics*. Hermeneutics may be defined as the art or practice of the interpretation of texts. It probably originated during the Reformation as a way to understand Biblical literature. Today, it may be seen as a way of analyzing the "necessary conditions for coming to any understanding of a text" (*Columbia Encyclopedia*, 2001–2005). Analyzing a text necessarily involves some way of doing it, some procedure, if you will. Derrida himself examined texts and discovered several important things (more about this later). Why should we, as researchers, have our work marginalized or excluded, simply because we choose to use deconstruction in much the same way Derrida did? If he analyzed texts with his deconstruction philosophy in mind, why can't we? The short answer is, of course, we can and we will!

DECONSTRUCTION ASSUMPTIONS

Before we get to a detailed discussion of how to use deconstruction as a research method, we need to establish some fundamental assumptions about its nature. Deconstruction can be said to have the following characteristics:

- celebrates difference and is obsessed with variety, plurality, otherness;
- believes that marginalizing, that is, excluding, ignoring, or demeaning an individual, group, or idea, is a frequent occurrence;
- argues that there is no complete and consistent system; therefore, no system has all or can discover all the truth;
- does not accept personal intentions or individual experience as significant in the creation of meaning;
- does not try to "root out" what a text is "really saying;"

- tries to show that the perspectives from which any text is analyzed are always shifting and unstable;
- challenges the idea that any scientific method and a logical consistency can lead to the discovery of conclusive truth; and
- rejects the notion that meaning and truth in a text are absolute or time-less, suggesting instead that meaning and truth are always dependent on our social, historical, and intellectual knowledge.

[Adapted from Ward (1997); Smith (1989); Bauman (1992)]

You may be thinking you will never understand deconstruction or be able to use it in communication research. You may feel this list attacks many of the things modern researchers did or found important. For example, if one can't find "truth," why bother with research at all? If "meaning" is never stable, why try to look for it in any text? Not to worry! Look again at the list. You will notice that it really doesn't say that "truth" and "meaning" do not exist, it says that a *single truth* or *single meaning* does not exist. This opens the door for you to consider a range of possible truths and meanings. Without just one truth or meaning, other voices can be heard, and other points of view can be considered. This makes it possible to see a text as richer and more revealing, particularly if we examine some of the thinking behind a particular interpretation. Remember, deconstruction is related to hermeneutics, and that means it is concerned with interpretation. Interpretation will almost certainly vary from person to person. It is this sort of variety that can be useful in coming to a more complete understanding of a text.

DECONSTRUCTING A TEXT

The procedure for using deconstruction as a research method will differ somewhat from the general procedures used for other research methods. It will not be necessary to state a problem. A problem statement could indicate some sort of bias, and, in any case, it is not deconstruction's aim to solve problems but to present a different reading of a text. Instead of a problem statement, you could *select a text to analyze*, that is, indicate the text which you are interested in examining. This could be any communication text, including an advertisement, a news program, a radio or television show, an Internet communication, a speech, a printed document, and the like. An ambitious project might attempt to analyze a series of advertisements, or a season's worth of a particular television program, or a week's worth of news programs, or a series of political campaign speeches.

You should, of course, *search the literature*, but you may not find much that is very helpful, that is, anything that has been done on your text of interest by communication researchers using deconstruction. Other research methods may have been applied to your text, and these studies may be of some interest. Once your study is complete, you may be able to point out how the results of other studies differ from or are similar to yours.

Posing a research question can be problematic, related as it usually is to a problem statement. Nevertheless, there is one general research question that will likely serve for all deconstruction research: What does deconstruction reveal about [text].

For example, if you are interested in deconstructing television advertisements for a household cleaning product, your research question might be something like this: What does deconstruction reveal about television advertisements for "Big Job Household Cleanser"? Do not be overly concerned that the research question is rather general. Deconstruction tries to avoid the trappings of mainstream social science/communication research which, Derrida believes, are closed and restrictive.

You are now ready to *examine the text*. Although you want to avoid doing so in a closed and restrictive manner, you still need to proceed in some sort of organized fashion in order to get the most from your analysis. It might be useful to analyze the text using the following set of questions, adapted from Ward (1997), Denzin (1994), and Sim and Van Loon (2001). The questions are posed in an attempt to reveal some of the issues that form the fundamental bases of deconstructive thinking.

1. Whose narrative is it? Who is telling the story presented in the text? What sort of story is it? Do you know anything about the author of the text? What general values seem to be suggested by the text? Does the text seem to have authority?
2. What conditions must be present for the text to be meaningful? Is any particular knowledge required to understand the text? Are there social, political, or economic issues that must be understood for the text to have meaning?
3. What is the structure of the text? In what form does it appear? Does the form seem to be appropriate for the message the text carries? Would the structure be familiar to all readers of the text?
4. Does the text present an intertextuality problem? What other texts might influence the present text?
5. Are binary oppositions present? Is one member of the pair favored over the other?

The last two items on this list need explanation. *Intertextuality* simply means the overlapping of texts. In other words, your reading of a text might very well be influenced by similar or related texts you remember. For example, if you are deconstructing the latest Harry Potter movie, your thinking would most likely be influenced to some degree by the other Harry Potter movies you have seen and perhaps even the Harry Potter books you have read. Add to that the possibility of your being influenced by what others have written or said about the Harry Potter movies and books and you can see that your analysis of the latest Harry Potter movie is neither pure nor objective, but influenced by other texts.

A *binary opposition* is two terms used in discourse to describe certain situations, individuals, and behaviors. Derrida believes Western culture depends heavily on binary oppositions and that they represent "hierarchies in miniature, containing one term that Western culture views as positive or superior and another considered negative or inferior" (VirtuaLit Critical Approaches). There are several common binary oppositions at work in contemporary discourse. Some of these are black/white, good/evil, false/true, high/low, normal/abnormal, and gay/straight, among others. Powell (1998) notes that "one member of the pair is privileged, freezing the play of the system and marginalizing the other member of the pair" (p. 103). Derrida "aims to erase the boundary between binary oppositions—and do so in such a way that the hierarchy implied by the opposition is thrown into question" (VirtuaLit Critical Approaches).

You will, of course, have jotted down your answers to the questions as you examined the text. You may have written them by hand or you may have typed them into a computer file. In any case, you should have a record of your responses to the questions you applied to the text. You are now ready to *draw conclusions*, right? Maybe. You should avoid drawing sweeping conclusions about your deconstruction of your text of interest. Remember, you are not generalizing your findings to any other text or group of texts. Mainstream social science researchers like to generalize their findings, feeling as many do, that they have discovered "truth" and captured "reality." As postmodernists, we know that absolute truth and reality probably don't exist and that any found truth or reality may be only one of many. Instead of drawing conclusions, you might simply wish to summarize your findings. You can safely point out what you found in the text you analyzed and suggest how it might or might not fit within a contemporary cultural context, but going beyond that is risky. Faulconer (1998) provides a useful perspective on what deconstruction can and cannot do:

> Deconstruction is used to show that a work does not adequately address something, not that it should have. Deconstruction does not assume that once its work has been done everything will have been included. That would be impossible. It doesn't even assume that its work will result in the inclusion of more than previously included; it doesn't assume that its work will make things better. That remains to be seen in each case. In sum, deconstruction doesn't assume that there is, even if only in principle, an end to the work of deconstruction. The point of deconstruction is to show where something has been omitted, not because of the blindness of the author . . . but because that is the way things are. There are always things I don't know, though in a very real way *that* I don't know them is part of what I know (p. 5).

WHAT ABOUT LOGISTICS?

In our discussion of other research methods, we have devoted considerable time to a consideration of the logistics, or precise details, necessary to complete a research project. Should you worry about logistics if you use deconstruction as a research method? Probably not. For deconstruction, you need only a text and a way of writing down what you found when you deconstructed it. Since, for our purposes, a text can be any communication, you would not likely have much of a problem accessing your text of interest. Note taking is a straightforward activity. You really need only a text, pencil and paper (or a computer), a quiet place to examine the text and write down what you find, and time to carefully read and consider.

Some texts might be easier to get than others. For example, suppose you wish to deconstruct television news coverage of the first day of the first U.S.–Iraq War in the Middle East, called Desert Storm. Copies of the news broadcasts of that first day are not readily at hand. You would likely have to visit the television news archives at Vanderbilt University in Nashville, TN, to view the news footage. On the other hand, if you were interested in deconstructing political communication and you used your home television set and VCR to videotape a speech by a politician who was running for president, you'd have the text in hand. Overall, the logistics of deconstruction are often easier to handle than those of other research methods once you have the desired text.

ADDRESSING THE RESEARCH QUESTION

You can now provide an answer to the research question posed at the beginning of your study: What does deconstruction reveal about [text]? Remember, you analyzed a particular text, and you will not be generalizing to other texts. Your answer will almost certainly be brief and related to the issues you discovered in your analysis of the text.

EVALUATING THE STUDY

Derrida might consider this step unnecessary. You did not need the cooperation of others to complete the project. You did not need a large budget to do the work. It will probably be difficult to find much that went wrong with the project. It is possible, of course, that you were unable to answer some of the key analysis questions about the text, but this is not necessarily a failing. Not all texts are stable and revealing; deconstruction of a text provides only temporary information.

DECONSTRUCTION IN ACTION: AN EXAMPLE

Because deconstruction is largely unknown as a research method in communication, you can't very well search the literature for a study using the method. You might like to try deconstructing a text, but would be interested first in seeing how someone else used the method. Some researchers somewhere have deconstructed texts of various sorts, but that work is probably not part of the communication literature. You would be more likely to find it in publications presenting research in English and literature. In other words, you need an example of a piece of communication research using deconstruction as the method of text analysis. The following example is presented to give you a general idea of the sorts of things deconstructing a text might reveal.

The Example

Medium: newspapers

Area of interest: sports

> Specific text of interest: coverage of the 2006 Men's and Women's NCAA College Basketball Tournaments, March 20, 2006, *USA Today*, Section C

Research method: deconstruction

General observations about text:

Page 1	• Large photo of action in a men's tournament game and accompanying story; specific games highlighted in red and yellow; 1/3 page; above fold
	• Small picture and story on results in women's tourney games; 1/8 page; below fold
Page 2	• Continuing story from Page 1 on men's tourney action and results; 1/2; page
Page 3	• Additional stories on men's action and columnist piece on television coverage of men's games; 1 page
Page 4	• Entire page presented men's tourney bracket, that is, game pairings plus two photos
Page 5	• Advertisement; 1 page
Page 6	• Story on women's tourney, including tourney bracket pairings; 1/2; page
	• Stories and summaries of men's games; 1/2; page
Page 7	• Stories and summaries of men's games; 1 page
Page 8	• Stories and summaries of men's games; 1/4; page
Page 9	• Men's game stories and statistics; 4/5; page
Page 10	• Stories and summaries of men's games; 1/4; page
Pages 11–16	• Devoted to stories on other sports and advertisements

Deconstruction Questions and Answers:

1. Whose narrative is it? Who is telling the story presented in the text? What sort of story is it? Do you know anything about the author of the text? What general values seem to be suggested by the text? Does the text seem to have authority?

Answers: The narrative is a series of stories reporting on the action and results in both the men's and women's college basketball tournaments. The stories are presented as sports news items and are written by several different reporters. The typical reader knows little or nothing about those writing the stories. The reporters' names are attached to the stories, but no other information is provided about who the reporter is. The stories seem to indicate that the games are important events in American cultural life and are deserving of considerable space in the newspaper. The stories seem grounded on the notion that athletic competition is a highly desirable activity and one that interests most readers. The fact that the stories appear in a well-known national newspaper gives them some authority. If a reader is well-acquainted with the world of sports, the stories provide interesting and accurate information about the tournament games.

2. What conditions must be present for the text to be meaningful? Is any particular knowledge required to understand the text? Are there social, political, or economic issues that must be understood for the text to have meaning?

Answers: The first condition that must be present for the text to be meaningful is that it must be written in an organized, coherent fashion, so that a reader can understand the language used and follow the storyline. Some sports knowledge is required for the text to be meaningful. A reader who is not interested in sports or does not understand sports, basketball in this case, would not find the text particularly meaningful. Athletic competition has social and economic implications, but these are not often obvious in sports stories. A knowledge of the social and economic implications of the games is not required in order for a reader to find the text meaningful.

3. What is the structure of the text? In what form does it appear? Does the form seem to be appropriate for the message the text carries? Would the structure be familiar to all readers of the text?

Answers: The text is comprised of several stories about basketball games. These stories are presented using a typical news-story structure. This means that there is an interesting opening sentence—a lead—to the story, followed by several supporting sentences. Details are provided as the story progresses. These details usually include game scores and quotes from both players and coaches.

A popular way to end the stories in this particular text seems to be a clever or revealing quote of some sort from someone who played, coached, or watched the games. The form seems appropriate for the message, and the structure of the text would be familiar to all newspaper readers, regardless of their level of interest in the games.

4. Does the text present an intertextuality problem? What other texts might influence the present text?

Answers: There is an intertextuality issue here. Although some readers of the text may find it to be their only source of information about the games, others may have seen the games on television, heard them on the radio, or talked about them with friends. A reader could be influenced by the overlapping nature of these texts. It is also possible that some readers have been following their favorite team in the tourney and are well acquainted with the team's performance this year and in past years. Other readers might not focus on a particular team but on the tourney itself, and may be influenced to some degree by this year's tourney in contrast to those of other years. Thus, the text cannot be isolated from other texts. Any interpretation of the present text must take into account the likelihood that the text's meaning may be influenced to some unknown degree by other texts with which the reader is familiar.

5. Are binary oppositions present? Is one member of the pair favored over the other?

Answers: There is a well-known binary opposition at work in this text. It is the male/female opposition. Although information from both the men's and the women's tournament games was presented, the men's games were clearly privileged by the news coverage. Information about the men's games was given 7 4/5 pages of space; information about the women's games was given only 5/8 of a page. To some readers this binary opposition may imply that the men's games are more important (and perhaps superior) to the women's games. This notion may occur subconsciously as it does elsewhere in the culture where this particular binary opposition is present.

SUMMARY OF FINDINGS

Deconstruction of *USA Today*'s reporting of the 2006 NCAA Men's and Women's College Basketball tournaments has revealed several things. First, the women's games seem to have been clearly marginalized. Although not ignored entirely, these games failed to receive even one page of total coverage, while the men's games received more than seven pages of total coverage.

Second, the text was quite good at highlighting differences, particularly in terms of the style and quality of the play of all teams, as well as differences among players and coaches. These differences seem to be celebrated and tied to a team's overall performance. Finally, meaning and truth were obvious in the text chiefly because the information was based on observable facts. However, the truth and meaning found in the text are temporary because new truth and new meaning will result when the winning teams in the tourney play again later in the week.

Author's Note: The deconstruction example presented earlier was to give you a general idea of how the methodology might be used to examine a text. If you were to use the method, you would want to do a more thorough job and perhaps examine other editions of the newspaper and their reports of the men's and women's basketball tournaments before you report your observations. You may feel that the summary of findings presented earlier was not specific with regard to where the text might have fallen short. But remember that deconstruction tells us only "what is," not what "should have been."

REVIEW QUESTIONS

1. **a.** Define content analysis.
   b. What are some of the advantages and disadvantages of content analysis?
   c. What is the difference between *manifest* and *latent* content?
   d. What is a unit of analysis?
2. Which sampling method seems most appropriate for a content analysis project? Why?
3. Distinguish between *recording* and *coding* in content analysis.
4. Why is intercoder reliability important in a content analysis project?
5. How does reader-response research differ from the other research methods you have studied?
6. What sorts of texts are appropriate for a reader-response study?
7. What unique challenges does a reader-response project pose?
8. Why are the questions asked in a reader-response study so important?
9. What is deconstruction?
10. What is the relationship between deconstruction and hermeneutics?
11. How is deconstruction uniquely postmodern in its approach?
12. What is a binary opposition and why is it important to deconstruction?
13. What general research question might well serve all deconstruction projects?

SUGGESTED ACTIVITIES

1. Search the communication literature in your university library for studies using content analysis as a research method. Compare several studies in terms of the communication texts examined, the research questions asked, the samples selected, and the coding instruments used.
2. Conduct a small, personal content analysis project involving some communication product. Content analyze two episodes of your favorite television program, for example. Or analyze the content of a series of text messages you received on your cell phone from a friend or relative. Develop a research question, identify your unit(s) of analysis, and record your observations on a coding sheet you designed. What conclusions can you draw from this simple exercise?
3. Make an appointment with a faculty member in your university's Department of English. Ask about reader-response research in his/her field. Then ask about whether he/she thinks the method could be applied to other academic areas and, if so, which ones?
4. Team with another member of your class and try your hand at deconstructing a text. Deconstruct the class syllabus or a class writing assignment. Examine the school newspaper and deconstruct the stories appearing on the front page.

CHAPTER 10

Feminist Methodology

By Kim Golombisky

I want to walk through life instead of being dragged through it.

—Alanis Morissette

"I'm not a feminist, but . . ." While most people support gender justice in principle, many are put off by the "F-word": *feminism*. This is thanks to the unappealing depictions of feminists we find in mass media and popular culture. Like feminist philosophies, "feminist methodology" is not well understood, perhaps because of prejudice toward the F-word. At its best, feminist methodology stimulates productive discussions about what we do as researchers, which is the aim of this chapter. The following sections clarify feminist methodology before discussing the importance of operational definitions in gender research. In doing so, this chapter also tries to dispel some misconceptions about feminism.

However, as if a chapter devoted to the F-word isn't shocking enough, several initial points need to be made in the interest of full disclosure. First, feminist methodology is not so much a specific method as it is a shared commitment to gender justice, which leads to the second point. What distinguishes feminist research is an honesty about its political agenda, namely its commitment to gender justice. Third, feminist *methodology*, by definition, is more interested in "methodology" (the principles that guide inquiry) than "methods" (the techniques of data collection), although an interest in methodology necessitates asking questions about methods. Because of these three points, this chapter mostly builds on what you already have learned about doing research.

A POSTMODERN PERSPECTIVE

Nevertheless, if the purpose of this book is to provide a new research perspective for navigating postmodern life, then feminist methodology offers an excellent option for students of communication. Fewer than 50 years old, feminist research is a contemporary of postmodernism. As academic endeavors, the two grew up together on college and university campuses. Like the era that produced them, feminist methodology and postmodernism both question what we think we know and how we know it. You can think of them each as inquiries into the process of inquiry. At the same time, like siblings, feminist methodology and postmodernism do not always see eye to eye. Yet, despite their disagreements, they are related and do influence each other.

For one thing, because both feminist methodology and postmodernism critique the sources and content of what we consider to be legitimate knowledge, they both represent "critical" perspectives. Emerging from the humanities or "humanistic" research traditions, critical scholarship quite literally is critical of unexamined ideological assumptions and beliefs guiding society and culture, such as the notion that men are superior to women. Yet, even though all feminist research is *critical* with regard to gender issues, it is important to recognize that not all feminist research is humanistic. Important feminist research comes out of the physical, natural, and social *sciences*, as well as the humanities, including, for example, rhetoric, history, and philosophy. In the communication arts and sciences, we can find humanistic and social scientific feminist research agendas. Indeed, we increasingly see feminist and postmodern researchers blending both approaches, another sign of postmodern culture. Moreover, not every postmodern or critical researcher is sympathetic to feminism, either. But feminist methodology and postmodernism do share a belief that all research is political to some extent. They also share skepticism toward research that claims universal truth, sometimes called "capital 'T' Truth."

Additionally, like postmodernism, feminist research is transdisciplinary, meaning postmodernism and feminism each transcend specific academic disciplines. Meanwhile, communication research is interdisciplinary, meaning it crosses borders into other academic areas in search of useful ideas, including those offered by postmodernism and feminism. The interdisciplinarity of contemporary communication arts and sciences is due, in part, to its historical origins in other disciplines, in both the humanities and the social sciences. Spigel (2004) observes that, "at its best, interdisciplinary research opens up questions that we might not ask within the confines of our own field" (p. 1211). Like any good researcher, feminism and communication both tend to be open-minded about the world in general and in considering others' ways of doing and thinking about things. It is helpful to remember that open-mindedness is an asset in research, although it may not feel like one when we try to synthesize the varieties of things we have learned into textbooks or courses called, for example, *research methods*.

DEFINITIONS

It may be surprising to learn that there is no such thing as a feminist method per se. Any research method is available for feminist research. *What is distinctive about feminist research is its commitment to improving the lives of women.* Dow and Condit (2005) write that "the moniker of 'feminist' is reserved for research that studies communication . . . from a perspective that ultimately is oriented toward the achievement of 'gender justice,' a goal that takes into account the ways that gender always already intersects with race, ethnicity, sexuality, and class" (p. 449).

Feminism

So it might be better to begin a discussion of feminist methodology with a working definition of "feminism." In her book *Feminism Is for Everybody*, hooks (2000) writes, "Simply put, feminism is a movement to end sexism, sexist exploitation, and oppression" (p. 1). If feminism is for everybody, then it is important to note that a commitment to improving the lives of women does *not* mean making things worse for men. "Male bashing" is a common, though inaccurate, first reaction to feminism. *For the present purpose, we will define feminism as a commitment to gender justice.*

Feminist Methodology

Defining "feminist methodology" is a bit more complicated because there are so many different kinds of feminists using various research methods from quantitative to qualitative. Again, readers should see parallels between the range of feminist research and the broad array of mass communication research. Harding (1987) helps make some sense of this difficulty in defining feminist methodology. She reminds us that research "method," refers to "technique," the practices involved in the actual doing of research, such as how to conduct a survey. Method, then, is different from research "methodology," which refers to the philosophical foundations underpinning the research process, such as empiricism driving the principle of observation. Harding further reminds everyone about "epistemology," which suggests that the knowledge we produce from research is limited by both the method (technique) and the methodology (perspective).

The word *epistemology* takes us back to the philosophical discussion in Chapter 2 about the nature of knowledge. Harding (1987) points out that all feminist research shares a common interest in epistemology. Until very recently, women mostly have been excluded from those who may know (scholars and experts) and those who may produce knowledge (researchers). Additionally, women and women's culture only rarely were considered suitable subjects of research. As a historical consequence, women's knowledge has been absent from what we believe we know to be true about the world. In other words, the sum of our knowledge may be partial, distorted, or simply wrong without considering women.

Since that is the case, then all research, regardless of method, will be improved by including and accounting for women, the other half of humankind. Thus, the knowledge that research produces will be more complete when it includes the perspectives of women. Feminist research accounts for women in all their diversity, and, because the ultimate goal of such research is to improve the status of women, feminist research is openly political. In fact, feminists and postmodernists both understand that all research is political to some degree, and so researchers would improve their work, and the transparency of research, with systematic self-examination—called "self-reflexivity"—and disclosure. All decisions about what to study and how to study have political dimensions. As Harding argues, responsible researchers bear in mind the critique of epistemology: All knowledge is limited by the standpoints of the people who produce knowledge. We need not give up our ideals, such as empirical observation. But we must recognize that researchers are fallible and be vigilant in identifying our faults and shortcomings.

In general, feminist methodology critiques the ways that our assumptions about gender tend to influence research and knowledge in subtle and not-so-subtle ways. In doing so, feminist methodology also tries to make visible some of the invisible assumptions and politics driving research. DeVault (1999) characterizes feminist methodology by three criteria: First, feminist methodology brings women and women's voices into the research process, thus knowledge. Second, feminist methodology critiques the research process in terms of power relationships to avoid doing direct or indirect harm to the people studied. Third, feminist methodology encourages research that benefits women and improves the societies in which women live.

Bringing women into the research process means including women as researchers as well as the subjects of research. It also means valuing what women have to say. Critiquing the research process goes beyond "do no harm." Being critical of the research process means relinquishing the sense that researchers are superior to their research subjects and are empowered with the right to control and manipulate the people they study. Conducting research that benefits women and improves the societies in which they live speaks to the feminist goal of "intervention" or positive social change, whether that change is immediate or more long-term. Research that directly and often immediately improves the lives of its human participants is called "action research," an increasingly popular kind of fieldwork among feminists and nonfeminists. So feminist methodology questions traditional ideas about and ways of doing research.

For example, until Janice Radway published her groundbreaking research on women and romance novel reading in 1984, romance novels were considered a frivolous, unimportant form of mass literature, unworthy of serious study. Part of the reason romance novel reading was considered trivial is because women comprised the majority of romance novel readers. People assumed romance novel reading was merely silly romantic escapism with no intrinsic literary or social value, which further denigrated this kind of fiction. Additionally, media experts and feminists alike tended to assume that romance novels duped women as passive audiences. Others criticized the genre for perpetuating stereotypical depictions of heterosexual white women interested only in finding true love.

Using multiple methods, including participant observation, surveys, depth interviews, and content analysis, Radway's (1984) research challenged many of these assumptions. First, her work helped to change ideas about the merit of studying popular culture's relationship to society. She approached romance novels as a profitable publishing industry with a cultural and economic impact on society. Her work also challenged the belief that women's media and women's media habits did not deserve serious analysis. Maybe most important, she treated the women she studied as the real experts. She listened carefully to what the women in her study said about their romance novel reading.

One of Radway's (1984) more spectacular discoveries found that the women in her study were active, indeed ingenious, audiences. As stay-at-home wives and mothers, the women in Radway's study revealed that they read romance novels as a creative way temporarily to tune out their families' never-ending demands on the women's time. Romance novel reading, according to the women, provided recreational downtime that fit well within but did not upset their families' household routines. Radway's research also proved that romance novel readers are not necessarily naïve audiences being influenced by content. Radway's research subjects processed the content in romance novels critically in unexpectedly resistant and unorthodox ways. At the same time, Radway's critical analysis noted that reading romance novels to throw up a temporary barrier between readers and their families did not change the domestic social context that led the readers to seek a barrier in the first place.

Today, Radway's (1984) book, *Reading the Romance,* is widely considered not just a milestone in feminist media research but also one of the earliest and best U.S. examples of a kind of media audience research called "reception studies." Radway's work provides an exemplar of the ways feminist methodology can contribute valuable knowledge to communication studies by reevaluating what we study, whom we study, and how we study.

To recapitulate, *feminism is a commitment to gender justice. Feminist methodology critiques the validity of knowledge that excludes women, and feminist research seeks to improve the lives of women.* With that background we can turn to the topic of feminist methods. DeVault (1999) writes, "For the most part, feminist researchers have modified, rather than invented, research methods" (p. 28). DeVault does note, however, that "feminist researchers have produced a distinctive body of writing about research practice" (p. 28).

Feminist Research Methods

One of the most influential contributors to this feminist body of writing about research practice is Reinharz (1992). She set out to answer the question, "What is the difference between feminist research methods and other research methods?" (p. 3). Her analysis of the best practices of feminist methods concluded with a list of 10 features. According to Reinharz, feminist researchers:

- share a perspective, not a method
- use multiple research methods creatively
- participate in an ongoing critique of nonfeminist scholarship
- engage feminist theory
- exhibit transdisciplinarity
- work for social change
- recognize diversity
- involve the researcher as a person
- involve the people being studied as individuals
- involve the reader as a person

Let's examine each of these features in greater detail:

FEMINIST METHODS SHARE A PERSPECTIVE, NOT A METHOD: This shared perspective is an interest in women and gender. Feminist methods name women, as individuals and as a social category, or gender as the object of study.

FEMINIST METHODS USE MULTIPLE RESEARCH METHODS CREATIVELY: Feminist researchers employ whatever methods are useful, often improving popular methods, reviving undervalued methods, or combining multiple methods at once. It is worth noting that mass communication and communication researchers also value the use of multiple methods. Triangulation refers to the research practice of studying something from several perspectives by using a number of different methods, such as Radway's (1984) study of romance novel reading.

FEMINIST METHODS PARTICIPATE IN AN ONGOING CRITIQUE OF NONFEMINIST SCHOLARSHIP: All feminist researchers are critics, even though not all feminist scholars employ critical methods. Feminist researchers are skeptical of knowledge that forgets to account for women and gender, research that excludes women, and methods that are not reflexive about possible bias against women.

FEMINIST METHODS ENGAGE FEMINIST THEORY: Feminist researchers are not satisfied merely to report on the status of women, although that is certainly useful knowledge. Feminist research methods engage and develop feminist theory to *explain* the status of women. Feminists agree with postmodern thinking that researchers tend to forget that academic theories can never represent universal truths. Feminists know too well the dangers of totalizing grand theory because women too often in history have been the objects of false, unjust, and even harmful theories about the "true" "nature" of women. But feminism is not yet willing to reject theory totally, even as feminism approaches theory with extreme caution. Rather, feminist thought treats theory as a kind of planned obsolescence. Any theory is only a partial, limited "model." In this view, we can think of theories as tools that function properly only as long as they stimulate fresh thinking. In other words, theories should be disposable by design.

The feminist refusal to reject theory stems from recognition that gender itself represents an array of theoretical concepts about women, over which women have had little power or control. Since gender is the mechanism by which women become a distinct social category, feminist methods of necessity are forced to deal with theories of gender. However, feminists are skeptical of mainstream gender theories because such theories so often have proven to be rather unscientific *justifications* for maintaining women's subordinate status. For example, nineteenth century medicine argued against the education of women on the basis that women were physically and intellectually inferior to men and that educating women would shrivel their reproductive organs. In this case, untested gender *theories*—women are inferior to men and education adversely affects women's reproductive organs—became the rationale for unjust social policy. In hindsight we can easily find such a claim insupportable and perhaps even humorous. But in the nineteenth century, the newly professional practice of medicine, which actively barred women from its ranks, not only employed theory and bad science to the detriment of women, but also had the *power* to do so. Reinharz (1992) writes, "Feminist social research utilizes feminist theory in part because other theoretical traditions ignore or downplay the interaction between gender and power" (p. 249).

FEMINIST METHODS EXHIBIT TRANSDISCIPLINARITY: There are a number of reasons for this happy accident, including an affinity for postmodernism, which is also transdisciplinary. Most obviously, however, women, thus gender issues, transcend disciplinary boundaries. Not to put too fine a point on it, women are ubiquitous. What is more, as a new field in the 1970s, women's studies drew its faculty members from among feminists working in other disciplines. This made university women's studies departments multidisciplinary from the start, a tradition that continues. Additionally, as a tiny minority often attacked for their politics, feminist scholars and researchers in university departments, including mass communication and communication programs, had to look to feminists in other fields for collegial inspiration and support.

But Reinharz argues there is a more pragmatic reason to encourage interdisciplinary feminist research and methods. If women's subordinate status is nearly universal across all human endeavors, including history, arts and humanities, politics, economics, the sciences, and so forth, then any vision of gender justice would do well to examine the interrelationships among these areas. For example, answering questions about the underrepresentation of women in sports media requires an understanding of not only news values and practices but also the psychology and sociology of sport, as well as the economics of professional and amateur athletics. As a mass communication researcher interested in women and sports, Creedon (1994) agrees that because communication is also a "hybrid discipline," it is compatible with transdisciplinary feminist research.

FEMINIST METHODS WORK FOR SOCIAL CHANGE: As you now know, feminist research seeks to improve the lives of women. Ironically, when researchers develop an agenda for public policy, professional practice, or business profit, we tend to label it "applied" research. But feminist research tends to get another less positive label: "political."

FEMINIST METHODS RECOGNIZE DIVERSITY: Feminist research methods recognize diversity because of the great diversity among women, in terms of age, race, ethnicity, disability, sexual orientation, religion, geography, education, socioeconomic status, and nationality, among others. It is impossible to make an unequivocal claim about all women without either misrepresenting or excluding some women. No claim about women as a group can be true of all women. Feminists use the term "standpoint" to refer to the researcher's obligation to identify her/his personal research blinders—limited perspectives and possible sources of bias—based on the researcher's own demographics, history, and circumstances (Hartsock, 1983, 1997). Additionally, feminist researchers must be sensitive to the standpoints of the women who participate as research subjects. Feminists use the term "intersectionality" to refer to the fact that all people have multiple identifications beyond gender that *influence* gender in different kinds of ways.

For example, African American women are subject to what is called the "double jeopardy" of both sexism and racism in ways that white women are not (Beal, 1970). African American women's experiences of sexism will be different because of their experiences of racism. African American women are always both women and black. Imagine a survey interested in women's experiences as public relations professionals. Now suppose this survey queried only white women but drew conclusions about *all* women working as public relations professionals. Such a survey overlooks the high probability of significantly different findings for African American women working as public relations professionals. In fact, research shows very different professional experiences for minority public relations practitioners (Kern-Foxworth, 1989; Len-Rios, 1998; Zerbinos & Clanton, 1993). Feminist researchers are particularly sensitive to diversity, standpoint, and intersectionality because of the prevalent pattern of generalizing the findings of research on white men to everyone.

FEMINIST METHODS INVOLVE THE RESEARCHER AS A PERSON: This feature refers back to standpoint. In the positivist and empirical research traditions, researchers have been allowed to fool themselves that their presence as *researchers* can be extracted from the processes and results of their work. This may lead to a false sense of confidence about results, along with a tendency to deflect responsibility for unintentional biases or abuses that may occur during research. Rather than trying to extract ourselves as researchers from the research process, feminist methods suggest that taking stock of ourselves as researchers, along with focusing on the ways we inadvertently may influence our own research, improves the quality of research in at least two ways. First, we may better identify our biases, and this would require us to take responsibility for not only our results but also our actions as researchers interacting with the people we research. Second, it allows us as researchers to use our lived experiences to guide our common sense and judgments—a perfectly reasonable and useful idea as long as we are being self-reflexive and transparent about our decisions.

FEMINIST METHODS INVOLVE THE PEOPLE BEING STUDIED AS INDIVIDUALS: As long as feminist methods require us to take personal responsibility for the outcomes of our work, then it is no great leap to treat the people we study with respect as individuals, instead of as "subjects," "data," or "statistics." Feminist *methodology* requires researchers to recognize and surrender their power over research participants and, hence, reduce the possibility of exploitation. But feminist *methods* go further to suggest that the people we study are valuable *partners* in research. Because all feminists are sensitive to power and hierarchies that create unjust social relations, much feminist thought focuses on ideas of collaboration and cooperation, even with the people who consent to help us accomplish our research. This may mean inviting participants to help craft the design of a study, a prerequisite in action research. Such an idea, however, may be useful in other kinds of research as well. On a smaller scale, it may mean allowing participants to review and edit their interview transcripts, which makes for good research practice anyway. This allows research participants some say in how research will represent them. If traditional nonfeminist research has tended to represent women unfairly, then feminist methods try to avoid unfairly or inaccurately representing anyone.

FEMINIST METHODS INVOLVE THE READER AS A PERSON: After considering and respecting everyone else involved in the research process, why not respect the people who serve as audiences for our research results, too? Beyond simple respect, there are additional reasons for thinking about our readers as involved with our research—long before they actually read printed copies of our work. First, it is important for researchers to remind themselves that they usually are crafting their research for a particular audience *as* they plan, execute, and write up their studies. As students of mass media and communication, we all understand the importance of crafting messages for particular audiences. On the one hand, crafting our research messages for particular audiences only makes sense. On the other hand, we would do well to remind ourselves that this process of crafting the message *during* research demonstrates just one way that researchers are never wholly impartial. In feminist methods, this is not a problem as long as we don't try to kid ourselves (or others) with a false sense of neutrality. Whom we are communicating with always influences how and what we communicate, whether we're talking to a friend, reporting a news story, or conducting research. Second, there is no guarantee that our audiences will interpret our work in the way we intend it. Like Radway's romance novel readers, research audiences are *active*. Moreover, thinking about audiences as individuals reminds researchers to recognize and consider diversity among these individuals. The life experiences readers bring to their reading influence how they interpret what they read. Feminist methods acknowledge the ever-present specter of the active individual "reader" throughout the research process.

None of these features alone or in combination necessarily distinguishes the presence of a feminist method. Simply studying women or gender does not make the research method feminist, either. But a research method need not exhibit all 10 features to become feminist. The best way to recognize a "feminist method" is that the researcher has adopted that particular label.

Yet feminist research is not necessarily good research. Although openly political, feminist methods—whether quantitative or qualitative—demand the same standards of rigor and accountability as all good research. Indeed, because the words *feminism* and *feminist* generate so much suspicion, feminist researchers need to be just as critical of their own work as they are of nonfeminist research. To be credible in the face of widespread misunderstanding and distrust, feminist research must be transparent in its practices, self-conscious about its limitations, and cautious about its conclusions.

USES

In practice, feminist methods can be appropriate in any kind of communication research. Because the goals are to account for women and women's perspectives, identify unfair centers of power, improve the status of women, and advance a more complete body of knowledge, feminist communication research covers the gambit from rhetorical or critical-cultural studies to interpersonal, organizational, or performance studies, and beyond. To offer some idea of what feminist media research looks like, we can break out roughly six often overlapping topical categories: (1) professional issues, (2) media channels, (3) media messages, (4) media audiences, (5) mass communication education, and (6) historical research.

Feminist research on professional issues in mass communication includes all the media-related professions, including journalism, telecommunication, advertising, and public relations. Specifically, feminist research is interested in these areas as careers, including hiring and promotion issues along with professional practices. Regarding hiring and promotion, feminist researchers may document the sheer numbers of women working in the professions, the roles they play, their advancement, their work environments, and their job satisfaction. For example, glass-ceiling research studies a phenomenon in which women are not promoted into top management at the same rates as men. Regarding professional practices, feminist researchers examine the ways professional ideology and routine may disadvantage women. For example, why is it so difficult for women to break into sports reporting and broadcasting?

Feminist research on media channels includes not only focusing on underresearched women's media but also asking questions about women's issues in mainstream media, such as why people assume women are not online gamers. Women's research on channels includes studying media for which women are the target audience, such as women's magazines, so-called women's cable channels, and radio stations formatted for women listeners. Women's media also include minority women's media and women-owned media. Feminist research on mainstream media channels asks questions about gender disparities in women's access to media as well as the flow of messages to women. For example, a feminist research project may study elderly or poor women's access to computers and the World Wide Web in order to examine the flow of Web-based healthcare information to these women.

You probably are most familiar with feminist research on mediated messages, which concentrates on the content of mass media. The feminist research agenda on media content includes documenting the numbers and diversity of women appearing in mediated messages, from television anchors to sitcom actors. But counting numbers of women is not enough. As Phelan (1993) is famous for pointing out, "If representational visibility equals power, then almost-naked young white women should be running Western culture" (p. 10). Beyond counting, feminist message research asks questions about the qualitative representation of women, including oral, textual, visual, and symbolic representations. "Symbolic annihilation" refers to the absence, trivialization, sexual objectification, or condemnation of women in mediated images and messages (Tuchman, 1978).

Feminist research on media audiences mainly focuses on women as media consumers—viewers, listeners, readers, and users—such as Radway's work. Durham's (2004) focus groups with South Asian immigrant adolescent girls revealed that these young women watch both U.S. and Indian television and film, and they do so critically. They are aware that the sexualized images they see in both countries' media have little to do with their own lives as ordinary U.S. high school students. The teens in Durham's study also revealed that the content of media from both their homelands and the United States makes them feel like outsiders because neither country's media reflects their particular cultural standpoints as young immigrant women of color in the United States. In addition to women as audiences, feminist audience research also may be interested in how men interpret mediated images of women, messages of interest to women, or women's issues.

Although women have been the majority students in mass communication classrooms since 1977 (Kosicki & Becker, 1998), feminist research on mass communication education is a relatively new area. Here the research agenda covers the numbers of women and minorities teaching mass communication, how teaching practices affect women and minority students (called *feminist* or *critical pedagogy*), and whether the curriculum and textbooks include the perspectives of women and minorities (Golombisky, 2002). If education is the process by which we pass on our knowledge, then feminist researchers ask if women and minorities are part of that knowledge. This research also asks if women and minorities are being prepared adequately to enter the media professions. Additionally, *all* mass communication students should be educated about gender and diversity issues in the media and media professions if we are to improve the future of mass communication.

Meanwhile, feminist historical research in mass communication examines the past for women's issues with respect to media professions, channels, messages, and audiences. Feminist media historians search for women missing from mainstream history, which tends to focus only on men. Feminist media historians also search for undocumented women's media history, such as women's professional organizations, women's media, and women-owned media.

If feminist research can employ any method in any area of communication research, and if feminist research is accountable to the same level of rigor as any communication research, then you may assume that this chapter is complete. Not so fast. In addition to problems and issues associated with using particular research methods in feminist research, there are issues and problems specifically associated with doing gender and feminist research. Many of these issues and problems are traceable to processes of human communication, specifically language, meaning, and interpretation. Unfortunately, one introductory chapter cannot cover every pitfall, dilemma, and annoyance that routinely arises in feminist research. So, for the purpose of this chapter, we will concentrate on operational definitions, as this is often the first and most serious set of difficulties in gender research. Fair warning, though, the discussion in the next section may "rock your world."

PROBLEMS AND ISSUES

Contemporary critiques of social science and research usually get around to discussing objectivity, subjectivity, and intersubjectivity. As you know, *objectivity* refers to the idea that researchers can refrain from influencing their research results. *Subjectivity* refers to individuals' standpoints and to intersectionality. That is, many factors contribute to an individual's uniquely subjective experiences and interpretations of reality. *Intersubjectivity* refers to how individuals with unique standpoints manage to agree on what counts as reality. In research, *intersubjectivity* means everyone agrees on the definitions of terms. If we are all unique subjects, then how do we manage to achieve intersubjectivity in order to agree on truth, fact, and reality? This is a standard epistemological question. Feminist methodology goes further to ask, "Who has been invited to participate in this debate about reality?" "Where are the women?" and "Who has the power to define women's reality?" There are no simple or locked-down answers to epistemological questions. But rather than thinking about reality as a postmodern figment of our imaginations, it is more productive to think about reality as the intersection between people's lived experiences and the ways that people use language to name and order those experiences. There certainly is a material world, but what it means depends on how individuals both experience and label it. Feminist researchers want to make sure that women get to participate in that labeling process and that the labels attached to women are fair by women's own perspectives. Simply put, feminists will quibble over words, and, by social science's own standards, they have good reason to do so.

Contrary to what some may think, the feminist interest in words and labels is not about being "PC" (politically correct) or policing others' use of language, thus infringing upon First Amendment rights. Instead, the feminist fascination with language reflects an interest in using words with precision. In the case of feminist research, fastidiousness in choosing words becomes a matter of operational definitions: being as clear and transparent as possible about terminology in order to achieve intersubjectivity. In what follows, we will rely on current feminist thinking to: (1) describe problems with biological determinism and essentialism, (2) conceptualize gender as performance, (3) clarify common gendered words, (4) critique research that presumes men represent the standard from which women deviate, and (5) discuss the complexity of measuring gender differences.

If feminist research focuses on women, then to begin at the beginning is to ask, "What is a woman?" To most this seems a silly question with an obvious answer. But before you write off the question as nonsense, let's play along with the exercise. Suppose you need an operational definition of "woman." There are many ways we could define a woman (or a man). For example, we could use the practice of birth assignment, although, believe it or not, medical science tells us that this method is imperfect. We could use birth certificates, although birth certificates are based on birth assignment and may be changed in courts of law. We could use chromosomes, although science tells us there are varieties of anomalies that don't prevent a person from living as either a woman or a man. Contemporary medicine also tells us that people may change their gender, *and* the legal system accepts such changes. Each method defines women in a different way, and none is perfectly reliable.

From a purely scientific perspective, there is no failsafe method for defining a woman—or man. *So contemporary feminist thought suggests a woman or a man must be self-defined.* In other words, a woman or a man is any-one who claims to be a woman or a man. In practice, of course, researchers don't make a habit of asking the people they research if they are women or men—or do they? Gender counts as basic demographic information in social science research. How many times throughout our lives are we asked to self-report gender by marking one of two options on forms and applications? While this exercise may cause some readers discomfort, there are reasons for having it within a broader discussion of doing research. Suddenly, we are forced to reevaluate our assumptions about women and men, to confront the ambiguity of language, and so to rethink the purpose of gender research.

First, illustrating the difficulty in operationalizing "woman" or "man" forces us to question our taken-for-granted assumptions about women, men, and gender. It also takes us back to the idea of intersubjectivity. We daily manage to get through life by simply agreeing that there are two groups of people, women and men, even though we really have no perfect way to define either group. In fact, it is important to note that definitions of women and men, female and male, feminine and masculine, femininity and masculinity are *always* interdependent and circular: What is femininity? The opposite of masculinity. What is masculinity? The opposite of femininity, and so on. Despite intersubjectivity, however, making unassailable claims about groups of people on the basis of gender becomes a little more precarious. Suddenly researchers need to qualify and limit the conclusions they draw about women and men, and differences between them. Learning to qualify gender calls into question making claims on the basis of race, too, along with other kinds of "differences." Thus, the entire concept of demographics begins to unravel at philosophical and ethical levels, even as demographics continue to be very useful at a practical level.

Second, such a realization illustrates the slipperiness of language. In fact, daily life in our social worlds becomes largely a matter of relying on intersubjectivity, agreeing to agree on the basis of little more than faith. There is no direct correspondence between the material world and language. The world simply exists, regardless of whether people are there to name it with words. Only people attach labels to the world and give those labels meaning. At the same time, language is slippery and imprecise. Language is also loaded with both denotative (explicit) and connotative (implied) meanings. Words always convey both less and more information than we intend. Whoever has the power to label also has the power to attach intentional and unintentional meanings to people and things. This further cautions researchers to be careful in wielding their power to define reality through language.

Third, unexamined assumptions about women and men along with the slipperiness of language have implications for the kinds of research questions we ask, for defining and measuring variables, and for our ability to generalize about populations. Words such as sex, gender, woman/man, female/male, feminine/masculine, and femininity/masculinity present not only definitional challenges but also causal ones. Social scientists often have used the words "sex" and "gender" as synonyms, and/or implied cause-effect relationships between the two words without providing operational definitions. Similarly, pairings such as female with feminine and male with masculine often imply necessary and/or sufficient causality between femaleness and femininity and between maleness and masculinity. But, for example, the existence of so-called masculine women and feminine men refutes the assumption that being female causes femininity or being male causes masculinity. The slipperiness of language can be downright vexing for the researcher's problem of operational definitions. Until the natural sciences provide more answers, the social sciences would do well to examine their assumptions about women and men and to deploy their terminology thoughtfully and transparently.

Contemporary feminist thought, already having grappled with these issues, offers communication research some help. First, feminism urges social science and humanistic research to avoid "biological determinism" and "essentialism," meaning the assumption that women's biology determines their *essential* "nature." *Biological determinism* and *essentialism* refer to the habit of "essentializing" women as biologically hardwired for their social roles and status. If the natural sciences and medical arts have yet to isolate some essential definition of biological sex, then social science and the humanities ought to avoid the whole subject. *Social* science, by definition, is not qualified to make claims about biology, anyway. Feminist research argues that social scientists should disqualify themselves from drawing conclusions about "nature," "biology," and "sex." Biological sex is irrelevant in social science. Indeed, social science ought to eschew the word "sex" altogether. "Gender" is the preferable word because it lacks biological—and sexual—connotations. Communication scholars may be as interested in "sex" as anyone else, but we *research* "gender."

Now we have begged another tricky question, "What is gender?" Contemporary feminist thought provides a working concept of gender that avoids biological determinism while accounting for gendered bodies, individual standpoints and intersectionality, self-determination, and power relationships that may enable or constrain self-determination. *Gender is a performance* (Butler, 1990, 1993, 2004). More specifically, an individual performs her/his gender. As performance, gender becomes something that people *do* (Rakow, 1986), which we can observe empirically without resorting to biological explanations. Individuals with agency to make choices perform gender with their bodies within the confines of their social and cultural contexts, which include others' gender performances.

Gender as performance sidesteps not only biological essentialism but also cultural essentialism. The second wave women's movement of the 1960s and 1970s coined the slogan, "Biology is not destiny." While this persuasive argument advanced women's legal rights, many came to interpret gender as a wholly social construction located outside of the body in language and symbolism. This divorced "sex" as nature/biology from "gender" as nurture/culture. Gender as purely nurture or culture, however, represents another kind of essentialism (Fuss, 1989). Gender as pure culture assumes that there is no relationship at all between sex and gender. But, again, we have no irrefutable way to prove such a claim, so we are better-off if we "just don't go there." Gender as performance allows us to account for individual embodied gender performances without resorting to either biological or cultural essentialism. Gender as performance asks how our cultural, social, and institutional beliefs and practices encourage, limit, and enforce different kinds of gender performances for different people in conjunction with our performances of race (including whiteness), ethnicity, disability, sexuality, socioeconomic status, and nationality, among others.

In addition to avoiding the word "sex," feminism advises prudence on the use of other common gendered terms. Current feminist thinking suggests that social science researchers should be cautious in using the words "female" and "male" because they, too, historically have been used to denote biological sex. If "female" and "male" seem appropriate, such as on a questionnaire, researchers should use them consciously with a logical rationale.

Furthermore, if "woman" applies to any individual who self-identifies herself as a woman, then a group of these individuals becomes "women." The plural word "women" stands for the demographic category, too, with the reminder that there are no "demographics" in nature. Demographic categories, while useful, are *man*made. The same principles apply to applications of the words "man" and "men." "The history of man," for example, becomes imprecise usage, not just because history should include women, too, but also because there is no single "man" who transcends and represents all men. A good researcher would ask, "Which man?" These may seem obvious rules of thumb, but agreeing on terminology, once again, becomes a matter of precision and establishing intersubjectivity.

Two other pairs of terms may cause problems: *feminine/masculine* and *femininity/masculinity*. While both pairs of words are gendered, they have no necessary relationship to biological sex, sexuality, or individual women and men. In fact, we regularly label nonbiological phenomena "feminine" or "masculine." For example, pink is a feminine color in our culture, although there is no basis in nature or science for labeling and applying it that way. Furthermore, applications of feminine/masculine and femininity/masculinity vary widely in interpretation and performance. History, anthropology, and sociology all tell us that the dividing line between the two genders constantly moves around depending on the era, culture, and society. Men wearing wigs, makeup, and lace symbolized socially constructed ideals of masculinity thus ideal masculine performances in eighteenth-century Europe. Researchers should proceed with caution when using "feminine," "masculine," "femininity," and "masculinity." These words require careful definition and qualification.

Another issue concerns an unfortunate linguistic idiosyncrasy of gendered terminology called "marking" the feminine, which results in the "semantic derogation" of women (Spender, 1985). All English language pertaining to *women* and *female*s is "marked" as not male, either denotatively or connotatively, and marking language for feminine forms also automatically marks it as the negative and derivative of unmarked masculine forms (Spender, 1985). *Semantic derogation*, literally, translates as making language derogatory. An example should clarify the problem. Research, researcher, and research subject represent masculine, neutral, and universal overarching categories, which may or may not also include women. For women or feminine forms to be explicitly present in language, we must mark our vocabulary as "not male," as in *women's* research, *woman* researcher, and *women* research subjects. Once we have marked language for the feminine form, it becomes a "special" subcategory that absolutely does not include men and automatically seems to be less important than the masculine, neutral, and universal form. Semantic derogation is why feminine forms are often deployed pejoratively, such as making fun of synchronized swimming, scoffing at romance novels, or ridiculing men as "sissies." The semantic derogation of women and feminine forms raises two kinds of troubles for feminist researchers, nonfeminist gender researchers, and researchers who simply study women. First, they have to be sensitive to the negative (derogative) connotations of the feminine language forms they use. Second, people tend to take their work less seriously just because the subject matter is marked as "not male."

The entire matter of terminology raises something of a paradox for feminist researchers who wish to improve the lives of "women." Feminists need the category of "women" in order to pursue their work. But feminists must acknowledge the categories of "women" and "men" as unstable scientifically speaking and a fiction demographically speaking. As deconstructionists would say, feminists use gendered words such as "women" or "men" "under erasure," meaning they simultaneously use them and recognize their limitations. Deconstruction purists would write "women" or "men" under erasure like this: ~~women, men~~.

Yet feminist scholars are fascinated by this human predilection to divide up the world into two types of gendered people, social rules (called *double standards*), things, and ideas, even though there are no perfectly reliable ways to do so. They are curious about the mechanism of binary gender—women and men, feminine and masculine. Why just two categories? Why do we seem so deeply invested in trying to make sure people, things, and ideas fit neatly into one or the other category? Why do culture and society expend so much time and energy nervously cataloging "differences" between women and men, instead of assuming similarities and focusing attention elsewhere?

This cultural impulse toward gender separatism and double standards raises other dilemmas for researchers interested in gender. First, for feminists, correcting the absence of women in research requires focusing on women, but focusing on women requires focusing on gender and participating in gender separatism. Focusing on women also risks semantic derogation. Gender researchers solve this dilemma by pointing out that they did not invent binary gender; they merely study a preexisting phenomenon that also has tended to exclude and undervalue women.

Second, how can gender research make claims about women or men in particular without reinforcing the great cataloging of gender differences and gendered double standards? In addition to being clear about operational definitions, the answer lies in examining our research questions for unsubstantiated assumptions about gender. Feminists argue that researchers, after avoiding essentialism and defining gendered terms, need to think critically about their research questions. The kinds of questions that we ask determine the kinds of answers that research can provide.

Nonfeminist gender research often begins with the presumption of "natural" gender differences between women and men, and then attempts to prove and explain those differences—which nearly always are measured using men as the standard. The underlying implied research questions, then, are usually, "How and why are women different?" Research almost never begins with the question, "How are men and women alike?" This phenomenon occurs in both the natural and social sciences. So, in the rare instances when women do show up in research, their purpose has been to prove that gender differences are natural and omnipresent and that women are different *from* men. This is a subtle but significant point. The presumption is that men represent the norm—meaning, literally, that men are normal. So women's differences *from* men represent deviance. Nonfeminist gender research tends to frame women as abnormal. Men equal the standard; women equal the deviation. Researchers must refrain from casting either gender as superior or inferior. Such evaluations are virtually impossible to prove.

Meanwhile, social scientists have continued to conduct research assuming that sex and/or gender are biological and/or synonymous and that they represent the independent variable causing women's differences from men, who represent the ideal type. More specifically for our purposes, Dow and Condit (2005) find that we are currently unable to generalize any conclusions about communication differences between women and men because "the literature shows unstable, context-specific, relatively small, and variable effects" (p. 453). Indeed, they write that communication research contradicts itself regarding the existence of "pervasive and strong differences between men and women" (p. 453). There are just too many other variables to control when measuring gender differences. It is extremely difficult to draw durable conclusions that cover all women or all men of all backgrounds in all contexts for all time. That is why gender researchers must qualify and limit the conclusions they draw about women or men.

It may be easier to think about the significance of Dow and Condit's finding in terms of the kinds of claims social science can and cannot make. In social science, there are only three kinds of things we can measure: *direct observables, indirect observables*, and *constructs* (Kaplan, 1964). Direct observables are phenomena that we can witness and measure directly, such as the percentage of women's names appearing as news sources in newspapers, although ambiguous names such as "Pat" cause some difficulties and require a transparent method for dealing with them. Indirect observables represent those things we can measure only indirectly, such as counting the number of times "female" is checked on questionnaires to surmise the number of survey respondents self-reporting as women. Direct and indirect observables are fairly straightforward and usually valid ways to make *limited* claims about gender. For example, because women's names appear less frequently than men's names in newspaper source attributions, we fairly may conclude that reporters use women less frequently than men as news sources. This conclusion makes a claim about professional practice, but it does not make any claims about the "nature" of gender or the innate qualities of women or men as news sources.

The third kind of measurement, constructs, is where social science can get into trouble with gender. Measuring IQ (intelligence quotient) is a classic example of a measurement based on neither direct nor indirect observables. IQ is a purely conceptual construction comprised of many dimensions (Babbie, 1992). Like demographics, there is no "intelligence quotient" in nature. IQ does not exist in the material world outside of the complex mathematical formulas (derived from and represented by words) used to calculate it.

To return to the issue of gender in media and communication research, there are three things to consider with regard to constructs. First, researchers must avoid using informal unrecognized constructs to define or measure gender differences. This is accomplished by carefully operationalizing gendered concepts and double-checking research questions for gender assumptions. Second, researchers must scrutinize any constructs they do deploy for gender bias. For example, Harvard psychologist Lawrence Kohlberg developed a widely accepted construct for measuring human moral development. In applying this construct, however, women often exhibited what his construct labeled as arrested moral development. Kohlberg's construct implies that women do not develop properly and are less moral than men. One of Kohlberg's research assistants, Carol Gilligan (1982), recognized that Kohlberg had developed and tested his construct using only men. The construct was limited to men's experiences and perspectives on morality, a clear case of accidental gender bias in a construct applied universally to women and men. Analysis of Gilligan's (1982) subsequent work on women's moral development suggests that any appreciable differences between women's and men's moral decision making have less to do with "essential" gender differences than gender performances learned through socialization. Third, researchers specifically interested in measuring gender must carefully conceptualize gender as a construct or when incorporating gender into constructs.

Communication researchers studying gender need to think carefully about their operational definitions, examine their research questions for biased and essentialist assumptions, and construct their instruments of measurement painstakingly. Based on their analysis of the state of the art in feminist communication research, Dow and Condit (2005) note the time has come to abandon "the simple dummy variables of male and female biological sex" (p. 454). They write that "the earlier era, in which sex or gender were taken to be simple highly coherent variables based on invariant characteristics that were uniform within groups, has passed" (p. 454). "Sex and gender are not simply variables deserving incorporation into equations, but are complex factors that require careful, sustained attention to their formation" (p. 454). Furthermore, we must pay much more attention to the "implications of cultural variability" in gender research (p. 455). Dow and Condit write that being a woman or a man has "meant different things for persons of different ethnicities, and masculinity and femininity have been performed in different ways in different cultures" (p. 455).

So what should we take away from this rather long discussion? Language does matter, especially in research. Self-report is the best way to operationalize women and men. Because "sex" has connotations of biological determinism, "gender" is a better word for communication research. Gender is best conceptualized as a performance or something people do, such as checking "female" or "male" on a questionnaire. The words "female" and "male" tend to signify biology, too, so communication researchers should tread lightly in using them. Preferable terms include *woman* and *man* for individuals and *women* and *men* for groups of individuals. "Feminine" and "masculine" are descriptive words applied not only to people but also to material objects (such as pink computers), social roles (such as weather girls), social practices (such as nurturing) and abstract ideas (such as femininity). Focusing on women and feminine forms invites semantic derogation (such as weather *girl* instead of *woman*). Therefore, researchers need to be alert when deploying such gendered words, especially marked feminine forms, to avoid unintentional denotative or connotative meanings. Furthermore, notions of "femininity" and "masculinity" vary, not only due to individual intersectionality and standpoint but also across contexts, cultures, and history. So, again, researchers need to apply them guardedly and transparently. Encapsulated, the problems and solutions we have covered form a set of recommendations for communication researchers interested in studying women, men, or gender:

1. Focus on gender, not sex, to avoid biological determinism
2. Conceptualize gender as performed
3. Operationalize women and men as self-identified
4. Examine research questions for essentialist assumptions about women, men, and gender
5. Deploy gendered terminology thoughtfully and transparently

6. Recognize that marked feminine word forms are subject to semantic derogation
7. Proceed with caution when measuring gender differences, particularly regarding constructs
8. Limit and qualify gender claims with intersectionality and social, cultural, and historical context

If you are still reading at this point, then you are to be congratulated because the ideas we have covered can be "mind-blowing" for the uninitiated. Contemporary thinking about gender is the product of feminist scholarship, performance studies in communication, and postmodern influences on social science. Despite these influences, contemporary approaches to gender are not yet widely recognized or understood, even as they continue to evolve under the ongoing critique of feminism, including feminism's own self-critique. And that is precisely the point of feminist research, to expose, analyze, and reconsider foundational assumptions and presumptions about gender, women, and men in order to improve our research methods and, ultimately, our knowledge.

IMPLEMENTATION

Since feminist research in communication may use any appropriate method available, it is difficult to lay out its process in any specific way. You should refer to the other chapters in this book for instruction on implementing particular methods. Like any researcher, however, feminist researchers first refine their questions, clarify their operational definitions, and complete the necessary preparations for implementing the study. Implementation depends on the peculiarities of the method or methods employed. Analysis and reporting follow implementation.

Upon examination, there is much to gain by adopting the principles of feminist methodology and the features of feminist methods, particularly in our postmodern era. Any research project improves with self-consciousness about operational definitions and self-reflexivity about the ways the work of researchers represents others' realities. Feminist methodology's recommendations to include women, do no harm, and improve society offer commendable research goals for anyone. Few could find fault with feminist methods, either, if their best practices include: being inclusive regarding minorities and women, using multiple methods creatively, critiquing what we do as researchers, treating unjust ideas about gender as disposable, being open to other disciplinary perspectives, working for the social good, and respecting the people involved in the research process, including the researcher, research subjects, and research audiences. Judged by what it does instead of its name, feminist research is an admirable project for any researcher. As hooks says, "Feminism is for everybody."

This chapter of necessity has oversimplified a broad and exciting field of inquiry. There are many brands of feminism, including, for example, postmodern feminists, and some suggest we always should speak of feminisms in the plural to avoid "essentializing" the many and sometimes incompatible kinds of feminist philosophies. But if the biggest problem for feminists is misinformation, then perhaps this chapter has helped the feminist research agenda in some small way. Interrogating the media-saturated, statistic-laden world we live in is everyone's right. For feminist researchers, it is a mission. For communication scholars, researchers, students, and professionals, it is a duty, albeit an exhilarating and gratifying one. Enjoy!

REVIEW QUESTIONS

1. What three initial points about feminist methodology distinguish it from other research methodologies?
2. What is the chapter's working definition of feminism?
3. How does the chapter define feminist methodology?
4. What three criteria characterize feminist methodology?
5. What 10 features characterize the best practices of feminist research methods?
6. What are self-reflexivity, standpoint, and intersectionality? Why are they important to feminist research?
7. Feminist media research tends to fall into what six categories?
8. What is the recommended operational definition of woman or man?
9. How does contemporary feminism define gender?
10. What is the problem with biological determinism and essentialism?
11. What is the problem with cultural essentialism?
12. Why is it important to examine research questions for gender bias?
13. To what does the semantic derogation of women refer?
14. What difficulties do researchers face in measuring gender differences?
15. Why is it important to limit and qualify claims about women, men, and gender as a result of research?

SUGGESTED ACTIVITIES

1. Critique some feminist research: Log on to one of your campus library's academic journal databases. Then do a keyword search for "communication and feminism" or "mass media and feminism." Scan some abstracts from your results, then choose and read an article you think looks interesting. (Hint: try to find an article with a recent date that uses one or more of the methods you have studied in this book.) Which, if any, of Reinharz's (1992) 10 best practices of feminist research methods does the article exhibit? In your opinion, how well does the article handle its operational definitions for gendered terms?
2. Learn about the status of women: Find out if your campus has the equivalent of a status of women committee or council. Ask permission to attend its next meeting, or invite one of its members to speak to your class about its efforts to improve the lives of women on your campus. Ask about the group's efforts to collect data about women on your campus.
3. Listen to women's stories: Take an oral history from a woman working in a communications field. Focus your research question on your narrator's professional or employment history. Before the interview, take some time to be self-reflexive: Journal a couple pages about your standpoint and the ways your standpoint may

influence your assumptions and expectations for the interview. After the interview, reflect on what your narrator's story has taught you and what you might do differently if given the chance.

4. Count the representation of women in media content: Conduct a content analysis of your campus student newspaper for its representation of women. Decide whether you will look at one issue, one week of issues, one month, or a more representative sample of issues over a long period of time. Justify your decision. Then develop a protocol for quantifying the ratios of women to men in terms of bylines and quoted news sources, along with news story references to women versus men in general. Also examine ratios of women to men in photographs. Last, look at the ratio of women to men on the newspaper staff, along with their ranks, positions, and titles. How will you handle situations in which someone's gender is unclear? Based on what you have learned about sampling, content analysis, and feminist methodology, what kinds of claims can you make about the results of your gender analysis of the student newspaper on your campus? What kinds of claims should you avoid making? What have you learned?

SECTION III

Writing a Research Report

No research project is complete until a written report is prepared. This section of the text will help you understand why a report is necessary and provide you with guidelines that will assist you in preparing an informative, clearly written report.

In Chapter 11, you will learn how to use references properly and how to cite them in the paper. You will also be reminded about the "mechanics" of writing, that is, correct grammar, spelling, punctuation, and the like. Chapter 12 will detail the proper order and content of the sections found in a research report.

Writing Style

English usage is sometimes more than mere taste,
judgment, and education—sometimes it's sheer
luck, like getting across a street.

—E. B. White

If you were to look up the word *style* in a good dictionary, you'd find numerous meanings for the word, depending on whether you applied it to life, clothing, or a particular way of speaking or behaving. But, all writers know that using a dictionary definition anywhere in any paper is taking the easy way out. It is often a mark of laziness, some critics say, for a writer to resort to a dictionary definition for some term or concept. It makes far more sense to define the words, phrases, or concepts you use in a singular fashion, that is, define them as they apply to your particular piece of writing or to your particular understanding.

WHAT IS WRITING STYLE?

We are going to define *style* this way: a distinctive manner of writing reflecting the proper use of language and a standard set of rules. This may seem like a rather narrow definition, but it will serve you well in the writing of a research report.

You are almost certainly a unique individual with your own particular writing style. You probably write in a way that makes you comfortable and that may mean you do not always follow standard rules of grammar, punctuation, spelling, and the like. In today's world of electronic communication, it is becoming increasingly difficult to motivate people to write correctly. Instant messaging is popular among computer users, and communications using electronic media are almost always abbreviated in some form and, some say, this sort of communication results in an overall degradation of the language. For example, during a session where you and another person are communicating via instant messaging, you might receive this: brb. For many people, this set of letters informs the receiver that the sender will "be right back," in other words, the sender is going to do something else for a moment, but will return soon.

This sort of shorthand may be acceptable for some electronic communications media, but it is totally unacceptable when such practices bleed over into standard, purposeful, written communication. You will likely ignore spelling, grammar, and punctuation in your instant messaging or cell phone text messaging activities, but you must not ignore such things when you are preparing any serious written document: a memorandum to be circulated in your workplace; a letter of application, resignation, or inquiry; an essay for a class you are taking; or even a friendly letter to a friend or relative. Above all, you must attend to matters of grammar, punctuation, and the like in a research report. There is much to learn about references and citation style. This chapter, however, does not provide everything you will likely need to know about reference and citation style. Nevertheless, this chapter does provide a basic framework for three popular styles.

If you wish your report to have any credibility or to be of any use to others, you must show that you know how to communicate in a way that reflects your education, experience, and expertise. In other words, you will need to communicate using a standard way many researchers use to insure that their work will be read and understood by other researchers. Let's call this standard *scholarly style*.

SCHOLARLY STYLE

Scholarly style has at least two characteristics. First, it uses language correctly. This simply means that it follows the basic rules of grammar. You may remember from the writing courses you took early in your college career that a paper (or other piece of formal writing) should have an introduction, a body, and a conclusion. What you may not recall is the requirement that the writing be composed of complete sentences, have proper punctuation, use clearly understood words or phrases spelled correctly, and the like. Moreover, the entire written document should be coherent and clearly organized.

It is not the purpose of this chapter to engage you in an extended discussion of grammatical structure, punctuation rules, or frequently misspelled words. Nevertheless, you may feel that a little review of the basic principles and practices would be in order. There are several dependable reference books that can provide helpful information. Many writers depend on Strunk and White's *The Elements of Style* (4th edition, Needham Heights, MA: Allyn & Bacon, 2000). This slim, well-respected volume has been around for decades and is an excellent source of information on the basics of grammar and style. It's often available in paperback and easily fits in the hand or pocket. It is inexpensive, but if you prefer not to purchase a new copy, you would do well to browse a used bookstore or two and find a previous edition of the book. The used book will cost a little less and will be quite useful.

If you need something a little more comprehensive, try *Essentials of English Grammar* by L. Sue Baugh (New York: McGraw Hill, 2005). This paperback usually sells for less than 10 dollars and presents a rather complete summary of the style issues that regularly confront writers.

It should be noted that both of these books have, as their foundation, the essentials of standard English grammar. Do not expect to find rules and suggestions there that deviate from clear, forceful, educated, correct, written communication. For example, in postmodern America almost all speech and much written communication violate the rule that a pronoun must agree with its antecedent in number. Look at the following statement. "Anybody can see for themselves that there is considerable violent content on television." This statement is grammatically incorrect. *Anybody* is singular, but *themselves* is plural. This sort of mistake is so regularly made in speech and written communication that it may have taken on some sort of validity, that is, it seems correct because people are using it. However, just because most people fail to speak or write correctly doesn't mean that a rule changes. Educated individuals use proper grammar. Hold yourself and others to high standards of written and spoken communication. Accept no compromises.

What if you feel you don't need a complete review of writing rules? Maybe you are a fairly competent writer and are simply wondering whether there are a few major things you should watch for in your writing. Actually, there are about 10 errors writers commonly make that result in their writing being less than effective. These 10 errors are easily summarized and just as easily corrected in your writing (See Figure 11.1).

The second scholarly style characteristic is the use of a standard, recognized way of citing and referencing sources used in a paper or research report. This simply means that there is a particular way in which one gives credit to the work of others if that work is used in any fashion in the paper or report. Why is it necessary to credit the work of others? There are two reasons. First, you do not want to plagiarize, that is, to present the original ideas and work of others as your work or ideas. Plagiarism is both unethical and unlawful. Referencing sources will separate your original ideas and work from the original work and ideas of others. Second, you will need to reference the work of others so that your readers may not only find that work and read it themselves, but also place your work in the context of what others have done.

There are several widely used, well-respected citation and reference systems. Communication researchers often use the practices detailed by the American Psychological Association (APA). Some communication scholars use one of two other useful systems: Modern Language Association (MLA) and the *Chicago Manual of Style*, commonly called "Chicago." Each of these systems will be presented in detail in the following pages.

Quick Style Checklist for Research Reports and Student Essays

1. *Format*   Is the report or essay titled? Is the author clearly identified? Does the report or essay meet the requirements of the assignment or the sponsoring organization (length, type size, margins, spacing, etc.)?

2. *Organization*   Does the report or essay appear to be clearly organized, that is, does it have an introduction, a body, and a conclusion? Does it logically proceed from one point to the next in making the author's argument?

3. *Paragraphing*   Is the report or essay composed of a series of well-developed paragraphs? A well-developed paragraph usually contains a main idea and three or more supporting sentences. Eliminate one-sentence paragraphs.

4. *Complete Sentences*   Check each sentence in the report or essay. Make sure each has a subject and a verb and expresses a complete thought. Avoid sentence fragments; avoid complete sentences connected by a comma.

5. *Subject-Verb Agreement*   Check each sentence in the report or essay. Determine whether the subject of the sentence is singular or plural. Check to see whether the verb in the sentence is singular or plural. Match them up.

> *Remember: The word media is plural and takes a plural verb. The singular form of the word is medium. For example, television is a medium, but radio and television together are media. Newspapers are a medium, but newspapers and magazines together are media.*
>
> *Incorrect: The media is a powerful force in American culture.*
> *Correct: The media are a powerful force in American culture.*

6. *Pronoun-Antecedent Agreement*   This is one of the most frequent style errors in American writing today. A pronoun must agree in number (singular or plural) with the noun to which it refers.

> *Incorrect: Everyone should remember to bring their books to class tomorrow.*
> *Correct: Everyone should remember to bring his/her books to class tomorrow.*
>
> *or*
>
> *Students should remember to bring their books to class tomorrow.*
>
> *Incorrect: The media should use its power carefully.*
> *Correct: The media should use their power carefully.*

7. *Punctuation*   Errors in punctuation almost always involve commas, semicolons, and colons. Of course, there can be problems with question marks, exclamation points, and periods, too, but errors involving these punctuation marks do not appear as frequently. There are specific rules for the use of the comma; do not follow the rule you may have heard in junior high school: a comma always goes where one pauses in the reading of a sentence. This

FIGURE 11.1   Style Checklist for Common Writing Errors

almost never results in the accurate use of a comma because no two people are going to read any sentence in precisely the same way and pause at the precise location where the rules require a comma. In general, do not use a lot of commas. They go after items in a series and after a long introductory (adverbial) clause; they also go before a coordinating conjunction in a compound sentence. There are other rules, too, but if these rules cause your head to spin, the simple solution is to use few commas. You will probably make fewer errors. Semicolons serve essentially the same function as periods (except where periods are used in abbreviations such as a.m. or p.m.). A colon indicates that a short list of items follows. Never use a colon right after a verb. Most reports and essays can get along rather nicely without semi-colons and colons.

8. *Apostrophe*   The apostrophe seems harmless enough but is often incorrectly used. An apostrophe is usually used to show possession.

> *Examples: John's research report was 50 pages long. Professor Jones's class was cancelled today.*

> *Exception: When the subject-verb combination it is becomes a contraction, it takes the form it's. When the pronoun it needs to show possession, only the s is added; it thus becomes* its.

> *Note: Singular words ending in s still require an apostrophe and another* s.

> *Example: Charles Dickens's best book is*
> David Copperfield.

> *Plural words ending in s require only an*
> *apostrophe.*
> *Example: The students' final essays are due Friday.*

> *Plural words not ending in s require both and apostrophe and an* s
> *Example: The women's focus group met last night.*

9. *Similar Constructions*   Several words have a similar construction, or at least a similar pronunciation when spoken. But there are differences. Do not confuse these words:

> *then . . . than*
> *to, too, two*
> *their, there, they're*
> *affect . . . effect*

10. *Spelling*   Spelling errors are some of the most damaging mistakes a writer can make. Computer word processing programs have a spell checker. These work well enough but not without possible errors. Take the time to read your report or essay and carefully check it for spelling errors.

FIGURE 11.1   (Continued)

APA Style

APA style* was developed by the American Psychological Association. This style has gained wide acceptance in academic circles. It is regularly used in psychology, of course, and is the style of choice in other social sciences, including communication.

In general, APA documentation style requires two methods of acknowledging sources in a research paper: (1) parenthetical *in-text citation*, and (2) complete documentation on the References page. For in-text citations, cite last names only, then the year, and—if appropriate—page number(s). Enclose this information in a set of parentheses.

Examples:

Smith (1997) has advanced the idea of combining the social sciences and mathematics to chart human behavior.
or
One study has advanced the idea of combining the social sciences and mathematics to chart human behavior (Smith, 1997).
or
Smith (1997) thinks we ought to "combine the social sciences and mathematics so that we can successfully chart various types of human behavior" (p. 76).

Notice that the first two examples are paraphrases of Smith's words; nevertheless, the ideas belong to Smith, and you must therefore give him/her credit for those ideas by providing a citation. The third example is a direct quote from Smith's work. This citation must include the number of the page where the quote may be found. Sometimes a close paraphrase requires a page number. Pay special attention, too, to the placement of the citation and the surrounding punctuation. These details are not trivial; they are extremely important in that they represent a standardized system recognized and understood by others.

Deal with multiple authors in a similar manner. For example:

Smith, Jones, and Wesson (1997) feel that a good way to chart human behavior would be to combine the social sciences and mathematics.
or
Some scholars believe that a good way to chart human behavior would be to combine the social sciences and mathematics (Smith, Jones, & Wesson, 1997).
or
Smith, Jones, and Wesson (1997) believe a good way to chart human behavior would be to "combine the social sciences and mathematics" (p. 76).

---

*APA style information was adapted from the following: Lester, J. D., & Lester, J. D., Jr. (1999). *The essential guide to writing research papers*. New York: Addison Wesley Longman.

If the author is not identified, the citation should include the first two or three words of the article or book title and, if appropriate, page numbers. For example:

> One source has questioned the results of the use of some drugs in the treatment of ailments in children ("Arthritis treatment," 1991).

or

> The American Medical Association (AMA) has questioned "the use of aspirin in the treatment of children's ailments" ("Arthritis treatment," 1991, p. 6).

Citations for books, magazines, newspaper articles, and similar printed material can usually be handled using the citation methods explained earlier. However, Internet sources present a different set of problems. Most Internet sources do not have page numbers, and you cannot list the screen numbers or page numbers from downloaded documents because printers and monitors differ. If the article you are using has an author and/or title, you can make use of that information to some extent. The important thing is to provide the reader with enough information so that the article can be easily found on the References page and, if the reader desires, located on the Internet. For example:

> Dove (1997) has made the distinction between the work required of state politicians and the work required of federal politicians.

or

> One source has noted the differences in the type of work required of state and federal politicians ("Legislative duty," 1997).

Notice that in the first example, the author is known (Dove) so his/her name is used and the Internet entry can be easily found in the References. In the second example, there is no author, but the article on the Web site is titled "Legislative duty differences at various levels." If you use the first two words of the title in the in-text citation, the title of the full article can be easily found in the References. Note also that the date (1997) was the date the article was written. You should use the date an article was written, if available. Some Internet articles do not indicate when an article was written or posted, so, if that is the case, you should substitute the download date. Thus, if we did not know that article was written in 1997, we would have to use the year we downloaded it for use in our research paper.

The *References* page appears at the end of your paper and contains an alphabetical listing of all the material you used and cited in the paper's text. For example:

Books: Author. (Date). *Title*. City of publication: Publisher.

> Carter, J. (1998). *An outdoor journal: Adventures and reflections*. New York: Bantam.

or

> Carter, J., Smith, B., & Jones, C. (1998). *An outdoor journal: Adventures and reflections*. New York: Bantam.

Journals/Magazines: Author. (Date). Article title. *Magazine or journal name*. Volume (Issue number), Page number.

> Kluger, J. (1997, August 4). Beyond cholesterol. *Time*, 150, 46.

or

> Misumi, J., & Fujita, M. A. (1982). Effects of communication in a closed setting. *Journal of Experimental Psychology*, 21(2), 93–111.

Newspapers: Author. (Date). Article title. *Name of Newspaper*, Section and page number(s).

> Troxler, H. (2003, December 20). State legislature and phone companies rip off the public. *St. Petersburg Times*, p. B1.

Internet: Author. (Date of original article or date of download). Title of article. *Name of Web site owner or sponsor*. URL address.

> Health care inflation: It's back! (1997, March 17). *Business Week Online*. Retrieved from www.businessweek.com/1997/11/b351452.html.

or

> Raver, A. (1999, August 27). Qualities of an animal scientist. *New York Times Online*. Retrieved from www.search.nytimes.com/search/daily/query/2?C1.

Note: Internet references are often a problem due to lack of information. At a minimum, a reference should include article title, Web site sponsor, authorship date or download date, and URL address.

Interviews/Personal Communication: Name of person. (Date of contact). Type of interview or communication.

> Clinton, W. J. (2004, January 15). Telephone interview.

or

> Clinton, W. J. (2004, January 15). Personal letter.

or

> Clinton, W. J. (2004, January 15). Personal interview.

or

> Clinton, W. J. (2004, January 15). E-mail message.

There are, of course, other sources that may be used in a research paper. These may include a government document, an advertisement, a broadcast interview, a cartoon, a thesis or dissertation, and so forth. If you need to use a source not covered by the guidelines listed earlier, ask your instructor for advice or consult the latest APA style manual. It is a good idea to consult the APA style manual on a regular basis anyway, because there are many variations in the basic APA citation and reference style. These variations are required because of the variety and differences apparent in the many available sources. There may also be some variation in the use of language and grammatical style based on the editorial needs of the various journals publishing scholarly work. In any case, you can see that proper citation and reference style depends on attention to precise detail. Punctuation, spelling, and format all matter. Current information about APA style can be found on the American Psychological Association Web site, www.apa.org.

MLA Style

The Modern Language Association developed MLA style.* It is regularly used in a variety of academic disciplines, including English and the humanities. It is well-known and can be used in other disciplines. You should check with your instructor to see whether MLA style is acceptable for the work you submit in his/her course.

MLA documentation style requires two methods of acknowledging sources in a research paper: (1) parenthetical *citation in the text*, and (2) complete documentation on the *Works Cited* page.

Citation in the text means identifying the source of any borrowed material immediately as it appears, right in the text of the paper. For example:

> According to Berman, adopted children "want to be connected with a past heritage or a genealogical history" (119).
> or
> Berman found that adopted children want to be connected to their past, their genealogical history (119).

Note that a citation is required regardless of whether you quote directly or paraphrase the material. If the material quoted has more than one author, you should adjust accordingly:

> According to Berman and Jones, adopted. . . .
> or
> According to Berman, Jones, and Smith, adopted. . . .

If the material you are quoting or paraphrasing has no author, it may be identified by mentioning the name of the publication from which it came, then using the first word of the title as a page reference. This will help the reader find the entry on the Works Cited page. For example:

> A survey published in *Consumer Reports* in 2001 found that only slightly more than half of respondents had home computers connected to the Internet ("Exploring").

Of course, Internet sources present some problems. As noted earlier, most Internet sources have no prescribed page numbers. You cannot use the screen numbers or page numbers of downloaded documents because

---

*The information on MLA style was adapted from the following: (1) Dees, Robert (2003). *Writing the modern research paper* (4th ed.). New York: Addison Wesley Longman; and (2) Lester, James D., & Lester, James D., Jr. (1999). *The Essential guide to writing research papers*. New York: Addison Wesley Longman.

computer screens and printers differ. If the article you are using has an author and/or title, you can make use of that information to some extent. The important thing is to provide the reader with enough information so that he/she can find the complete reference on the Works Cited page and can ultimately, if desired, find the article on the Internet. For example:

One bank showed a significant decline in assets despite an increase in the number of depositors (Wachovia Bank Annual Report 2002).

or

CEO John Smith reported a significant decline in assets for his bank although the bank had an increase in the number of depositors (Annual Report 2002).

The *Works Cited* page appears at the end of your paper and contains an alphabetical listing of all the material you used and cited in the text. For example:

Books: Author. *Title*. City of publication: Publisher, Date of publication.

Welch, Evelyn. *Art and Society in Italy*. New York: Macmillan, 1997.

or

Welch, Evelyn, Joyce Stone, and Sally Salisbury. *Art and Society in Italy*. New York: MacMillan, 1997.

Journals/Magazines: Author. "Title of Article." *Name of journal or magazine* Volume. Issue (Date of publication): Page number.

Cann, John, and Deborah Smith. "Volcanoes and the Oceanic Crust." *Earth News* 18.2 (2001): 61–66.

Newspapers: Author. "Title of the Article." *Name of newspaper as it appears on masthead* Date of publication: Section and page numbers.

Shields, Sharon. "Mothers March on Jail for Justice." *Tampa Tribune* 15 Dec. 2003: Metro 2.

Internet: Author. "Title of Article." Name of Web site owner or sponsor: Date downloaded URL address.

Link, Richard. "Territorial Fish," *Environmental Newsgroup*. 22 Dec. 2003 (www.aquaria.freshwater.com).

Note: Internet references are often a problem due to lack of information. At a minimum, a reference should contain the article title, Web site sponsor, download or authorship date, and URL address.

Interview/Personal Communication: Name of person. Type of interview/communication. Date of interview.

Safire, William. Telephone interview. 30 Dec. 2003.

or

Safire, William. Personal interview. 30 Dec. 2003.

or

Safire, William. Personal letter. 30 Dec. 2003.

or

Safire, William. E-mail communication. 30 Dec. 2003.

There are other sources often used in a research paper. These include a government document, an advertisement, a broadcast interview, a cartoon, a letter, a thesis or dissertation, and so forth. If you plan to use a source whose citation/reference style is not covered by the examples presented earlier, ask your instructor for advice or consult *The MLA Handbook for Writers of Research Papers*. As with APA style, MLA style has many variations in its basic citation and reference style. Please remember that precise details are important in citations. Current information about MLA style can be found on the Modern Language Association's Web site, www.mla.org.

Chicago Style

Writers who prefer footnotes or endnotes rather than in-text citations often use the style of documentation recommended in the *Chicago Manual of Style*.* This style, often called "Chicago" for short, is popular in the humanities and other academic fields.

Chicago documentation requires three steps: (1) in the text of the paper, a *number*—often a superscript—is placed after a phrase, clause, or sentence that you need to document; (2) each note number is linked to a *footnote* or *endnote*; and (3) every source cited or used is listed alphabetically in Works Cited list. Endnotes (listed in order, and numbered and placed on a separate page) are more common than footnotes and easier to manage—though some computer word processing programs can arrange footnotes at the bottom of a page automatically. Individual endnotes and footnotes are single-spaced, with double spaces between each entry. You should select either endnotes or footnotes; do not mix them.

Because endnotes and footnotes are quite comprehensive, a Works Cited list may be optional. If additional works are consulted, that is, examined by the researcher but not specifically cited in the paper or report, the reference list may be presented as a *Bibliography*. In any case, check with your instructor (or publisher or the organization sponsoring your research) to find out what is required.

In-text numbering for *endnotes*, that is, placing a superscript number at the point of reference and providing the complete citation on a separate page, can usually be easily accomplished with the help of your computer word processing program. Just click on the proper icon or tab on the toolbar—often the

---

*Information on Chicago style adapted from the following: Ruszkiewicz, John, Walker, Janice R., & Pemberton, Michael A. (2003). *Bookmarks: A guide to research and writing* (2nd ed.). New York: Addison Wesley Longman.

"insert" tab—and indicate you would like an endnote. The word processing program should respond and number your citations sequentially. For example:

> "Fourscore and seven years ago, our fathers brought forth on this continent, a new nation, conceived in liberty and dedicated to the proposition that all men are created equal."(1)

Footnotes, of course, appear at the bottom of the page on which the superscript number was placed. The proper citation for the endnote or footnote based on the previous example is the following:

> 1. Abraham Lincoln, *The Gettysburg Address*. (Gettysburg, PA: November 19, 1863).

The basic format for endnotes and footnotes is as follows:

> Full name, "Title," *Title of book, magazine, journal, newspaper* (Publication data): Page number.

Here are some examples:

> Brian Urquart, *Gregory Peck: An American Life* (New York: Norton, 2003): 225.

> Alice Moulakis, "Storm Chasers Never Rest." *Newsweek* (October 4, 2001): 51.

> Don Kelsey, "Teaching English in the Secondary School." *English Journal* (Autumn 1994): 66–67.

> Jim Rivers, "Communicating with the Public," *St. Petersburg Times* (6 January 2004): D1.

Camilla Benbow, "Pay Equity in Business." *Current Business News* (15 November 2001). Available from www.cbn.com/news/656ab.html.

Please note this last entry. As you already know, referencing Internet material is often problematic. Again, the key is to provide as much information as possible, but make sure there is enough information in a citation to enable a reader to access the material. It is not enough just to list a Web site address and nothing else. You should not use Internet material from which you cannot get a good citation.

If you are presenting a Works Cited page or a Bibliography, you should note that the entries on these pages are only slightly different from the footnote or endnote entries. For example:

Footnote:

Don Kelsey, "Teaching English in the Secondary School," *English Journal* (Autumn 1994): 66–67.

Works Cited entry:

Kelsey, Don. "Teaching English in the Secondary School." *English Journal* (Autumn 1994): 66–67.

Notice that for Works Cited, the author's name has been reversed. This allows you to place the entries on the reference page in alphabetical order by the author's last name. Notice also that the main elements in the entries in Works Cited are separated by periods, not the commas used in the footnotes.

Many sources can be used in a research paper, of course. If you plan to use a source not covered by the guidelines listed earlier, ask your instructor for advice or consult the *Chicago Manual of Style.* This is particularly important because Chicago style appears to allow for more variations on its basic format than do other styles. Current information about the *Chicago Manual of Style* can be obtained online at www.chicagomanualofstyle.org.

CHAPTER 12

Report Format

True ease in writing comes from art, not chance, As those move easiest who have learned to dance.

—ALEXANDER POPE

Communication using the written or printed word is still important in the twenty-first century. With all the ways we have to communicate electronically, one might assume that writing normally required in an academic or research setting would have risen above the old-fashioned handwritten or typed word. After all, we have a plethora of electronic ways to communicate: text messages, e-mail, cell phones, and the like.

There may not be much of a conflict here. A researcher can make good use of electronic devices to communicate information either to a large audience or to a smaller, specific audience. Many scholarly journals, for example, are available online as well as in the standard printed-on-paper format. Some journals are online only. In any case, a research report can easily be typed into a computer text file then printed out for circulation in paper form. That same text file can be burned on a CD and shared with any number of people. It would, of course, be impractical to try to distribute information about your research study by text message or cell phone. But you could do it in an e-mail message if you attached the text file to the message.

WHY WRITE A REPORT?

Research activity can be a little tiring, particularly if you have spent long hours reading, taking notes, talking with people, or traveling here and there to gather your data. Once the data have been gathered and analyzed, and once you have addressed the study's research questions, you may feel that the project is over. After all, the study is complete and your questions have answers. Case closed, right? No, your work is not finished. You may remember the flowchart presented in Chapter 4. If you refer to it, you will notice that the final step in the research process is writing the report.

Why do you need to write a report? Why couldn't you just summarize or list your study's findings in a page or two and be done with it? Well, there are several reasons for writing a complete, detailed report about your research study. One relates to the scientific method, discussed in Chapter 1. Although postmodernists do not place much faith in the science metanarrative, the scientific method, or at least parts of it, can be useful in helping us understand contemporary issues and get answers to our questions. Of particular interest here is the scientific method's belief that research should be both public and cumulative. By that we mean that your study's results should be available for others to read, think about, and possibly comment on. Your study may add something to what we already know (or think we know) about how the world works, how people behave, what people think, how people communicate, or how influential the media are. The only real way for you to communicate your study's results and meet these objectives is to prepare a research report.

In order to communicate the full extent of your research effort and place the results in their proper context, you must present a clearly written, detailed account of your study. A one- or two-page summary of your results will not provide others with the information needed to fully understand your work. Others will want to know how the study was done, what problems and successes you had, and what conclusions you drew from the data you gathered and why. This cannot be accomplished in anything less than a complete, final research report. A precise format for the research report will be presented in this chapter.

WHO IS THE AUDIENCE?

The kind of report you write may very well depend on who will be reading it. In other words, who is the audience? Who will be reading the report and perhaps using the information in it? If the report is for a class, your instructor is your audience. He/she will read the report and assign it a grade or evaluate it in some other way. Thus, you will need to make the report conform to the guidelines for the project set down by the instructor.

If an organization of some sort has sponsored the research and the report is to be submitted to that organization, you can consider the mid- and upper-level management of that organization to be your audience. This will likely include the financial officer who approved the money given to you to do the project. Others may read the report, but management will most likely be the first reader and may use the report as a basis for making decisions.

If you are writing for a trade publication, your report might be a little different from those required for the audiences noted earlier. Merrigan and Huston (2004) define a trade publication as a "written publication aimed at practitioners in a particular business or industry" (p. 290). Practitioners may or may not be familiar with precise research terminology. They will most certainly want to know what your study means to the real world in which they work.

If your study results are likely to be published in the popular press (magazines, newspapers, etc.), your report will be "aimed at the general public, largely without regard to the readers' fields of academic study or particular occupations" (Merrigan & Huston, p. 290). The general public is almost certainly unfamiliar with research terminology and will probably only want to know what your study means for everyday life.

If your study is for the academic community, that is, intended to be published in a scholarly journal or placed in a library or online for reading by other researchers, you will likely be writing for an informed audience. This audience will understand research methods and research terminology and may be interested in not only what the study means in terms of life, but also what the study means in terms of theory and research.

For purposes of this text, let us assume that your research report will be read by your instructor (a member of the academic community) or by other academic researchers. We will, therefore, be mostly concerned about writing a report for an academic audience.

THE TRADITIONAL FORMAT

By the time students get to college, they have had many opportunities to write essays or reports of various types. It is often easy to recall what your high school English teacher told you about the proper format for any written report or essay. He/she most likely said that a good essay or report has three parts: an introduction, a body, and a conclusion. You were probably urged to write a first, "rough" draft, revise it, then write a final draft and submit it for evaluation. This simple format is easy to remember, but students often found it difficult to follow, particularly if they did not know precisely what was supposed to be in each of the report's sections.

Occasionally, a teacher would take a more colloquial approach to formatting by telling students to use the following plan: "tell 'em what you are going to tell 'em, then tell 'em, then tell 'em what you just told 'em." Clever, but not very practical, at least in terms of knowing what specific information is required in any particular report section.

However, when students get to college, they often face a more disciplined form of writing in the introductory English classes all students must take as part of their general requirements. These courses often have names like English 101. This 101 designation usually indicates that the course will cover the basics of writing, particularly the type of writing required of college students. Once a student declares a major field of study, he/she may find that the writing required in that field is somewhat different from the writing mastered in English 101.

A SPECIALIZED FORMAT

In many of the social sciences (communication included), research reports follow a more detailed plan than the introduction-body-conclusion format that is popular in secondary schools. There is some variety, of course, in the specific elements required in each discipline. Nevertheless, the same basic overall format can be recognized in almost all social science fields. One reason for the similarities is that it is easy for any researcher to read a report and understand what was done. A communication researcher can read a research report prepared by a researcher in sociology or psychology, for example, and have a fairly clear understanding of almost all of the research procedures and techniques used as well as how the data were gathered.

Regardless of the discipline you are writing for, you must write your report using a recognized reference and citation style. Those presented in Chapter 11 should serve you well. Follow their guidelines precisely. It is also a good idea to avoid using the first person pronoun "I." Instead of saying "I decided to do a telephone survey," say "A telephone survey seemed the most efficient way to gather data from the target audience." Consult an appropriate style manual for additional information on using the proper voice in a research report.

A thorough research report will contain at least 9 and possibly 10 elements. Here they are in the order in which they should appear in the research report:

Title Page

Abstract

Table of Contents

Introduction

Literature Review

Methodology

Results

Discussion

References

Appendix

There is widespread agreement among researchers that this standard format be followed where possible. As previously noted, a report using this format will be highly accessible to other researchers. Nevertheless, this format may change somewhat depending on the reference/citation style you selected. Your instructor may have yet another format that she/he prefers.

Some researchers have put their own spin on the standard format. Tinberg (2003), for example, suggests that a research report have six elements: Inquiry, Scholarship, Research, Reflection, Presentation, and Action (p. ix). Tinberg explains that in the "Inquiry" element, one should frame a question or pose a problem. Presenting a problem or posing a question would be part of the "Introduction" element noted earlier in our suggested format. Further, Tinberg believes that the "Scholarship" portion of the report should contain information on what has been done before in the research area, that is, a summary of the literature already available on the subject (p. xix). This, of course, matches the "Literature Review" element of our suggested format. The same sort of correspondence exists among the elements suggested by Tinberg and the elements provided in this text's suggested format. If you read other research methods texts, you will likely find some variation from field to field and from researcher to researcher regarding the labeling of the various parts of a research report, but the content of each of those parts is strikingly similar.

A SECTION-BY-SECTION EXPLANATION

We have been calling the various parts of a research report its "elements." That term seemed useful early in our discussion. However, let us now begin to refer to each part of a research report as a "section." It really doesn't matter what you call the many parts of a research report, but, for our present purposes, the word *section* seems to convey the notion that it is an important and fully developed part of the overall report. It is important to understand just what information should appear in each of the sections of a research report. Therefore, each will be discussed in some detail.

There is little to be concerned about in preparing the *title page*. It should contain the title of the report or name of the project, the name of the person preparing the report and contact information for that person, the date the report was prepared or submitted, and the name of the sponsoring organization (if applicable). The placement of the items on the title page will likely depend on the reference/citation style you are using. Consult the appropriate style manual for precise information on the title page. You can see the logic behind each of the items required on the title page. A reader needs to know the title of the project or report because this is a general indicator of the subject to be covered in the report. Additionally, a reader needs to know who wrote the report, how that person may be contacted (usually a business address or perhaps an e-mail address), when the report was completed or submitted, and who sponsored the project (if applicable).

The *abstract* appears early in the research report, but it should probably be among the last things the researcher writes. An abstract is a brief description of the research project and a quick summary of the results. It usually contains 200 words or fewer. This means, of course, that key aspects of the study must be presented, but presented succinctly. Other researchers will likely consult the abstract to see whether the information in the research report is of enough interest to them to be worth their time to read the entire report. Writing the abstract is not easy; it requires you to focus on the most important parts of the project in terms of method and results and report significant information concisely. The abstract is best written near the end of the project when all data are in and analyzed, when conclusions have been drawn, when research questions have been answered, and when recommendations have been made.

Like the abstract, the *table of contents* should be one of the last pages the researcher prepares. This is, of course, because the report must be 100% complete before an accurate list of page numbers can be compiled. The table of contents simply lists each section of the report in the order in which it appears in the report and provides a corresponding page number for the beginning of that section.

The *introduction* will likely be the first section of the report that will challenge the researcher's writing skills. The introduction should do several things. First, it should clearly identify the specific subject of the research. For example, simply saying that your study deals with "violence on television" is not enough. You should be more specific: "This study used content analysis to examine incidents of violence on Saturday morning network television cartoon programs." This gives the reader important information on precisely what your study was about. Second, the introduction might present and discuss a particular problem and/or pose a general question that needs an answer. If the research is sponsored by an outside organization, the involvement and interest of the organization should be explained. Third, the introduction should provide information about the importance of the study to individuals, organizations, or the culture in general. In other words, it should answer the famous "So what?" question. Why was the research needed and by whom? What use might be made of the results? It is probably safe to assume that a reader does not know a lot about your research area, so you must assist the reader by providing clear, specific information about your research topic and its importance or usefulness. Avoid wide-ranging discussions of issues and situations that have little relevance to your project. In other words, do not inflate this section, but use it as an opportunity not only to provide the reader with important information about the basis for your research study but also to interest him/her in reading the entire report.

You may recall that one of the steps in the research flowchart presented in Chapter 4 was "develop a research design." It might be useful to reread the passages in Chapter 4 relating to literature searches. The *literature review* is a part of the design process and summarizes the results of your search of the literature. It describes what other researchers have found about your topic or subject and focuses on questions that have yet to be answered or issues that need further exploration. A literature review is most often helpful when it identifies recent research about your subject. Discussing studies that are more than 20 years old can provide a reasonable foundation for your research, but discussing what has been done recently puts your subject or topic in a contemporary context.

A literature review that merely strings together synopses of the articles you have read will probably be of little value. A more meaningful literature review will organize the articles, either by topical area or perhaps by chronological order—if that chronological order has some significance in the development of information about your topic. For example, a chronological order might be appropriate for a violence study if the literature search revealed that a number of early studies produced essentially the same results, but later studies produced different results. You could show how the literature reflects these changes.

Remember that the literature review should provide the broad context for your study. This is important because later sections of the report, particularly the results section—perhaps even the discussion section—will need to connect your findings to the findings of others. Your study should find its proper place among the other studies that have been done on your topic.

Some researchers use the literature review as the opportunity to pose their study's research questions. This makes some sense. After all, if you have just completed a comprehensive literature search, you likely have found that there are questions to be answered and/or issues to be explored. Posing your study's research questions at the end of the literature review will show the reader that you have attempted to address some of the shortcomings of the previous research. Other researchers prefer to pose their research questions in the next section of the research report.

The *methodology* section of the research report can begin by posing the present study's research questions. The section might begin with statements like these: The literature review in the previous section revealed three issues yet unresolved; therefore, the following three research questions are posed . . . .

If you have already noted your research questions in the literature review, you are ready to begin explaining in detail what methods you used in your research, how and why these particular methods were decided upon, and how these methods were employed. This section of the report should be a step-by-step account of how you did the work. Each step should have a justification, that is, some reason for doing it. For example, why did you decide to do a mail survey instead of a telephone survey? Or why did you decide to convene three instead of four focus groups? What method did you use to identify focus group subjects and why was this method appropriate? While your readers might want to accept your word that such-and-such a decision was the appropriate one or that this-or-that method was the best one to employ, they cannot simply take your word for it unless they understand the reasoning behind each of your decisions.

Things get a bit more complicated in the *results* section of the research report. In this section, you should provide an organized summary of your data. You may wish to prepare visual aids, that is, tables or figures, to illustrate particular findings. Summarize all the data you gathered. The way you summarize your research results may depend to a large degree on the research methodology you used. A survey, for example, is likely to generate quantitative data and these data can often be summarized in what some researchers call descriptive statistics. You may remember from Chapter 3 that as postmodern researchers, we do not place a lot of faith in the mathematical analysis of data. Nevertheless, it is usually quite useful to summarize your numerical data in terms of frequencies and percentages.

If you have qualitative data that might be generated by focus groups, your summary of research results will be different. You should refer to Chapter 5, which explains the method your study used, for additional information about how to analyze the data resulting from that particular method.

Many researchers enjoy writing the *discussion* section of a research report because it provides an opportunity to interpret their research findings. In other words, they get to say what they think the results mean. This calls for careful judgment. You should not assume that the data answered all your research questions, though that's possible. More than likely, some of your questions will have a satisfactory answer, but others will not. You should begin this section of the research report by restating the study's research questions. Then, take one question at a time and determine whether your study's results provided a reasonable answer to it. Refer frequently to the data to support your answer to each question.

Once you have satisfactorily addressed the study's research questions, you can place your study's results in the overall scheme of things, that is, where your study fits with everything else that has been done and everything else we know about your subject or topic. This is where you can connect your study to those you summarized in the literature review. You also have a little freedom here to speculate just a bit beyond the boundaries set by the data you gathered. You can do this by pointing out the strengths and weaknesses of the study and/or how your results seem to be pointing in a new direction. Avoid sweeping generalizations, but do not be afraid to think outside the box, as some businesses are fond of saying. In other words, the reader needs to know the meaning of what you've found, how it fits with what else is known, and where research activity should go from here.

The *references* page is next in the report. This page should not be all that challenging to prepare if you have been keeping good records of the sources you used in the paper. Remember the literature review section? The references page should provide a complete citation for each of the studies, articles, books, and so forth that you cited in the literature review or elsewhere in the report. Entries here are listed alphabetically and require precise punctuation and capitalization. Consult Chapter 11 in this text or a standard style manual for details.

It is possible, perhaps even likely, that you will need an *appendix*. Stark and Roberts (1998) believe you should place material in an appendix if placing it in the main body of the report would be distracting, or if the material is not essential to the report but would be of interest to some readers (pp. 263–264). For example, if you have done a survey, you could include a copy of the questionnaire in the appendix. If you've done a historical study, you could place a list of individuals you interviewed in the appendix, together with the dates and times of the interviews. Some of this information would likely be elsewhere in the report, but it is often helpful to see overall summaries of activities or copies of work documents used in the research effort. Be careful not to throw everything in the appendix. It is not a catch-all section, but it can be successfully used to provide supplemental information about your research project, particularly if that information bears heavily on how things were done.

SOME LIKELY VARIATIONS

A research report does not have to follow the *exact* format described earlier. The format is flexible enough to accommodate a variety of modifications. If you are doing a thesis or a dissertation for an advanced degree, your college or university will likely suggest a format for these documents that may be similar to the one described earlier. Some researchers like to have a *conclusions* section. This usually follows the discussion section. However, in many cases a discussion section will include the conclusions you have drawn from your study's results. In short, section labels may not mean very much. A research report's meaning derives chiefly from the quality of the research process and the clarity of the report.

Since we are now well into the electronic age, you may wish to include a CD with a PowerPoint presentation of some sort which explains your research project and illustrates its findings. Or you may wish to provide a series of transparencies suitable for use on an overhead projector. You could include a video or audiotape presenting your results or explaining some of your research activities. These additions are fine and may be welcomed, especially by organizations outside the academic community. But if your report is for a scholarly audience of other researchers, you would likely do well to avoid the glitz and glamour of postmodern technology. Use it if you wish, but use it judiciously.

SECTION IV

Applications

You are now ready to apply what you have learned in the previous sections of this book. In the chapters just ahead, you will have the opportunity to use some of the methods and procedures researchers in communication commonly use. You will be asked to work with other students in conducting a group research project. You will also be asked to prepare an individual research proposal or, if your instructor so determines, actually conduct a research project.

CHAPTER 13

An Individual Research Proposal

"Begin at the beginning," the King said, gravely,
"and go till you come to the end; then stop."

—Lewis Carroll

In order to demonstrate that you understand communication research methods and to give you some practice in using some of the terms, concepts, and procedures you have learned, your instructor may ask you to prepare an individual research proposal or she/he may ask you to plan and actually conduct a research project.

Let's deal with the proposal-only option first. In this option you are not being asked to actually conduct a research project. As you already know, conducting a research project takes considerable time and money. As a student in a one-semester research methods course, you may have neither the time nor resources to conduct a real project. You may have to do that later if you pursue an advanced degree. But for present purposes, you can *plan* a research project. The planning of a project will enable you to demonstrate that you understand research methods and could, if necessary, actually carry out a real research project.

THE INDIVIDUAL RESEARCH PROPOSAL

Your research proposal should have six major sections. Each is explained in some detail in the pages which follow. Remember that this option does not require you to execute the project, that is, actually do the research. But you will be preparing a plan that could, at some point in time perhaps, be carried out with little or no change to the plan. You will be following the research flowchart, but some steps in the process may be combined or eliminated given the special nature of this assignment.

Your proposal should begin with an *introduction*. You should state the topic you have selected or been assigned and provide a description or explanation of the topic. For example, if you are assigned the topic "Media Coverage of the World Series," you would have to explain what that is, when and how it occurs, and what the results are for those involved. Assume your reader knows little about your topic; therefore, you will need to provide enough background information on your topic for the reader to make sense of your proposal. If you feel it is necessary to narrow your topic somewhat—suppose you'd like to do something on "Media Coverage of the Final Game of the 2008 World Series"—make sure your reader understands how and why you have narrowed the topic.

The second section of the proposal is the *literature review* in which you provide the reader with up-to-date information gathered in your search of the literature about your topic. You will particularly want to report what other researchers have done on the subject as well as whether there have been any recent developments in what we know about the topic. In this portion of the proposal, you will have the opportunity to become proficient in at least two of the citation/reference styles you have studied. Search the literature on your topic using the process outlined in Chapter 4. You should have a minimum of 15 different sources, and no more than 5 should be from the Internet. It is important that you limit your Internet use. It is often difficult to determine the validity of Internet information, so use online information sparingly. Please note, however, that some scholarly journals, newspapers, magazines, and research studies are available online, and these are usually reliable sources of information. But it is almost always appropriate to use printed materials since most have been through an editing process and are often more reliable than information you might find on "Joe's Blog." In any case, use a variety of sources, including books, magazines, newspapers, scholarly journal articles, interviews, and the like. Concentrate your search on material recently published; however, some topics may require you to go back several, perhaps dozens, of years. If you have questions about this, ask your instructor.

Please observe all citation/reference guidelines when writing this section of the proposal. You have studied three reference/citation styles. You should select two of these. This means that you will need to present *two versions* of the literature review in the proposal. One should be in APA style since that is the norm in communication. You may select either MLA or Chicago for the other. You should write the literature review the first time using APA, then rewrite it using one of the other styles. In most cases, the wording of the literature review will remain much the same, but the citation/reference style will be different. Submit both of these versions as the second section of the proposal.

The third section, *proposed new data-gathering plan*, is an important one. First, you will need to state the study's research questions. The literature review may have helped you identify new questions about your topic. What information about your topic appears to be missing in the literature review? What is it that we still don't know about the topic? In what areas of the topic is the literature too old or outdated to be of much use in understanding the topic? You should propose at least two or three new research questions.

Next, specify in some detail exactly how you would go about getting the information, that is, the data, needed to address the research questions. You should use one of the methods you are familiar with, but it should be a method that will provide you with the information you need. For example, if you are examining media coverage of the final game of the 2008 World Series, and you are particularly interested in what the audience thought of the media coverage, you would probably want to do a survey or conduct a focus group. The historical method would probably not provide you with enough of the right kind of data for you to successfully address your research questions. Be creative, but be practical. It would not be worthwhile to suggest, as part of a proposal on the influence of movie stars on American life, that interviews be conducted with Brad Pitt and Angelina Jolie. There is almost no chance that either of these celebrities would be available for you to interview.

Please provide a step-by-step plan for getting new information about your topic. Indicate when and how this information would be gathered, by whom, and how it would be recorded. Provide examples of questionnaires, focus group discussion points, interview forms, and so forth that you would use in the data-gathering process.

The fourth section of the proposal is something new. It is not part of the research flowchart process but is presented here to provide you the opportunity to suggest how your study results might be made public. Let's call this section *proposed media format*. Assume you have gathered new information which has answered your research questions and shed new light on your topic. Consider now just how you would like to communicate this information to the public. Should it be in a newspaper article? A magazine article? A news release? An online Web site piece? A tri-fold brochure? A scholarly journal? A speech at a regional conference? In other words, how would you disseminate your findings? Once you have selected a way in which to report your findings, explain why you made this particular choice and how it uniquely fits your topic.

The *budget* section (fifth section) of the proposal should detail the money necessary to carry forth the proposed project. Review the discussion of budgetary issues in Chapter 4. You should have as many of the following budget categories as are appropriate for your proposed study: personnel, materials and supplies, office space/hardware/utilities, travel, and miscellaneous. Your particular project may require other budget cate-gories. Remember that a budget is a list of *anticipated* expenditures. Be as ac-curate as you can in estimating the cost of the project.

The final (sixth) section of the proposal will include the *References* (APA) and *either Works Cited* (MLA) or *Endnotes* (Chicago). Review Chapter 11 style or consult the appropriate style manual. Remember that precision, that is, attention to detail, is an important part of reference style.

Once the body of the proposal is complete, you can prepare the *title page* for the document. The title page should contain the title of your pro-posed project, of course, as well as your name, the date, and the name of the person, organization, or institution for whom the proposal has been prepared. More information about what should be on the title page can be found in Chapter 12.

Your Research Proposal Topic

You or your instructor may decide on an appropriate topic for your individ-ual research proposal. Since you are studying communication, your topic should have some connection to those areas of interest and study that com-prise the discipline. The following list of topics is presented to give you (or your instructor) a starting point. Some of the topics listed may not interest you; others might have high interest.

The Columbine shooting incident

The Watergate scandal

The Atlanta Olympic Games bombing incident

Hate Web sites

Gun control

Militia groups

Liberal bias of the media

The 2000 presidential election in Florida

The Princess Diana accident

U.S. immigration policies and practices

Terrorism

Super Bowl advertisements

Telemarketing/National Do Not Call registry

Tobacco advertising and teens

Alcoholic beverage advertising

The Exxon Valdez incident

The contaminated Tylenol scare

The Air Florida disaster

The Three Mile Island incident
The Jenny Jones Show murder
Talk radio
Controversial music lyrics
Student-run college radio stations
The films of Michael Moore
Political correctness
Campus speech codes
Migrant workers in California and Florida
Economic impact of sports franchises
Feminism
Sexual harassment
The death penalty
Body piercing/tattoos
The abortion controversy
Gay marriage
Fast food practices
Hells Angels
Public access television
Television's reality shows
Teens and video games
Rap music/hip-hop
Audio books
Product placement in movies and television shows
College newspapers
The Valerie Plame incident
Journalists in war zones
Satellite radio
Journalistic plagiarists (Glass, Blair, etc.)
Radio shock jocks
The Danish Muslim cartoons
E-mail spam
Homeland security
Hurricane Katrina
Prescription drug advertising
The ValuJet crash

Love Canal

HDTV

Internet bloggers

Computer hackers

Binge drinking

The Vice President Cheney shooting incident

The Duke University lacrosse team incident

The 2008 Democratic presidential nomination campaign

School shootings: Virginia Tech and Northern Illinois

The paparazzi and Britney Spears

Paris Hilton and celebrity culture

Cable network talk shows

The 2007–2008 Hollywood writer's strike

The 2008 U.S. visit of Pope Benedict XVI

It is clear from a cursory examination that most of these topics are media-related and lend themselves to some sort of historical research. Nevertheless, these topics present an opportunity to use other research methods, particularly because one of the purposes of the individual research proposal is to enable you to design a project that will add new information to what we already know. Take, for example, student-run college radio stations. If you want to know how college radio stations got started and what it was like for early stations, you will want to take a historical approach. But you could also survey present-day student-run college radio stations or perhaps conduct focus groups on a campus where a student-run station was highly popular. In this way you would find out not only what is presently being done, but also what students who listen to the station think about it.

If you are not interested in a topic connected to media, you might wish to prepare a proposal on a topic related to rhetorical criticism, interaction analysis, performance studies, or some sort of naturalistic inquiry. Your instructor may assign you a topic or he/she may ask you to select one that is of interest to you. The important thing here is that you select a topic not only because you like it, but also because you have questions about it worth investigating. In other words, an investigation should stem first from questions or concerns you have and second from topics that interest you. You certainly would not want to do a research project on a topic that is of no interest to you; however, if you are a careful observer of media or a careful listener in various communication situations, questions should pop into your mind about what you've seen or heard. These questions often lead you to a specific topic.

Once you have settled on a topic, your instructor may ask you to narrow your topic area and focus on a researchable aspect of the topic. He/she may also ask you to provide a brief, written statement explaining how you arrived at that particular topic.

THE INDIVIDUAL RESEARCH PROJECT

The second option offered by this chapter requires you to plan and execute a research project. The first step in this process is preparing a research proposal. You should use the information in the previous section "Your Research Proposal Topic" to assist you. You will, of course, need to modify the process described earlier just a bit. It is not necessary to provide two versions of the literature review. One version will do nicely. You may also omit the *proposed media format* section of the proposal. If you are going to conduct a research project, you will likely write a final report suitable for submission to a scholarly journal or perhaps an online journal or newsletter. You can also eliminate the "budget" section from your proposal, although it would be a good idea to think about what it will cost to do the project.

Once your proposal is complete, present it to your instructor for approval. She/he may want you to make some changes in the proposal. You should make the necessary modifications promptly and resubmit the proposal for approval. Once you receive approval, you can begin to conduct the project. Follow the process outlined in the *proposed new data-gathering plan* section of the proposal. You should regularly consult the chapter in this book dealing directly with the research method you wish to employ. If you are using a method not addressed in this text, ask your instructor where sources of information about your method can be found. Find these sources, read them carefully, and employ methods correctly.

In Chapter 4 we discussed the importance of the logistics or precise details of a research project. Each research method has its own special set of logistics. You will now be faced with handling the many details required of researchers. Gathering, recording, organizing, and analyzing data are all processes requiring careful attention to detail. Be precise in how you perform each of these tasks. Refer to this text or to other texts for helpful information. It is almost always appropriate to ask your instructor for advice. She/he will not do the project for you but will likely suggest ways in which things can be done. Look again at the flowchart in Chapter 4. Are you following each step in the research process?

When you are ready to write the report, read Chapter 12 again. You can follow the report-writing guidelines there, or your instructor may ask you to write the report in the format she/he specifies.

## CHAPTER 14

A Group Research Project

> *Knowledge isn't wisdom, and we aren't here just to stuff ourselves with facts and figures. We are given this life so we might earn the next; the gift is a chance to grow in spirit, and knowledge is one of the many nutrients that facilitate our growth.*
>
> —DEAN KOONTZ

Although many research activities are conducted by individuals, some projects may require a group effort. This chapter will provide a general outline for a group research project. Unlike the previous chapter where you were asked to plan or conduct an individual research project, this chapter will enable you to work with others, design a small-scale research project, carry out the project, prepare a written report, and make an oral presentation about the research activity.

PROCEDURE

The group project plan presented in the pages just ahead will attempt to follow the research flowchart. Some modification of the normal research process may be necessary, given the nature of group work and classroom activity. The suggested group project plan has 11 steps. Each will be explained in some detail.

The first step is, of course, to *form the research groups*. Your instructor may elect to assign you to a group, or he/she may allow students to form groups on their own. Your instructor will determine how many students will be assigned to each group. The typical number of students in a group ranges from four to six. The number of students in your group may depend on the number of students in the class or on your instructor's preferences.

Next, each group should *elect a group leader*. It is not the job of the leader to do all the work. A group leader should be active in establishing deadlines, sending out reminders, and, in general, coordinating the work of the entire group. It is a good idea for group members to share e-mail addresses and telephone numbers. Most likely, the research activity will have to be conducted outside of class hours and contact information will be vital in getting the cooperation and participation of all group members. At the first meeting of the group, each member should indicate his/her strengths. For example, if one of the group members has a particular interest and skill in computer graphic design, it might be useful to suggest he/she be in charge of putting together the final report, or in preparing visuals for the oral presentation.

The group should next *pose a communication-related research question.* Research projects often have more than one research question, and multiple questions could be posed by a group, but posing only one question often helps the group focus its research activity. Your instructor can provide guidance on the issue of research questions. The question(s) should be specific enough to be answered by a limited research effort. For example, consider the following question: What are the media use habits of the university's administrators, faculty, staff, and students? Such a project could be done, of course, but it involves four different populations. The participation of administrators, faculty, and staff might be problematic, given their various work schedules and responsibilities. Students would likely be more accessible. Therefore, it would be a bit more practical to pose a limited research question: What are the media use habits of students at this university?

One or more members of the group should be assigned to *search the literature.* If the research question is the one suggested earlier, you will not likely find any literature dealing with precisely this issue at your university. You might, however, find that researchers at other universities have conducted studies on the media use habits of college students. What about the media use habits of high school students? Elementary students? Recent college graduates? What has been done and written in these areas? You will need some context in which to place the results of the study your group is conducting.

The literature search may have revealed some information that requires the group to *revise the study's research question.* This step may not be necessary, but the literature may suggest a particular approach or a particular emphasis that your group might wish to use. If this is the case, spend a little time refocusing the research question so that it will meet your needs for the project.

The group's next task is to *develop the research design.* This means selecting the methodology that will be used to gather the information, that is, the data, you will need to successfully answer your research question. Is a survey the best way to gather the data you need? Would focus groups be more appropriate? All group members should be involved in the discussion of the methodology. Be ready to explain clearly why the method selected is the most appropriate one for the project. Next, develop a detailed plan for employing the method. Which group member will be responsible for what part of the research effort? For example, if your group wishes to use a survey, who will draft the questionnaire, who will pretest it, and who will prepare the revised questionnaire and produce multiple copies of it for group use? Remember, the logistics of any research project are important. A project can

Group Name:_____

Instructions: Write the name of each group member in the spaces provided below, then indicate the strength of that individual's contribution to the group research effort. Please use a 1 to 5 scale, with 1 meaning "little or no contribution," and 5 meaning "important and significant contribution." Sign your name at the bottom of the page. Your ratings will be kept confidential.

Name	Rating
_____	_____
_____	_____
_____	_____
_____	_____
_____	_____
_____	_____

Comments:

_____

_____

_____

_____

Your Signature

FIGURE 14.1 **Group Research Project Member Evaluation Form**

rise or fall depending on whether each and every detail has been handled in a precise, appropriate fashion. Chapter 4 of this text contains additional information that may be helpful to your group in designing the study.

The group is now ready to *execute the project*. Follow the detailed plan developed in the previous step. Each group member should have some responsibility in this part of the project. Remember that keeping accurate records of the data gathered is important. If a survey, handle completed questionnaires carefully. Assign one group member as the official "collector" of the completed questionnaires. Each group member should submit the completed documents to this person as soon as possible. If you are conducting focus groups, preserve the notes or other data that the sessions generated. If the notes are handwritten, convert them to typed copy. Do not allow notes, observations, or other hand-recorded data to lie around and "get cold" before they are turned into typed copy. Save all material whether you think you will need it or not.

At least two members of the group should *organize and analyze the study results*. Tabulate and summarize the data on the questionnaires if your group has conducted a survey. If your group conducted a focus group session or two, summarize (and possibly compare) the results. In short, you will need to have a clear idea of what your study found. Additional information about analyzing study results can be found in each of the specific methodology chapters (Chapter 5, 6, and 7) in this text.

The group is now ready to *address the research question*. Hopefully, you will be able to provide a reasonable answer to your question. Your answer should be supported by the data gathered. In some cases, your group may not be able to provide a complete answer to the question; nevertheless, the question should be answered as completely as possible. It might also be useful to pose new questions or new issues that have been raised by your study.

All group members should help *write the report*. If two group members conducted the search of the literature, those members should write that section of the report. If others were involved in other aspects of the project, they should contribute to the report by writing up their parts of the project. It is often most efficient if one individual accepts the responsibility for collecting the various parts of the report written by group members and "pulling them together" into a complete, coherent document. This is not easy. Individuals have different writing styles. The report writer should have considerable editing skills and be able to blend the various documents into a complete whole. Remember that a final research report, at minimum, contains the following elements: title page, introduction, research questions, literature review, methodology, results, discussion, and reference list.

Most researchers do not have to *deliver an oral report* on their research projects unless they are presenting their research findings at a conference of some sort or making a formal presentation to a funding agency. However, it is important that your entire class hear about your project: what you did, why you did it, how you did it, what you found, and what it all means. All group members should participate in this activity. Use visual aids as appropriate. Admit the project's weaknesses and point out its strengths. Be ready to answer questions about your project.

GROUP EVALUATION

Some students complain about group work. One of the chief objections is that some students in a group do a lot of work and others do little or nothing, yet the group often receives a single grade that applies equally to all group members. It is usually not possible for your course instructor to monitor all group activities. She/he must sometimes rely on the group members' evaluation of each other in order to get a clear understanding of who contributed to the project and who did not. If your instructor chooses to use an evaluation tool as part of his/her overall assessment of the total group activity, some use may be made of the evaluation form in Figure 14.1. However, your instructor may have some other way to evaluate the contributions of group members.

A successful group project can go a long way toward helping you understand the complexities of research activity. It can also leave you with a sense of satisfaction and a willingness to engage in future research.

REFERENCES

Appignanesi, R., & Garratt, C. (1995). *Introducing postmodernism.* Cambridge, England: Icon Books.

Approaches to reading and interpretation. Reader-response criticism. Available from www.assumption.edu/users/ady/HHGateway/Gateway?Approach.

Ashley, D. (1994). Postmodernism and antifoundationalism. In David R. Dickens & Andrea Fontana (Eds.), *Postmodernism and social inquiry* (pp. 53–75). New York: The Guilford Press.

A student's approach to the second law and entropy (2006). Retrieved from www.entropysite.com/students_approach.html.

Avery, R. K. (1987). Agendas for mass communication research. In Jay G. Blumler & Michael Gurevitch (Eds.), *Mass communication review yearbook* (Vol. 6). Newbury Park: Sage Publications.

Babbie, E. (1992). *The practice of social research* (6th ed.). Belmont, CA: Wadsworth.

Babbie, E. (2002). *The basics of social research.* (2nd ed.). Belmont, CA: Wadsworth/ Thomson.

Background of reader response theory. (2008). Retrieved from http://mrstubbardsclass. homestead.com/Reader_Response_Theory.doc.

Bajkiewicz, T. E., & Smith, J. E. (2007). When the inbox breaks: An exploratory analysis of online network breaking news e-mail alerts. *Electronic News, 1*(4), 197–210.

Bauman, Z. (1992). *Intimations of postmodernity.* New York: Routledge.

Beal, F. (1970). Double jeopardy: To be black and female. In R. Morgan (Ed.), *Sisterhood is powerful: An anthology of writings from the women's liberation movement.* New York: Random House.

Berelson, B. (1952). *Content analysis in communication research.* Glencoe, IL: The Free Press.

Berger, C. R., & Chaffee, S. H. (1987a). The study of communication as a science. In Charles R. Berger & Steven H. Chaffee (Eds.), *Handbook of communication science* (pp. 15–19). Newbury Park: Sage Publications.

Berger, C. R., & Chaffee, S. H. (1987b). What communication scientists do. In C. R. Berger & S. H. Chaffee (Eds.), *Handbook of communication science* (pp. 99–105). Newbury Park: Sage Publications.

Berman, M. (1988). *All that is solid melts into air.* New York: Penguin Books.

Berube, M. (1994). *Public access: Literary theory and American cultural politics.* New York: Verso.

Blumler, J. G., & Gurevitch, M. (1987). The personal and the public: Observations on agendas in mass communication research. In Jay G. Blumler & Michael Gurevitch

(Eds.), *Mass communication review yearbook* (Vol. 6, pp. 16–21). Newbury Park: Sage Publications.

Brennen, B. (1996). Toward a history of labor and news work: The use of oral sources in journalism history. *The Journal of American History, 83*(2), 571–579.

Brown, F. L., Amos, J. R., & Mink, O. G. (1975). *Statistical concepts: A basic program.* New York: Harper & Row.

Brown, R. H. (1995). Postmodern representation, postmodern affiliation. In R. H. Brown (Ed.), *Postmodern representations.* Urbana, IL: University of Illinois Press.

Burt, E. (1998). Challenges in doing women's history. *Clio: Newsletter of the History Division of the Association for Education in Journalism and Mass Communication, 31*(1), 17–19.

Butler, C. (2002). *Postmodernism: A very short introduction.* Oxford, NY: Oxford University Press.

Butler, J. (1990). *Gender trouble: Feminism and the subversion of identity.* New York: Routledge.

Butler, J. (1993). *Bodies that matter: On the discursive limits of "sex."* New York: Routledge.

Butler, J. (2004). *Undoing gender.* New York: Routledge.

Capra, F. (1982). *The turning point.* New York: Bantam Books.

The Chicago manual of style (15th ed.). (2003). Chicago: University of Chicago Press.

Clarke, J. N., & Binns, J. (2006). The portrayal of heart disease in mass print magazines, 1991–2001. *Health Communication, 19*(1), 39–48.

Cohen, H. (1994). *The history of speech communication: The emergence of a discipline, 1914–1945.* Annandale, VA: Speech Communication Association.

Columbia Encyclopedia. (2001–2005). Columbia University Press. Available from www.bartleby.com/65/he/hermeu.html.

Connor, S. (1989). *Postmodernist culture* (2nd ed.). Cambridge: Blackwell.

Conti, K. D. (1995). Oral histories: The most overlooked public relations tool. *Communication World, 12*(6), 52–53.

Creedon, P. J. (1994). *Women, media and sport: Challenging gender values.* Thousand Oaks, CA: Sage.

Creswell, J. W. (2007). *Qualitative inquiry & research design: Choosing among five approaches.* Thousand Oaks, CA: Sage.

Czitrom, D. J. (1982). *Media and the American mind.* Chapel Hill: University of North Carolina Press.

Davis, D. K., & Jasinski, J. (1993). Beyond the culture wars: An agenda for research on communication and culture. *Journal of Communication, 13*(3), 141–149.

Dees, R. (2003). *Writing the modern research paper* (4th ed.). New York: Addison Wesley Longman.

Delia, J. C. (1987). Communication research: A history. In Charles R. Berger & Steven H. Chaffee (Eds.), *Handbook of communication science* (pp. 20–98). Newbury Park: Sage Publications.

Denzin, N. (1994). Postmodernism and deconstruction. In D. R. Dickens & A. Fontana (Eds.), *Postmodernism and social inquiry*. New York: Guilford Press.

Denzin, N. K. (1991). *Images of postmodern society: Social theory and contemporary cinema*. Thousand Oaks, CA: Sage Publications.

DeVault, M. L. (1999). *Liberating method: Feminism and social research*. Philadelphia: Temple University Press.

Dibean, W., & Garrison, B. (2001). How six online newspapers use web technologies. *Newspaper Research Journal, 22*(2), 79–89.

Dow, B. J., & Condit, C. M. (2005). The state of the art in feminist scholarship in communication. *Journal of Communication, 55*(3), 448–478.

Dupagne, M. (1993). Gender differences in predicting productivity of faculty. *Journalism Educator, 48*(1), 37–45.

Durham, M. G. (2004). Constructing the "new ethnicities": Media, sexuality, and diaspora identity in the lives of South Asian immigrant girls. *Critical Studies in Media Communication, 21*(2), 140–161.

Ellis, B. G. (1999, August). *A comparative analysis of a successful approach for rescuing the undergraduate media research course from termination as measured against the traditional teaching modalities*. Paper presented to the Teaching Standards Committee, AEJMC annual convention in New Orleans.

Emery, M., & Emery, E. (1988). *The press and America: An interpretative history of the mass media* (6th ed.). Englewood Cliffs, NJ: Prentice-Hall.

Entropy. (1996). *American heritage book of English usage*. Retrieved from www.bartleby.com/64/C004/024.html.

Faulconer, J. E. (1998). Deconstruction. Brigham Young University. Retrieved from http://.jamesfaulconer.byu.edu/deconstr.htm.

Fawer, A. (2005). *Improbable*. New York: HarperTorch.

Feyerabend, P. (1993). *Against method*. New York: Verso.

Flew, A. (1984). *A dictionary of philosophy* (Rev. 2nd ed.). New York: St. Martin's Press.

Foucault, M. (1988). In Colin Gardin (Ed.), *Power/knowledge: Selected interviews and other writings*. New York: Pantheon books.

Foucault, M. (1998). In James D. Faubion (Ed.), *Aesthetics, method, and methodology*. New York: The New Press.

Frey, L. R., Botan, C. H., & Kreps, G. L. (2000). *Investigating communication: An introduction to research methods* (2nd ed.). Boston: Allyn and Bacon.

Fuss, D. (1989). *Essentially speaking: Feminism, nature and difference*. NY: Routledge.

Gilligan, Carol (1982). *In a different voice*. Cambridge, MA: Harvard University Press.

Golombisky, K. (2002). Gender equity and mass communication's female student majority. *Journalism & Mass Communication Educator, 56*(4), 53–66.

Gubrium, J. F. & Holstein, J. A. (1997). *The new language of qualitative method.* New York: Oxford University Press.

Gubrium, J. F., & Holstein, J. A. (2003). *Postmodern interviewing.* Thousand Oaks, CA: Sage Publications.

Harding, S. (1987). *Feminism & methodology: Social science issues.* Bloomington and Indianapolis: Indiana University Press.

Harman, W. W. (1988). The postmodern heresy: Consciousness as causal. In R. Griffin (Ed.), *The reenchantment of science: Postmodern proposals.* Albany: State University of New York Press.

Hartsock, N. (1983). The feminist standpoint: Developing the ground for a specifically feminist historical materialism. In S. Harding & M. Hintikka (Eds.), *Discovering reality* (pp. 283–310). Boston: Reidel.

Hartsock, N. (1997). Standpoint theory for the next century. *Women & politics, 18*(3), 93–102.

Heylighen, F. (1993). Epistemology, introduction. In F. Heylighen, C. Joslyn, & V. Turchin (Eds.), *Principia cybernetica web* (Principia Cybernetica, Brussels). Retrieved from http://pespmc1.vub.ac.be/EPISTEMI. htm.

Hirschman, A. O. (1987). The search for paradigms as a hindrance to understanding. In Paul Rabinow & William M. Sullivan (Eds.), *Interpretive social sciences: A second look.* Berkeley: University of California Press.

Hokikian, J. (2002). *The science of disorder: Understanding the complexity, uncertainty, and pollution in our world.* Los Angeles: Los Feliz Publishing.

Holsti, O. R. (1969). *Content analysis for the social sciences and humanities.* Reading, MA: Addison-Wesley.

Honderich, T. (Ed.). (1995). *The Oxford companion to philosophy.* New York: Oxford University Press.

hooks, b. (2000). *Feminism is for everybody.* Cambridge, MA: South End Press.

Howells, C. (1999). *Derrida.* Malden, MA: Blackwell.

Hust, S. J. T., Brown, J. D., & L'Engle, K. L. (2007). Boys will be boys and girls better be prepared: An analysis of rare sexual health messages in young adolescents' media. *Mass Communication & Society, 11*(1), 3–23.

Ivory, J. D. (2006). Still a man's game: Gender representation in online reviews of video games. *Mass Communication & Society, 9*(1), 103–114.

Kamhawi, R., & Weaver, D. (2003). Mass communication research trends from 1980 to 1999. *Journalism & Mass Communication Quarterly, 80*(1), 7–27.

Kaplan, A. (1964). *The conduct of inquiry.* San Francisco: Chandler.

Kern-Foxworth, M. (1989). Status and roles of minority PR practitioners. *Public Relations Review, 15*(3), 39–47.

Kiernan, V. (2003). Diffusion of news about research. *Science Communication, 25*(1), 3–13.

Kivikuru, U. (2006). Top-down or bottom-up? Radio in the service of democracy: Experiences from South Africa and Namibia. *The International Communication Gazette, 68*(1), 5–31.

Kniffel, L. (2005, December). StoryCorps oral history project: Listening as an act of love. *American Libraries*, 42–45.

Kosicki, G. M., & Becker, L. B. (1998, Autumn). Annual survey of enrollment and degrees awarded. *Journalism & Mass Communication Educator, 53*, 65–82.

Krenz, C., & Sax, G. (1986). What quantitative research is and why it doesn't work. *American Behavioral Scientist, 30*(1), 58–69.

Krueger, R. A., & Casey, M. A. (2000). *Focus groups: A practical guide for applied research.* Thousand Oaks, CA: Sage Publications.

Krippendorff, K. (1969). Introduction to Part I. In G. Gerbner, O. R. Holsti, K. Krippendorff, W. J. Paisley & P. J. Stone (Eds.), *The analysis of communication content: Developments in scientific theories and computer techniques* (pp. 3–16). New York: John Wiley & Sons, Inc.

Krippendorff, K. (2004). *Content analysis: An introduction to its methodology* (2nd ed.). Thousand Oaks, CA: Sage.

Lambert, F. L. (2005). *Entropy is simple—if we avoid the briar patches.* Retrieved from www.entropysimple.com/content.htm.

Len-Rios, M. E. (1998). Minority public relations practitioner perceptions. *Public Relations Review, 24*(4), 535.

Leshan, L., & Margenau, H. (1982). *Einstein's space and Van Gogh's sky.* New York: Collier Books.

Leslie, L. Z. (1998). The troubled waters of communication research: A position paper. *Journal of the Association of Communication Administration, 27*(2), 108–118.

Leslie, L. Z. (2000). *Mass communication ethics: Decision making in postmodern culture.* Boston: Houghton Mifflin.

Lester, J. D. & Lester, J. D., Jr. (1999). *The essential guide to writing research papers.* New York: Addison Wesley Longman.

Lincoln, Y. S. (1998). The ethics of teaching in qualitative research. *Qualitative Inquiry, 4*(3), 315–327.

Lombard, M., Snyder-Duch, J., & Bracken, C. C. (2005, June 13). Practical resources for assessing and reporting intercoder reliability in content analysis research projects. Retrieved April 27, 2008 from http://www.temple.edu/sct/mmc/reliability/.

Lynd, S. (1993). Oral history from below. *Oral History Review, 21*(1), 1–8.

Lyotard, J. (1992). Answering the question: What is postmodernism? In Charles Jenks (Ed.). *The postmodern reader* (pp. 138–150). New York: St. Martin's.

McChesney, R. W. (1993). Critical communication research at the crossroads. *Journal of Communication, 43*(4), 98–104.

McCombs, M. E., & Shaw, D, L. (1972). The agenda-setting function of the mass media. *Public Opinion Quarterly, 36*, 176–187.

McLeod, J. (2000, Spring). Lurching toward and into the 21st century. *CT&M Concepts, 29*(2), 1, 7.

McLuhan, M. (1964). *Understanding media: The extensions of man.* New York: McGraw Hill.

Merrigan, G., and Huston, C. L. (2004). *Communication research methods.* Belmont, CA: Wadsworth/Thomson.

Miller, D. C. (1991). *Handbook of research design and social measurement* (5th ed.). Newbury Park, CA: Sage Publications.

Morgan, D. L. (1988). *Focus groups as qualitative research.* Sage University Paper Series on Qualitative Research Methods (Vol. 16). Beverly Hills, CA: Sage Publications.

Nelson, J. (1987). Postmodern meaning of politics. Paper presented at the annual meeting, American Political Science Association, Chicago, September 3–6.

Nice, L. (2007). Tabloidization and the teen market. *Journalism Studies, 8*(1), 117–136.

Nord, D. P. (2003). The practice of historical research. In Guido H. Stempel III, David H. Weaver & G. Cleveland Wilhoit (Eds.), *Mass communication research and theory.* Boston: Allyn and Bacon, 362–385.

Norris, C. (1996). *Deconstruction theory and practice* (Rev. ed.). New York: Routledge.

Nunnally, J. C. (1978). *Psychometric theory* (2nd ed.). New York: McGraw Hill.

O'Sullivan, T., Hartley, J., Saunders, D., & Fiske, J. (1983). *Key concepts in communication.* New York: Methuen & Co.

Pfeil, F. (1988). Postmodernism as a "structure of feeling." In Cary Nelson & Lawrence Grossberg (Eds.), *Marxism and the interpretation of culture.* Chicago: University of Illinois Press.

Phelan, P. (1993). *Unmarked: The politics of performance.* London and New York: Routledge.

Poindexter, P. M. (1998). A model for effective teaching and learning in research methods. *Journalism and Mass Communication Educator, 52*(4), 24–36.

Poindexter, P. M., & McCombs, M. E. (2000). *Research in mass communication.* Boston: Bedford/St. Martin's.

Postman, N. (1999). *Building a bridge to the eighteenth century.* New York: Alfred A. Knopf.

Postmodernism in daily life. (1996). Downloaded from http://www.crossrds.org/subjct.htm.

Powell, J. (1998). *Postmodernism for beginners.* New York: Writers and Readers Publishing.

Qualitative social science research methodology. Downloaded from www.faculty. ncmc.edu/toconnor/308/ect09.htm.

Radway, J. (1984). *Reading the romance: Women, patriarchy, and popular culture.* Chapel Hill: University of North Carolina Press.

Ragin, C. C. (1994). *Constructing social research.* Thousand Oaks, CA: Pine Forge Press.

Rakow, L. (1986). Rethinking gender research in communication. *Journal of Communication, 36*(4), 11–26.

Randle, Q., Davenport, L. D., & Bossen, H. (2003). Newspapers slow to use web sites for 9/11 coverage. *Newspaper Research Journal, 24*(1), 58–71.

Ransford, H. E., & Butler, G. (1982). Teaching research methods in the social sciences. *Teaching Sociology, 9*(3), 291–312.

Reinharz, S. (1992). *Feminist methods in social research.* New York and Oxford: Oxford University Press.

Rice, G. (2000). War, journalism, and oral history. *The Journal of American History, 87*(2), 610–613.

Riffe, D., & Freitag, A. (1997). A content analysis of content analyses: Twenty-five years of Journalism Quarterly. *Journalism & Mass Communication Quarterly, 74*(3), 515–524.

Riffe, D., Lacy, S., & Fico, F. G. (2005). *Analyzing media messages: Using quantitative content analysis in research* (2nd ed.). Mahwah, NJ: Lawrence Erlbaum Associates.

Rifkin, J. (1989). *Entropy: Into the greenhouse world.* New York: Bantam Books.

Rosenau, P. M. (1992). *Postmodernism and the social sciences.* Princeton, NJ: Princeton University Press.

Rousmaniere, K. (2004). Historical research. In Kathleen deMarrais & Stephen D. Lapan (Eds.), *Foundations for research: Methods of inquiry in education and the social sciences.* Mahwah, NJ: Lawrence Erlbaum Associates.

Royle, N. (Ed.). (2000) *Deconstructions: A user's guide.* New York: Palgrave.

Rubin, R. B., Rubin, A. M., & Piele, L. J. (2005). *Communication research: Strategies and sources* (6th ed.). Belmont, CA: Wadsworth.

Ruszkiewicz, J., Walker, J. R., & Pemberton, M. A. (2003). *Bookmarks: A guide to research and writing.* (2nd ed.). New York: Addison Wesley Longman.

Sardar, Z., & Van Loon, B. (1997). *Introducing critical studies.* Cambridge, England: Icon Books.

Scheurich, J. J. (1997). *Research method in the postmodern.* London: The Falmer Press.

Shafer, R. J. (1980). *A guide to historical method.* Homewood, IL: The Dorsey Press.

Shipman, M. (1997). *The limitations of social research.* New York: Longman.

Sim, S., & Van Loon, B. (2001). *Introducing critical theory.* Cambridge, United Kingdom: Icon Books.

Sipe, D. (1991). Media and public history: The future of oral history and moving images. *Oral History Review, 19*(1–2), 75–87.

Smith, H. (1989). *Beyond the postmodern mind*. Wheaton, IL: Quest Books.

Spender, D. (1985,). *Man made language* (2nd ed.). London: Pandora.

Spigel, L. (2004). Theorizing the bachelorette: "Waves" of feminist media studies. *Signs: Journal of Women in Culture and Society, 30*(1), 1209–1221.

Stacks, D. W., & Hocking, J. E. (1999). *Communication research* (2nd ed.). New York: Addison-Wesley Longman.

Stake, R. E. (1994). Case studies. In Norman K. Denzin & Yvonna S. Lincoln (Eds.), *Handbook of qualitative research*. Thousand Oaks, CA: Sage Publications.

Stark, R., & Roberts, L. (1998). *Contemporary social research methods* (2nd ed.). Bellevue, WA: MicroCase Corporation.

Strinati, D. (1995). *An introduction to theories of popular culture*. New York: Routledge.

Strunk, W., Jr., & White, E. B. (2000). *The elements of style* (4th ed.). Needham Heights, MA: Allyn & Bacon.

Stucky, N. (1995). Performing oral history: Storytelling and pedagogy. *Communication Education, 44*(1), 1–14.

Tan, A. S. (1981). *Mass communication theories and research*. Columbus, OH: Grid Publishing.

Terkel, S. (1970). *Hard times: An oral history of the Great Depression*. New York: Avon.

The Museum of Broadcast Communications. (2005). Lone Ranger. Retrieved April 15, 2008 from http://www.museum.tv/rhofsection.php?page=287.

Thomas, S. (1994). Artifactual study in the analysis of culture: A defense of content analysis in a postmodern age. *Communication Research, 21*(6), 683–697.

Tinberg, H. (2003). *Writing with consequence*. New York: Addison Wesley Longman.

Tuchman, G. (1978). The symbolic annihilation of women by the mass media. In G. Tuchman, A. K. Daniels & J. Benet (Eds.), *Hearth and home: Images of women in the mass media* (pp. 1–38). New York: Oxford University Press.

Tuchman, G. (1994). Historical social science: Methodologies, methods, and meanings. In Norman K. Denzin & Yvonna S. Lincoln (Eds.), *Handbook of qualitative research*. Thousand Oaks, CA: Sage Publications.

VirtuaLit Critical Approaches. Definition of reader-response criticism. Bedford St. Martins Publishers. Retrieved from: http://bcs.bedfordstmartins.com/Virtualit/poetry/critical_define/crit_reader.html.

Walonick, D. (n.d.). *General systems theory*. Retrieved from www. survey-software-solutions.com/walonick/systems-theory.htm.

Ward, G. (1997). *Postmodernism*. Chicago, IL: NTC/Contemporary Publishing.

Watt, J. H. (1997). *Using the internet for quantitative survey research*. Downloaded from www.swiftinteractive.com/white-pl.htm.

Wiersma, J. (1988). The press release: Symbolic communication in life history inter-viewing. *Journal of Personality, 56*(1), 205–238.

Wilson, N. J. (1999). *History in crisis?* Upper Saddle River, NJ: Prentice Hall.

Wimmer, R. D., & Dominick, J. R. (2006). *Mass media research: An introduction* (8th ed.). Belmont, CA: Thomson-Wadsworth.

www.noogenesis.com/pineapple/blind_men_elephant.html.

www.physicalgeography net/fundamentals/chapter4.html.

http://plato.stanford.edu.

www.surveymonkey.com

Yow, V. R. (1994). *Recording oral history: A practical guide for social scientists.* Thousand Oaks, CA: Sage.

Zerbinos, E., & Clanton, G. A. (1993). Minority practitioners: Career influences, job satisfaction, and discrimination. *Public Relations Review, 19*(1), 75–91.

Zettl, H. (1998). Contextual media aesthetics as the basis for media literacy. *Journal of Communication, 48*(1), 81–95.

Zukin, C. (2004). Sources of variation in published election polling: A primer. American Association for Public Opinion Research (AAPOR). Available from http://.aapor.org/bestpractices.

INDEX